WRITING
NEW MEDIA
Theory and Applications
for Expanding
the Teaching of Composition

Writing
New Media

Theory and
Applications
for Expanding
the Teaching
of Composition

Anne Frances Wysocki
Johndan Johnson-Eilola
Cynthia L. Selfe
Geoffrey Sirc

UTAH STATE
UNIVERSITY PRESS
Logan, Utah

'

Utah State University Press
Logan, UT 84322

Copyright 2004 Utah State University Pressw
Manufactured in USA

Cover and interior design by Anne Frances Wysocki

Library of Congress Cataloging-in-Publication Data

Writing new media : theory and applications for expanding the teaching
of composition / Anne Frances Wysocki ... [et al.].
    p. cm.
Includes bibliographical references.
  ISBN 0-87421-575-7 (alk. paper)
1. English language--Rhetoric--Computer-assisted instruction. 2.
Online data processing--Authorship--Study and teaching. 3. English
language--Rhetoric--Computer network resources. 4. Report
writing--Study and teaching--Data processing. 5. English
language--Rhetoric--Study and teaching. 6. Report
writing--Computer-assisted instruction. 7. Mass
media--Authorship--Study and teaching. 8. Report writing--Computer
network resources. I. Wysocki, Anne Frances, 1956-
  PE1404.W7275 2004
  808'.042'0285--dc22
                        2003026881

CONTENTS

acknowledgments

The ever-challenging and invigorating thinking of our colleagues—in composition, computers and writing, literacy, rhetoric, and technical communication—sparked us into this book. Thank you all.

We also owe thanks to Michael Spooner at Utah State University Press, whose endless and patient encouragement nourished this book into being.

— *AFW, JJ-E, CLS, GS*

This book would not have been possible without the generous and always productive ideas of Cindy Selfe, who—at the 2000 Thomas R. Watson Conference on Rhetoric and Composition at the University of Louisville—thought that bringing the work of the four of us together might provide (because of the varieties of our approaches and backgrounds) useful support for others approaching new media from writing studies.

But also I must thank Dennis Lynch, without whom...

— *AFW*

Thanks to Underdog and Spork.

— *JJ-E*

PREFACE

what is in this book...

- Each chapter in this book provides rationales for opening a writing classroom to new media in particular ways.

- Because we believe that practice and theory clasp like hands, each chapter is followed by classroom and homework activities that grow out of, and in turn have shaped, the rationale. The activities we offer are all activities we have used and tested.

- The activities include teacher's notes, steps for assignments, and (if appropriate) handouts and assessment strategies; the activities are designed to help people in various levels of writing classes both analyze and produce new media texts.

- We didn't compose these chapters for you to move in order through them; instead, we hope you will find in one (or more) an opening that contains sense for you, a place to begin or continue.

a short set of reasons for why what is in this book is in this book

We've composed this book because of conversations we've had with each other, with other teachers, and with people in our classes. It's a current commonplace to acknowledge that writing is changing and that the look and functioning of texts are changing. Our conversations have been about how to respond responsibly—about how and what to teach—amidst the changes, about how people in our classes understand the changing textual landscapes, and about how they (and we) can be confident, effective, and ethical within that landscape. Our conversations—and this book, then—are about how we can understand these circumstances not as passive observers but as active, reflective, responsible composers.

Each of us necessarily approaches the situation differently: we each have different backgrounds, educations, and institutional settings, and so we each open our writing classrooms to the potentials of new media in ways that fit for us. And so, just as we believe there is no one "theory of written composition," we believe there is no one correct way into new media, no one grounding theory, no one "right" set of approaches. We are hoping, therefore, that the range of approaches we spread before you provides openings for you, too: we hope that one of our approaches—or some mix—provides you with directions of thought and theoretic groundings that spark with how you work. We also hope that the classroom and homework activities we describe engage you with their possibilities, so that you can modify them for the particular conditions of the people, technologies, administrations, and classrooms where you work.

I was caught by how he took
the musical phrase and seemed to find a new
way out, the next note was never the note

you thought would turn up and yet seemed
correct.

[...] What Monk banged out was the conviction
of innummerable directions. Years later
I felt he'd been blueprint, map and education:

no streets, we bushwhacked through the underbrush;
not timid, why open your mouth if not to shout?
not scared, the only road lay straight in front;

not polite, the notes themselves were sneak attacks;
not quiet—look, can't you see the sky will soon
collapse and we must keep dancing till it cracks?

from Stephen Dobyns, "Thelonius Monk"

Readings need to be defended in social settings if they are to be made
consequential, and social settings generate maxims of conduct that one may
not breach without cost. Successful readers are those who understand and
exploit such maxims most effectively. [...] One possible characterization of
the present book, indeed, is that it constitutes a primer of the kinds of
knowledge a person needed in early modern Europe in order to succeed in
his or her reading: knowledge of the circumstances and personnel involved
in making and distributing books, of the history and nature of printing
itself, and of the shifting bounds of civility guiding distinctions between
valid and illegitimate interpretation.

Adrian Johns, *The Nature of the Book*

OPENING
NEW MEDIA
TO WRITING:
openings & justifications

Anne Frances Wysocki

Do you miss that thick richly-printed rug that (apparently) used to be under your feet, the one into which (for at least several of the past centuries, as various theorists describe it) you could lose yourself in contemplation of its well-ordered and contained patterns? It's the rug that was pulled out from under you (and from under all the rest of us who teach writing in one form or another) within the last 15-20 years, predicted and described and shaped in words like those in the following quotation, from Jay Bolter some ten years ago now, from the introduction to the first edition of *Writing Space*, where Bolter claimed that "the printed book"

> seems destined to move to the margin of our literate culture. The issue is not whether print technology will completely disappear; books may long continue to be printed for certain kinds of texts and for luxury consumption. But the idea and the ideal of the book will change: print will no longer define the organization and presentation of knowledge, as it has for the past five centuries. This shift from print to the computer does not mean the end of literacy. What will be lost is not literacy itself, but the literacy of print, for electronic technology offers us a new kind of book and new ways to read and write. (2)

Or, much more recently, here is Gunther Kress, writing in the preface to his book *Literacy in the New Media Age*, claiming that we are at a

> moment in the long history of writing when four momentous changes are taking place simultaneously: social, economic, communicational, and technological change. The combined effects of these are so profound that it is justifiable to speak of a revolution in the landscape of communication. [...] Social changes are unmasking the structures and frames which had given a relative stability to forms of writing over the last two hundred years or so. Economic changes are altering the uses and purposes of the technology of writing. Communicational change is altering the relations of the means by which we represent our meanings, bringing image into the center of communication more insistently than it has been for several hundred years, and thereby challenging the dominance of writing. Lastly, technological change is altering the role and significance of the major media of dissemination. (9)

The chapters in our book do not argue with these comments; we may disagree with the periods of time mentioned or the particularities of the changes described or the drasticness that can be so psychologically compelling, but we do take as given that writing is changing. Writing is always changing (to see changes, we only need compare William James's books to those of Dr. Phil, or *The Rake's Progress* to *The X-Men*, or a metal matrix of the letter Q for the printing press to a software Postscript Q), but part of what has changed the warp and woof that used to seem so steady underneath us is precisely that we are now aware of the warp and woof, that we are aware of the complex weaves of writing as a material practice. Writing would not seem so different from what it was 30 or 300 years ago, really, if all that composed it was simply the words we hear in our heads when we read or if we define writing as being able by any means to make lettershapes visible to someone else as words. But we do understand, now, that writing, like all literate practices, only exists because it functions, circulates, shifts, and has varying value and weight within complexly articulated social, cultural, political, educational, religious, economic, familial, ecological, political, artistic, affective, and technological webs (you can name others, I am sure); we know that, in our places and times, writing is one of many operations by which we compose and understand our selves and our identities and our abilities to live and work with others. And so teachers of writing tend to be alert to how a change in any articulation of that long list above of webs of practice and institution sends waves of change shimmering elsewhere, including—necessarily—through our experiences of self and world: we know, for example, that changing the number of people in a class from 18 to 25 will change how we teach and the kinds of pedagogic relations we can develop with people in the class; we know that changes in testing requirements for college admission change the color of who is in our classes and hence who earns PhDs (see Crain, for example, on such changes at the City University of New York). The four of us—Cynthia Selfe, Geoffrey Sirc, Johndan Johnson-Eilola, and I—have written this book, pulled its chapters together, precisely because what we know as teachers of writing (of composition, of literacy, of rhetoric, of technical communication) is what enables us to see changes now occurring and is also what prepares us to shape change, actively and with care, in accord with what we know to be effective and just and necessary in our classroom practices and theories.

What we offer in this book is not, cannot ever be, a new complete rug to replace the old one shaped by writing, as though that rug ever existed as anything but an imaginary comfort. What we offer in this book is necessarily the equivalent of carpet scraps, some tentative weaves, bits and pieces of matting and colorful materials for you to consider and, if they seem at all useful, to arrange as they fit for you now. What we offer are some openings—some ranges of active possibilities—we each see in this particular time of change, openings that allow and encourage us to shift what we do in our thinking and classes so that we do not forget, so that we make actively present in our practices, how writing is continually changing material activity that shapes just who we can be and what we can do.

Let me move, then, from the broadly introductory to the more specific, by laying out five particular and connected openings that I, as a teacher of composition and rhetoric, now see for my practices:

1   The need, in writing about new media in general, for the material thinking of *people who teach writing*
2   A need to focus on the specific materiality of the texts we give each other
3   A need to define "new media texts" in terms of their materialities
4   A need for production of new media texts in writing classrooms
5   A need for strategies of generous reading

These openings are not precisely the ones my fellow writers in this collection see, but there are overlaps and similarities—and so I hope that my words can serve as some ground and introduction for the following chapters.

The first three openings I wish to consider involve what Bruce Horner, in his introduction to *Terms of Work for Composition: A Materialist Critique*, calls "the materiality of writing" as it exists for writing teachers and people in writing classrooms. Horner provides a long listing of what might constitute that materiality, so let me then give you his list, which is impressive and so requires a long repeat:

> That materiality may be understood in terms of writing technologies, an attribute of writing now being given renewed attention because of the recent shift from the technologies of paper and pen to computer software and hardware. Or it might be understood more broadly to refer to a host of socioeconomic conditions contributing to writing production, such as the availability of certain kinds of schooling, number of students in writing classes, student financial aid (and the need for it), public health, access to time and quiet. Yet more broadly, the materiality of writing might be understood to refer to networks for the distribution of writing, controls over publishing (in whatever forms), and global relations of power articulated through these. And it may be understood to include the particular subjectivities— the consciousness—produced by the conditions of "postmodern," "post-Fordist," and other socioeconomic conditions. Similarly, the materiality of writing may be understood to include social relations—say, between students and teachers in the writing classroom; relations of race, gender, class, ethnicity, sexual orientation, generation, and region, among others within the classroom and/or the larger social

realm; "personal" (e.g., familial) relations—and the lived experience of the history of these relations to which any act of writing may be seen as responding. The materiality of the work of teaching composition can be understood to include physical classroom conditions (size, heating, furniture, lighting, number of students); the teacher's physical health and office and library resources; clerical support, teaching load, salary and job security; intra- and interdepartmental relations between composition staff and other faculty; characteristics of the student population; relationships between the academic institution and state and commercial institutions; relations among members of the Composition "profession" and between those members and other organizations and constituencies; and teachers' lived experience of the history of those relations to which any act of teaching may be seen as responding. (xviii–xix)

Horner gives two cautions after his listing: first, that the listing should help us recognize that "no representation of teaching or writing can exhaust the full range of their materiality" (xix) and, second, relying on Giddens's theories of structure, that the listing should remind us that agency and structure are interdependent. We have agency, that is, in so far as we recognize how we are positioned by and hence can work with and within our particular historically-situated and contingent material structures, all the ones that Horner lists and all the ones my own more abstract lists above imply. Because the structures into which we have grown up are neither necessary nor fixed, they can be changed when we forge new positions for ourselves among them or when we construct new relations between the different structures that matter to us.

Teachers of writing recognize that writing classes can easily decontextualize writing such that agency and material structures look independent. The way school can seem separated from other institutions (the ones that constitute the "real world") can keep the work of classrooms from seeming that it has any value or purpose outside the class or the requirements of a degree schedule, and people in writing classes can for that reason among others (like the architectural isolation of classrooms and campuses from other social spaces) often feel they are writing by themselves, as isolated, separated individuals with no particular social, cultural, or historical location. Many writing teachers in the last decades have worked to develop classroom practices that help people in their classes see—through what they write—their particular locations in time and place, and hence how they are shaped by but can in turn shape those locations (and themselves) through textual work. Think here, for example, of the literacy inventories, literacy anecdotes, and autoethnographies that Linda Brodkey describes and shows us how to use so that their composers can see "that their personal histories are also cultural histories" (209). Think of the service learning classrooms in which "literacy itself is both the service and the subject of investigation" (Julier 144), making it possible for us to see connections among the practices of service—and, importantly, the practices that make such service necessary—and of literacy with the hope that, as Bruce Herzberg puts it, we might find it "possible not only to question and analyze the world, but also to imagine transforming it" (317). Think also of the work teachers of technical communication do in contextualizing technology so that we do not see and use composing technologies as neutral tools without effect on what we write, on who reads what we write, or on who we become through writing: as James Porter, for example, reminds us,

> every act of writing in the workplace involves the exercise of power. In some cases, this exercise of power can be unfair, manipulative, exclusionary, harmful, or illegal—and technical communicators have to be alert to the ways in which their online writing can do harm, can oppress, can represent unfair use of others' work. ("Legal Realities" 67)

It is this kind of thinking, action, and advocacy—focused specifically on texts and how situated people use them to make things happen in all kinds of contexts—that I believe needs to expand to new media work, as I describe through considering my five possible openings for how what we know about writing can usefully affect how we approach new media.

> *(Notice, too, for the moment, that I have just mentioned "new media" for the first time, without defining the term; I will define it in a section several pages ahead, in the context of the larger arguments I am making.)*

OPENING 1

THE NEED, IN WRITING ABOUT NEW MEDIA IN GENERAL, FOR THE MATERIAL THINKING OF PEOPLE WHO TEACH WRITING

I have not argued here and will not argue that we need to open writing classes to new media. There already exists plenty of such reasoned arguments (on why to incorporate the visual aspects of texts, for example, see Faigley; George; or Stroupe; on approaching literacies through multiple modalities, see the New London Group or any of the works of Kress alone or with van Leeuwen). Many people already include various visual- or Web-based activities in their classrooms, and, besides, it is impossible to pretend that the lives of the people coming to school have not been shaped by texts that don't look or function like academic essays. Instead, I want to argue that **new media needs to be opened to writing**. I want to argue that writing about **new media needs to be informed by what writing teachers know, precisely because writing teachers focus specifically on texts and how situated people (learn how to) use them to make things happen.** Such consideration is mostly lacking from existing writing about new media.

I do not pretend to have read everything that describes itself as being about new media, but what I have read from outside the areas of rhetoric, composition, literacy studies, or technical communication breaks into two broad categories: there is writing about how to analyze or design isolated individual texts and there is writing about the broad contexts and functioning of media structures in general. There is little or nothing that bridges those two categories to help composers of texts think usefully about effects of their particular decisions as they compose a new media text, to help composers see how agency and materiality are entwined as they compose. I do not want to be seen here as saying or implying that what has been written so far about new media is useless—far from it: there is a tremendous amount of thoughtful, sustained, and exciting research and speculation about new media (see, for example, the "Print Resources" section at the back of this book). It is just that *there is little concrete encouragement for the kinds of embedded and embodied practices writing teachers, from much practice and reflection and theorizing, know are necessary to help students—and teachers, and others—have any kind of alert agency with and within the structures of their composing lives.*

There is little or nothing about how with new media we make visible positions that engage others, that are structured so that they can give the socially-tied satisfaction and encouragement of producing "complex representations that invite argumentation" (Brodkey 201). There is little or nothing, for example, that encourages someone composing a Web page to think about how and why, in her place and time, her choices of color and typeface and words and photograph and spatial arrangement shape the relationship she is constructing with her audience and hence shape how the audience is asked to act—as active citizens? as passive consumers?—while it engages with the Web page, and there is consequently little that asks audiences to consider the behaviors and attitudes they are encouraged to take as they read such Web sites. There is little or nothing that asks composers and readers to see and then question the values implicit in visual design choices, for such design is often presented as having no value other than functionally helping readers get directly to the point. There is little or nothing to help composers and readers think about how the defense- and commercial-tied history of computers has shaped the logic of computer architecture and hence the logic of much computer software—and hence the structures of thinking supported and encouraged by the design of so much software people use to compose: how many word-processing or Web page composing software packages do you know that encourage scribbling, doodling, writing outside the margins, or writing in anything but straight lines?

There is a tradition within literary scholarship that reminds us how, in the particular physical constructions and means of production involved in some literary productions,

> the physique of the "document" has been forced to play an aesthetic function, has been made part of the "literary work." That is to say, in these kinds of literary works, the distinction between physical medium and conceptual message breaks down completely. (McGann, "Textual Condition" 77; see also McGann "Composition as Explanation," or Holland)

That tradition has been carried into digital texts, with, for example, Hayles, who reminds us in a study of both print and digital texts that

> Technological effects can no more be separated from literary effects than characters can be separated from the writings that contain and are contained by them. [...] Focusing on materiality allows us to see the dynamic interactivity through which literary work mobilizes its physical embodiment in conjunction with its verbal signifiers to construct meanings in ways that implicitly construct the user/reader as well. (130–131. Also see Kirschenbaum on the materiality of a particular digital text.)

What I want to argue is that it is not just within literary or aesthetic texts that textual materiality works in the ways McGann and Hayles describe: this materiality—which takes part in the construction of readers—occurs in all texts we consume, whether print or digital, research essay or technical instruction set. And this material functioning occurs when we *produce* any text as well, and needs to be supplemented with the broader understanding of materiality that Horner describes.

This, then, is why it matters for writing teachers to be doing more with new media: writing teachers are already practiced with helping others understand how writing—as a print-based practice—is embedded among the relations of agency and extensive material practices and structures that are our lives. Writing teachers help others consider how the choices we make in producing a text necessarily situate us (or can try to avoid situating us) in the midst of ongoing, concrete, and continually up-for-grabs decisions about the shapes of our lives. Writing teachers can thus fill a large gap in current scholarship on new media; they can bring to new media texts a humane and thoughtful attention to materiality, production, and consumption, which is currently missing.

To be alert to such materiality also matters because it helps us use our various composing technologies as justly and thoughtfully as possible. For example, when teachers of writing first started using synchronous and asynchronous discussion software in their classes, in the 1980s, they noted how people in class who rarely spoke in face-to-face discussions contributed to the online discussions. The first writing about such software attributed the ease of contribution to how identity seemed to be hidden online, or could be shifted and played with, as though the design of the software itself caused people to try out different identities with the result that quieter people "spoke" more online and males (for example) tried on what they considered to be female voices (or at least female names). Quickly, however, the same writers and others began to note how online discussions did indeed reveal aspects of identity, just in different ways than to which we'd been accustomed, and that people could be just as easily silenced online as off—because online discussions were just as much entwined with other social and cultural practices as writing with pen and paper. Susan Romano, for example, in describing a class in which Anglo and Latino students used synchronous discussion software to consider readings about Latino culture, told how the Latino students did not speak out online as

Latino because of how critical the Anglo students were of Latino culture; Romano wrote that

> Possibly the silent students were learning nothing about the social structures that support inequalities that they did not already know, and perhaps this textualized, networked conversation constituted not lessons about systems of power but a recapitulation of old lessons already learned. (n. pag.)

Similarly, Pamela Takayoshi, after analyzing women's reports about their experiences in synchronous discussions, argued that

> we must be aware that the problem of voice for women in academia is rooted at deeper level than can be addressed simply through implementing a new medium. Just because women are offered a "safe" space in which to speak does not mean they will know how to do so. [...] Patterns of interaction deeply entrenched within a patriarchal system cannot be undermined simply by offering access to a new medium. If we simply move away from traditional discourse forms that shortchange women without analyzing the ideologies that inform their formation and staying power, we run the risk of those ideologies becoming dominant once again in another form. (32)

Responding not to discussion software but to what we see on computer screens in general, Cynthia Selfe and Richard Selfe pointed out how the graphical user interface—the "GUI" of folder icons and desktops—seemed to be intuitive to many of us only because it came directly out of specific but long-woven Western-business practices of organization and structure; they show how what is intuitive to some, however, means that others "often learn that they must abandon their own culture or gender and acknowledge the dominance of other groups" (494) when they use such interfaces. What these examples indicate is that we cannot take new technologies as simply and automatically and necessarily new or positive or automatic: new technologies are always designed out of existing technologies and out of existing material economies, patterns, and habits. If our intentions are to teach so that people in our classes learn possible routes to agency through composition, then what these examples indicate is that we can be most effective in teaching when we see, and so can teach about, how our compositions only ever work within and as part of other, already existing, structures and practices.

There needs to be more of this sort of critique for new media, which shows us—because of its attentiveness to the particular material ways we use communicational technologies and media—that new technologies do not automatically erase or overthrow or change old practices. If there are openings for change in new media, we can take advantage of them if we are attentive not only to what is new but also, necessarily, if we are attentive to what is old and hanging on (and hanging on, especially, quietly, in places that do not call attention to themselves). This is the kind of work that teachers of writing are prepared to do precisely because of how they see texts as complexly situated practice embedded in the past but opening up possible futures. There needs to be more of the sort of just-described critique for new media, that is, not only so that teachers of writing can develop considered classroom practices for teaching the analysis and composition of new media texts but so that what teachers of writing know about the embedded materiality of any text can contribute to the current discussions about and making of new media.

What we offer in this book, we hope, moves toward such critique. Each of us writes from theoretic positions that guide us, and we offer specific and concrete classroom practices—growing out of theory and our particular experiences in classes—for approaching teaching about and with new media. For example, in her first chapter in this collection, "Students Who Teach Us," Cynthia Selfe describes for us the life and work of a young man who hasn't done well in school (who has, in fact, left school) because, first, his background didn't shape him to value what many of us do about school and second, because—even though his spelling and grammar brought him failing grades—he found success (and satisfaction) in composing Web pages; he does not need formal credentialing to be taken seriously as a developer of Web sites embodying and constructing Black identities, and Selfe likewise takes his success seriously, to help us see concretely how in a "postmodern world, new media literacies may play an important role in identity formation, the exercise of power, and the negotiation of new social codes" (49), and she then describes classroom activities to help us see for ourselves how we have become who we are within the various and shifting social-technological contexts that have been the spaces of our lives since birth. Geoffrey Sirc argues in his chapter that the people who share classrooms with him tend to find more engagement with, and "publish passionate writing" about (144), the "most exciting cultural media available" (136)—hip hop—especially when they are not restricted to the standard essay; given their understandings of the effects and authorities of different kinds of communication, and given their desire to construct texts that move each other, these composers find possibilities in texts other than those we might usually teach—and Sirc provides descriptions of assignments that have helped these composers build such texts. My own later chapter in this book is an argument for how, if we are to more thoroughly see the visual aspects of our texts, we can do this without bringing along old, unquestioned, and invisible articulations between visual arrangements and ideas about gender (and, by implication, race) that most of us now find unpalatable; I then offer activities, growing out of my arguments, that aim to help me and others see how visual arrangements both carry values and shape our relations with texts and each other. In his chapter, Johndan Johnson-Eilola shifts the focus from people in our classrooms and the workings of the visual to the courts whose decisions shape intellectual property law, to show how the law both embodies and contributes to changing notions of what constitutes authoring, authors, texts, originality, and copying; Johnson-Eilola argues that, as a result of several recent cases, we should be shifting between thinking of a text as a "coherent whole" and thinking of it as a set of "marketable chunks" (207)—

databases—whose nodes can be linked and unlinked into whatever combinations work for the at-hand circumstances, and the assignments Johnson-Eilola describes are aimed precisely at helping "students (and teachers) learn to question the 'original'/'copied' dichotomy" (225) as well as "who is represented in their own work, and how they represent others" (230).

In each of this book's chapters, then, we work to make visible, first, how larger material structures are woven into the practices of new media as we compose texts and, second, how we can work with those structures as we compose.

OPENING 2

A NEED TO FOCUS
ON THE SPECIFIC MATERIALITY
OF THE TEXTS
WE GIVE EACH OTHER

8½" x 11" white paper or black ink hasn't often seemed like a choice for writers in our classrooms—or for us. Our composing technologies of typewriter and of early printers for computers (designed to replicate our typing habits) often have come pre-shaped to take only that size page and to print in black. But now we can purchase desktop laser printers that can be loaded with regular, legal, or tabloid size paper and we can purchase color ink jet printers that have been designed to allow us any choice of color that their inks can combine to make (and that can print on various sizes of glossy or watercolor paper). The introduction of digital technologies has widened the range of choices of material for anyone working with a computer and with laser or color printers, such that including photographs or color illustrations or multiple typefaces in any on-paper composition is easy; the range of choices for anyone constructing texts that are meant to stay on screen can seem even wider: we can modify the size of the onscreen window through which audiences see a text, choose animation as the primary mode for conveying an argument, or structure a text so that audiences can choose a path for moving through its parts.

I want to argue that these results of digitality ought to encourage us to consider not only the potentialities of material choices for digital texts but for *any* text we make, and that we ought to use the range of choices digital technologies seem to give us to consider the range of choices that printing-press technologies (apparently) haven't. I want to consider how any material we use for communication is not a blank carrier for our meanings, is not a blank that contributes nothing to how readers understand. Instead, I believe that we have a time of opening here, a time to be alert to how these choices of material very much articulate into the other structures that shape writing and our lives— and that being alert to these choices can help us shape changes we might want.

The kind of materiality on which I focus here is the first materiality Bruce Horner names in the above long quotation about writing, when he names "writing technologies," those of paper and pen and computers. In her book *Writing Technology: Studies on the Materiality of Literacy* (which Horner cites as his source for naming this kind of materiality), Christina Haas discusses why these technologies are so often overlooked when we attend to the practices of writing—a result, in part, of how our writing technologies are meant to be invisible so that we can overlook them in order to get to the tasks at hand but also of how "writing, in its essential nature, is somehow imagined to exist independently of and uninfluenced" by technology (34). In response, Haas observed people composing with pen and paper and composing with computers, and her various studies gave her ground for arguments like the following, which comes out of one of the studies:

> The computer system used here facilitated certain kinds of writing activities—for example, the production of intact prose. This increased facility is probably due to the greater responsiveness of the high-speed system used by these writers. Similarly, the greater tangibility (and possibly legibility) of pen and paper made the creation of diagrammatic, conceptual notes easier when writers used that medium. Because the technologies allowed or even invited certain kinds of notemaking activities, they also, then, allowed or invited the thinking that is required by those activities. By supporting one kind of physical activity rather than another, technologies can affect writers' thinking processes in very real ways. (115)

Few writing teachers are in position to change the design of computers or pen and paper to better facilitate the kinds of thinking we might favor, in line with Haas's arguments, but we are in positions to encourage thoughtful decisions both about using computers or paper and pen in various stages of composing processes and—importantly—about the material designs of texts using those different technologies.

I focus on the communication technologies we use, and on the communication objects we build with them, precisely because our work as teachers and writers would not exist without them and yet we are so often unpracticed at considering how they too take part in shaping who we are—which is perhaps why, when writers do turn their attentions to them, these writing technologies can seem to take a much larger part in shaping, even determining, who we are; it is for such kinds of deterministic claims that McLuhan and other "medium theorists" have been criticized (see Deibert 26–31 for a summary of and response to such critiques). I do not think that the particular materials we use—and their particular instantiations as academic journals, comic books, online news services, or tombstones—determine who we are or what we do because (as the previous pages describe) the webs in which our texts circulate and have effect are complex and often un-tease-apart-able articulations of the social, cultural, religious, economic, political, affective, intellectual, and so on; neither do materials have essential instantiations, such that, for example, paper can only appear as 6" by 9" bound and printed books. But, to take a hand-sized bound book as an example, there seems to be little doubt that the appearance of such ready-for-reading-by-a-single-person books connects somehow to the emergence of (the very idea and the practices of) individual identity in Western Europe in the 16th through the 18th centuries. What is open to question is the quality of connection between object and identity: was the appearance of portable books—which people could read by themselves, quietly—alone sufficient to cause individuality and hence (for example) the rise of the democratic state (as McLuhan or Saenger, for example, tell it) or is how such books appear alongside and within certain domestic and political structures what enabled there to be separations of practices into the public and the private (as Habermas tells it)? It ought to be obvious that I come down on the vaguer side of connection, that I do not think we can with any confidence state the exact lines of cause and result—but that is not to deny that the particular shapes and arrangements and materials of our communications contribute to how we see ourselves in what we make and to how others take in what we give them.

Imagine, for example, that this book now before you were bound in leather or in large fish-like scales. Imagine that you were reading this online. Imagine that this ink were violet instead of black, or that this was a video of me speaking (or signing) these words. Imagine that this book were 2' on each side and printed with letters 1" high, facing you on a lectern in a dark wood-panelled room. Imagine that this chapter were appearing paragraph by paragraph in an Instant Messenger window. Each of those changes in the material instantiation of my words would change your attitude toward this text, certainly, but would also (I think) do more than that.

I have written elsewhere—in a chapter on visual rhetoric in another book—about how I think the material presentations of texts do more work than simply create a mood or direct readers' eyes through a text. In that other writing, I asked readers (as I asked you in the preceding paragraph) to imagine other than the conditions at hand, in order to consider how the visual presentation of most books "fits into and reinforces our cultural practices of authority, standardization, and mass production":

> Imagine that the book you now hold in your hands were presented on motley pieces of newsprint and notepaper, each chapter written in different colors and handwritten (some of this handwriting large and loopy; some small, tight, and left-leaning). […] What would you think of this book were it to call such visual attention to itself? Consider the imagined other book, and consider what seriousness and authority you would grant it; consider then how important is the repetitive visual presentation of the pages of this book as they are actually printed, the repetition tied to and impossible without cultural taste for mechanical standardization and reproduction… and ask yourself what other values you see adhering to the visual presentation of this book as it is now, in your hands. ("with eyes" 184)

Precisely because the texts we give each other are produced within the articulated cultural webs I've been describing, they re-present values that shape and are shaped by those webs. If we value efficiency but do not attend to how the design of texts embody values, then our texts most often will default to being efficient, and they will be efficient not only in production and distribution but also in the visual layouts and other material choices that help us read through them quickly—and that then reinforce for us, take part in teaching us, that efficiency is a good to be repeated.

It is when we see but do not notice, over and over, what our texts—as parts of the material structures in which we live and work—embody and how they articulate to other practices that we are most likely to learn, without noticing, what to value and how to behave. As Bourdieu, in these roundly alliterative words, argues:

> That part of practices which remains obscure in the eyes of their producers is the aspect by which they are objectively adjusted to other practices and to the structures of which the principles of their production is itself the product. (79)

For Bourdieu, that is, it is what we don't see that allows our practices and products to connect with each other in ways we may neither intend nor like and to shape the ways in which they are connected—and hence to shape what we are capable of doing and knowing. And so it is important to keep in mind, as Horner reminds us (130–133, for example), that agency comes precisely in being alert to the "social forms" (as Giddens names them) in which we move, in understanding where and how we and our practices fit, and hence where and how we have room and opportunity to make change. Haas reminds us again and again that "although technological effects are very real, they can be small, subtle, even paradoxical" (18)—and it is the whole effort of her book to show not only that such effects are real but that we can learn to be attentive to them. It is worth our while, then, as teachers of writing concerned about who we and the people in our classes are, and about how we act towards and with each other, to be attentive to those aspects of texts—such as their material designs—that haven't before been accessibly visible to us.

The technologies of the printing press were never static, and could have gone in other directions than those that made the reproduction of photographs, illustrations, charts, and graphs or of non-rectangular text shapes more technically difficult or expensive than the reproduction of linear type. Texts such as Mallarmé's *Un Coup de Dés,* or Derrida's *Glas,* or Kristeva's *Stabat Mater,* or Mayakvosky's *For the Voice*—all of which predate digital typesetting—ought to remind us that, prior to the apparent flexibility of layout that digitality has given us, writers who published through a printing press could push for layouts other than the linear lines of type that we associate with academic writing. I want to argue that these possibilities of other choices—along with how newer technologies have shifted the economies of publishing so that writing and layout needn't any longer be separate functions—ought to show us, finally, that our media really are modes, to use Kress and van Leeuwen's terminology. That is, in their words, "a mode is that material resource which is used in recognisably stable ways as a means of articulating discourse" (*Multimodal*

In *Multimodal
Discourse*, some of
the examples Kress
and van Leeuwen
give of modes in use
include architecture,
color, language (27);
gesture and taste
(28); writing (29);
furniture (32);
photography,
etching, card paper,
layout (60).

Discourse 25); a mode "is the abstract organization of a specific material drawn into semiosis" (*Multimodal Discourse* 27). Kress and van Leeuwen make a distinction between media and mode because they believe that media are possible; that is, they believe that there can be aspects of a text that contribute no meaning to the text. I disagree—the material stuff of our texts may sometimes seem not open to individual choice (as 8½" by 11" white paper often does not), but that means the choice has already been made for us, in the accumulation of changes and decisions that have led to us using our material technologies as we do.

Instead of believing that there are media that contribute nothing to our reading, I hope that we can see this time of change—when digitality gives us a position for questioning what had earlier seemed like a natural silence of media—as a time for asking questions like the ones below to broaden our understanding of the texts we give each other and hence of our selves:

- How might the straight lines of type we have inherited on page after page of books articulate to other kinds of lines, assembly lines and lines of canned products in supermarkets and lines of desks in classrooms? How might these various lines work together to accustom us to standardization, repetition, and other processes that support industrial forms of production? (Think, in parallel and for example, of arguments various writers have made about connections between the development of the city grid system and the development of democracy in Ancient Greece; see Fleming for an overview and thoughtful consideration.)

- How might the quiet emphasis on perspectival sight (over all other of our senses) of reading and books—and now computer screens (designed, after all, by people raised to be book-readers and -writers)—shape us as sensual embodied beings?

- How might the visual appearance of most academic texts of the previous century—texts most often without photographs or illustrations or varied typography—have encouraged us to value (or devalue or repress) the visual in the circulation of academic and other "serious" writing? Is it perhaps because we have banished photographs and illustrations and typography from such texts that they have seemed appropriate for—and been able to play such a large part and continually return in—texts for children and advertising and other commercial work?

- What potentials for thinking and argument and position do we lose when we most often think that attention to the layout of words on the page is appropriate for only functional (instructions and manuals) or aesthetic/poetic texts?

By being alert to this opening for considering the material of our texts—whether the material comes to our eyes as light shining through a screen or as light reflecting off paper or stone or the flesh of a tattoo—, we open possibilities for new arrangements, new articulations with other of our material practices. How would a text look, for example, that embodied the values of generosity, or slow rumination, or full-hearted justice—and what might we learn about ourselves in the processes of making and learning to read such texts?

This opening to change requires experimentation and patience with what might seem strange since it means calling attention to what previously functioned quietly, invisibly. This opening might give us more room for play because it gives us perspective for seeing and working alertly with a wider range of the material potentials of our texts.

OPENING 3

A NEED TO DEFINE
"NEW MEDIA TEXTS"
IN TERMS OF
THEIR MATERIALITIES

Because I believe we ought to strive to be alert to the varied materialities of our texts—to the particular materials we choose as we build concrete texts as well as to the wide range of structures Horner lists and suggests and in which the texts we make circulate and have weight—I desire to define (finally) new media differently from how the term has been defined in other places. I think **we should call "new media texts" those that have been made by composers who are aware of the range of materialities of texts and who then highlight the materiality: such composers design texts that help readers/consumers/viewers stay alert to how any text—like its composers and readers—doesn't function independently of how it is made and in what contexts. Such composers design texts that make as overtly visible as possible the values they embody.** Considering new media texts in this way, I think and hope, helps us see where openings for agency are within the new media texts we compose.

Under this definition, **new media texts do not have to be digital**; instead, any text that has been designed so that its materiality is not effaced can count as new media. New media texts can be made of anything (and in this book you'll see exercises that encourage producing or interpreting texts on paper as well as on screen); what is important is that whoever produces the text and whoever consumes it understand—because the text asks them to, in one way or another—that the various materialities of a text contribute to how it, like its producers and consumers, is read and understood. If what is important to us is the possibility of agency within the varied and variably articulated structures within which we live, then attending to the particular material qualities of texts is yet another opening for shaping change in those structures.

By considering new media texts in light of materiality, certain matters appear from different and, I think, useful perspectives:

• If we shift from seeing the apparently growing emphasis on the visual in our culture and time not as the automatic result of new technological ease but rather as a historically situated process, then we can situate that emphasis within ongoing vacillations in our understandings of how words and visual representations function and relate. WJT Mitchell, for example, reminds us (so that we can be critical of it) that there "is an ancient tradition, of course, which argues that language is the essential human attribute: 'man' is the 'speaking animal,'" and "man" in that equation, of course, is very much meant as a gendered, raced, and concrete noun, such that another equation is produced with the implied leftover terms: "The image is [therefore] the medium of the subhuman, the savage, the 'dumb animal,' the child, the woman, the masses" (24). If we wish less rigid ideas about gender, class, and who counts as human, then one strategy is to try disarticulating the various terms in the two equations and rearticulating them in other ways—which means working not only with ideas about gender and humanity but also with words and visual representations. For example, if we attend to how we have inherited a tradition of serious texts that refrain from having much of the visual about them while popular magazines and children's books are uncontainedly visual (see, for example, Kress and van Leeuwen, *Reading Images* 185), then we can consider how the above equations—and hence our understandings of words and visual representations—fit smoothly into the rise of consumer culture that uses visual representations to create unselfconscious and uncritical consuming desires: if we understand visual representations to work underneath the radar of language and rationality, then we need subjects who (at least for the time that they are engaged with the colors and moves of magazines and television commercials) do not see visual representations rationally or critically. (Or, perhaps, in this separation of the visual from the verbal there are processes at work that support what Kress and van Leeuwen claim, that "visual media […] form an alternative to writing and can therefore be seen as a potential threat to the present dominance of verbal literacy among elite groups" [*Reading Images* 16].) If we want, then, to imagine and build other possibilities for our selves as women and men who do not think and feel with such disconnection, one place to start is in rearticulating how we use words and other visual possibilities in our texts. We can experiment with building arguments that use photographs or drawings instead of words, for example, (as both Cynthia Selfe and I describe in our various chapters), and we can experiment with alphabetic texts whose visibility is more foregrounded in typographic and layout choices. Such rearticulations—because they are rearticulations not only of words and visual representations but of all those other terms that have previously been linked to them—provide *openings* for new possibilities for seeing selves that are connected within and to new structures.

• If we think of "interactivity"—a buzzword for describing something about readers and digital texts—not as an isolated property inherent to digital texts but rather as naming an apparent difference between reading online texts and reading print texts, then we can see it as a term about the relations readers (are encouraged to) have with texts, given the ways texts and textual technologies are structured. "Human-computer interactivity" has been defined as being what happens when someone clicks any link in a Web page or as "two conscious agencies in conversation, playfully and spontaneously developing a mutual discourse, taking cues and suggestions from each other as they proceed" (Stone 11). Lev Manovich, in *The Language of New Media*, turns away from the term because he considers it both too broad and too restrictive:

> When we use the concept of "interactive media" exclusively in relation to computer-based media, there is the danger that we will interpret "interactivity" literally, equating it with physical interaction between a user and a media object (pressing a button, choosing a link, moving the body), at the expense of psychological interaction. The psychological processes of filling-in, hypothesis formation, recall, and identification, which are required for us to comprehend any text or image at all, are mistakenly identified with an objectively existing structure of interactive links.
>
> This mistake is not new; on the contrary, it is a structural feature of the history of modern media. The literal interpretation of interactivity is just the latest example of a larger modern trend to externalize mental life, a process in which media technologies—photography, film, VR—have played a key role. (57)

By seeing the term within the larger material contexts of how readers/viewers are conceived, Manovich's words ask us to hold in mind how "interactivity" is a contested term as well as how what it is meant to represent is neither new nor unproblematic. Manovich's arguments hang on his particular understanding of internally existing thought, with which we may or may not agree—but his arguments portray how a process that can seem unique to digital texts can be more complexly connected to other ways we understand who we are and how we function, and can encourage us to ask what is at stake—and for whom—in the naming and definings of "interactivity." Manovich's words can encourage us to consider the various and complex relations we can construct with readers through the ways readers are asked to move through texts we build, whether that is by turning pages, clicking links, making conceptual connections between a photograph on one screen and a poem on another, or solving a puzzle that opens the gate to the next level of a gametext. Again, there are openings here for exploring who we might be within the relations we can build with others through the particular materialities of the texts we build.

• Being alert to how agency and materiality entwine can also help us see how the definitions we use—and hence how we understand our technologies—might obscure the agency we do have. For example, Manovich defines "new media" in the context of the

> translation of all existing media into numerical data accessible through computers. The result is new media—graphics, moving images, sounds, shapes, spaces, and texts that have become computable; that is, they comprise simply another set of computer data. (20)

Notice that there are no human agents in that definition, with the implication that the process of translation is natural and inexorable. Such a definition, used logically, can then be the undergirding for how Manuel Castells, for example, in a hyperbolic moment, sees the "information communication system" as

> a system in which reality itself (that is, people's material/symbolic existence) is entirely captured, fully immersed in a virtual image setting, in the world of make believe, in which appearances are not just on the screen through which experience is communicated, but they become the experiences. All messages of all kinds become enclosed in the medium because the medium has become so comprehensive, so diversified, so malleable that it absorbs in the same multimedia text the whole of human experience, past, present, and future… (I: 404)

Again, there are no human agents here, just the apparently natural logic of all representational modes of communication (somehow) becoming one. Such words and definitions can imply—through leaving us out—that we have no effective place here, that we can tinker and make things and play but it will not matter, really. The alternative is not to swing to the opposite position then, either, to act as though—if somehow we would only wake up and get busy and all become corporate CEOs with good stock options—we can have infinite agency. To recognize the materiality of our practices and settings is to recognize that practices and settings and structures are temporally contingent, as are we, and that who we are and what we do and what the structures around us are depend on how we understand and work on and within where we are now—and with where we would like to be. We can only see ourselves within the texts we make and give to others if we understand those texts (and how and where and with what we work as we produce them) to be connected to us through our various material relations.

I've just listed possible openings that result from thinking of new media texts as those in which we keep materiality foregrounded. There are of course then *closings* that result from what I propose:

• Under the definition I offer not just any computer-screen text counts as "new media": just because a newly published textbook (for example) has an online component does not mean that what is online is "new media." Just because there are the (relatively) new technologies of computers and printers and scanners and cameras and sound recorders and personal digital assistants and cell phones does not mean that those new technologies (as my earlier example of online discussion software shows) *cause* us to produce texts that break away from or ask us to think and act differently than print technologies—as they articulate into other material practices—did and do. Technologies are not responsible for texts, we are, within the limitations of what different technologies afford—and those limitations are always less restrictive than we might think, as Andrew Feenberg, for example, shows in his analyses of various communication technologies. My reason for defining new media texts in terms of materiality instead of digitality is to help us hold present what is at stake: to look at texts only through their technological origin is to deflect our attentions from what we might achieve mindful that textual practices are always broader than the technological.

- Under this definition, neither is it "new media" simply to have a text that incorporates text and sound and graphics and animation and photographs or illustrations in some combinatorial ratio other than that of a traditional academic or literary text. I have argued against this definition above because it too much covers over human involvement in the processes of doing things with texts. I am trying to get at a definition that encourages us to stay alert to *how* and *why* we make these combinations of materials, not simply *that* we do it.

- I am not trying with this definition to discount that digitality has mattered in all that we do with texts, for that would be to deny that our textual practices articulate to their material/technological instantiations. I cannot deny that it is easier now with computers than it was with printing presses to compose, produce, and distribute texts using combinations of the alphabet, photographs, video, sound, color, and animations. What is important is that the material particularities of our technologies and our texts take on whatever weight and meanings they do because they exist within the wider and shifting temporal structures in which we act. Our particular technologies do matter, and we do need to attend to new technologies and processes—because these technologies take shape in context of everything else that matters to us. They are in our worlds and they have weight—but we probably ought not give up our own agency by acting as though technologies come out of nowhere and are autonomous in causing effects.

For all those reasons, I hope you are persuaded that it is more useful—and more agency-holding—to think of "new media texts" as texts where we keep their materiality visible, both as we work to make them and as we hold them before us.

OPENING 4

A NEED FOR PRODUCTION
OF NEW MEDIA TEXTS
IN WRITING CLASSROOMS

Several years ago, in an interview concerned with the processes of writing, Stuart Hall discussed how we have conceived identity in an oppositional tension; in talking, Hall developed a position that works the sides of the tension into each other:

> There is one sense of identity as a fixed position, and another idea that identity is relative to the extreme. There is now a third position in the debate because I think those people have moved away from identity as process and have sometimes gone right over to the point where identity is nothing at all; it's a kind of open field where one just sort of occupies a particular identity out of habit. So it is that there is no fixed identity, but it's not that there's just an open-ended horizon where we can just intentionally choose. What that means is that there is no final, finished identity position or self simply then to be produced in the writing. Any cultural practice plays a role in the construction of identity. While it's true that you may have a very clear notion of what the argument is and that you may be constructing that argument very carefully, very deliberately, your identity is also in part becoming through the writing. (qtd. in Drew 173)

For Hall, that is, "we therefore occupy our identities very retrospectively: having produced them, we then know who we are" (qtd. in Drew 173).

It is not that we find our selves in work that we do because there was a unified self that preceded the work and that only needed being made present somehow; it is rather that the work makes visible to us what and where we are at that time: "I think only then" (continues Hall) "do we make an investment [in the produced position], saying, 'Yes, I like that position, I am that sort of person, I'm willing to occupy that position" (qtd. in Drew 173). One could also just as easily say, 'No, I do not like that position… how can I rework it?'— but in either case the position has to be produced before it can be so judged.

And I argue that—because in acknowledging the broad material conditions of writing instruction we then also acknowledge the contingent and necessarily limited structures of writing and writing instruction—people in our classes ought to be **producing** texts using a wide and alertly chosen range of materials—if they are to see their selves as positioned, as building positions in what they produce .

All that I have asserted and argued in the last pages ought to point to this conclusion—but let me add more.

In *Alternative Modernity,* Andrew Feenberg argues that we live within what he calls "system-congruent design," using the automobile as an example:

> The interlocking requirements of cars, urbanism, the petrochemical industry, production and consumption systems, and […] the defense industry, all form a system dictating a specific lifestyle. (229)

All elements of this system have been designed to fit together uniformly—and as a result, for Feenberg, the lives we lead within a culture that values such design are uniform, our day-to-day tasks similar to those of everyone around us as we in the morning (most of us, and to give small examples of the similarity of our lives) leave the homes or apartments where we live with immediate family, warm up our cars to go to work at similar times, listen to the radio or CDs or cassettes on the way, and then later, heading home, buy our food in large markets while our cars sit in the large lots out front; into such a system also fits the unvisually marked 8½" by 11" pages I mention in this writing, whose own design articulates, I suggest, to this "system-congruent design" Feenberg describes. In contrast to "system-congruent design," Feenberg speaks of "expressive design," of "the positioning of technologies at the intersection of multiple standpoints and aspirations" (229–232), and his book includes several examples of technological practices (experimental medicine, videotex in France) forced, by users, to be so flexible: once those who use an object (like a page of text…) understand how the object connects into systems that work counter to their ends, they can then start to work to experiment with and construct other and differing connections. In his earlier book, *Critical Theory of Technology*, Feenberg also discusses how our relations with the objects of technological systems can be made less uniform: he discusses how such objects can be made to seem less sterile to use, less isolating and alienating, if we recognize "the human significance of vocation, the acquisition of craft": with craft,

> the reciprocity of the relation of subject to object is recovered. […] In vocation, the subject is no longer isolated from objects, but is transformed by its own technical relation to them. This relation exceeds passive contemplation or external manipulation and involves the worker as a bodily subject and member of a community in the life of the objects. (189–190)

In addition, there is for Feenberg the importance of "aesthetic investment": "All traditional cultures produce and ornament simultaneously in order to reinsert the object extracted from nature into its new social context" (190). Feenberg argues for this notion of craft—for people to take up the careful, individual, crafted making of objects—in order to work against the standardization of our industrial corporatized world; he sees this kind of making as a way for differing positions to be constructed in contrast to the mass-produced. Such crafting requires one to gain expertise, but—more importantly for me— this notion of craft contains a particular sense of relationships among the maker of an object, the thing made, the users of the object, and the social context in which the object is made. Under Feenberg's conception, when someone makes an object that is both separate from her but that shows how she can use the tools and materials and techniques of her time, then she can see a possible self—a self positioned and working within the wide material conditions of her world, even shaping that world—in that object.

And so I write here that, if we do want to understand compositions as allowing us to see our positions, then it would be useful to think about—and teach—

composition of page and screen as a material craft under the terms I've just described. When we see our writing as objects—objects to be seen, to be physically manipulated—and not, for example, as attempts to get abstract thought present in the most immaterial means possible (as is how I think we have often taught writing), then we can consider the kinds of embodied, temporal positions that we need to be able to see.

The analysis of new media texts is important, necessarily, for it is in analysis that we see the produced positions of others. But the production—crafting—of new media texts is equally important, too, for it is how we produce and can see our own possible positions within the broad and materially different communication channels where we all now move and work with others.

OPENING 5

A NEED FOR STRATEGIES
OF GENEROUS READING

I do not want the instructions on my kitchen fire extinguisher to ask me to stop to think about how the instructions compose me as a rational, modern, gendered, raced, classed, fire-fearing, early 21st century individual. I hope, in fact and of course, never to have to read the instructions (or, rather, never to have to read them as fire nears, since I have read them, in peace, at ease, and critically, and have forgotten them) and I hope that the fire extinguisher is transparently useful without them: in the case of fire, I want to believe that immediate communication is possible, that the designs of this device reveal its function to anyone, me, my partner, or any visiting 10-year-old.

One solution to my concerns, of course, is for my partner and me to practice using the fire extinguisher so that we memorize its functions through bodily action, and then—since a fire extinguisher is allowed but a single use—to replace it. That is, we can acknowledge that new and/or unfamiliar objects always require familiarization and time for learning…

… as will the kinds of new media texts I describe here. Texts that alert us to their materiality go against much that we have been taught: all the writing handbooks on my shelf, for example, instruct students to print their texts on 8½" by 11" paper with one inch margins and a serifed 12 point typeface; none of the handbooks give students reasons for these material presentations but rather just present these instructions as though these material decisions are not and have never been decisions but are natural.

If we are serious about seeing our positions in the texts we make for each other, then we'll need strategies for generous reading, strategies that include but also help us look beyond the naturalized rules and guidelines for how we present selves in print. We already have the strong seeds for this practice, in how ask we people in our classes to describe why they have chosen the strategies they have to position themselves in their writing; we need extend such questioning to productions that include other materials. And we need acknowledge that texts we receive from others can look and function differently from those to which we've become accustomed, and this is where generosity too must enter, so that we approach different-looking texts with the assumption not that mistakes were made but that choices were made and are being tried out and on.

We do not have to become experts in different production technologies to be able to teach this generosity, nor do we have to teach production technologies. What I would hope we teach is an alertness to how different technologies of production—of writing, of photograph, and so on—have the status and position-building weights and possibilities they do because of how they fit within the broad but contingent material practices and structures in which we all live. What I would hope we teach is an alertness to how the various modes available to us can be used in various ratios and combinations to craft and try out positions. What I hope we would teach is a generosity toward the positions that others produce, no matter how awkward-looking or -sounding, and that through our readings we help each other achieve positions that are the most responsibly produced we can.

If we do want something new to come out of new media—if we want to achieve abilities to see and hear voices that we traditionally haven't, and to open composition even more to those whose ways with words and pictures don't look like what we know and expect—then generous approaches to texts that look different, and practice in making texts that look different and that therefore position us differently, seem to me worth exploring.

The exercises on the following pages, like the other exercises following the other chapters in this book, grow out of the above considerations and are meant for you to use as makes sense given with whom and where you work: please try them out if they look useful, and modify them to work for you.

ACTIVITY 1

MATERIALITIES OF SEEING

TEACHER NOTES

GOALS

Because using our eyes is just something we do, seeing can seem a natural thing, unmediated by other practices. It is not. We learn what is worth seeing and what to pay attention to and not, and there is much our eyes do not take in. The purpose of the exercises here is to help us see how seeing is not immediate and depends very much on the larger contexts in which we live; this is a way of becoming alert to the material results of our perceptual practices.

TIME

The activities listed below are fairly short and discrete; they require 15-30 minutes of discussion (after a bit of homework or some other kind of classroom event). These activities can be woven into longer assignments that include readings about sight (see the list of print resources in the back of this book for such readings) and/or the production of research projects on how sight and literacy entwine (for example), but these assignments can also be used as quick and discrete activities to vary a class routine and raise questions that help give broader contexts to the day-to-day work of a writing class.

LEVEL

These various activities work well at all levels because they ask us to consider aspects of seeing and working in the world that we most often don't consider.

EXERCISES

EYE-WITNESSING

This is a quick and usually entertaining—but highly instructive—activity. Arrange ahead of time for someone to interrupt your class in an unexpected way: have someone run in to shout a question ("Where's Kim? Have you seen Kim?") and then run out quickly, or have someone run in and up to a window to shout at someone outside and then just as quickly leave. While this is happening, you as teacher look a little non-plussed, but do not get involved: let the interruption pass and go back to what you were doing before. After 10-15 minutes, ask the class what they saw during the interruption. Ask them to describe what happened, and ask them to describe exactly the people who were involved.

The range of responses will most likely be surprising. When I have done this in class, people will disagree over the gender, age, and race of the interrupters, and over who said what—and can be very insistent on holding to what they saw even though there are such wide differences.

After listing all that everyone saw, ask why there might be such differences. How does what they have observed—that eyewitness accounts can be so different—change their ideas about how they see? About the validity of the eyewitness accounts of others? Why do they think eyewitness accounts—in trials as well as in various kinds of writing—carry the weight they do? (The purpose of this discussion isn't to achieve fixed conclusions about sight but rather to help us understand how sight is not as fixed and easy a sense as we might believe and how, just as with written texts, an audience's responses to the visual aspects of texts cannot be predicted with great certainty.)

THE ATTENTIONS OF A VISUAL WORLD

Ask people in your class to choose a two-hour stretch of a weekend day and to record every visual text they see in that period of time: ask them to write down everything they see that has been designed to catch their eyes and persuade them towards some thought or action (including but certainly not limited to purchasing). (They can do this in their own homes, as they move through the kitchen or bathroom, or they can do this walking across campus or through their town or city; this is not an activity to do while driving.)

When students come back with their written observations, ask them to discuss why they encounter so many things that ask visual attention of them. How do they decide what to be attentive to? What sorts of things draw their attention immediately—and why? What sorts of actions and ways of thinking do they think they learn from this kind of visual environment (for example, do they look carefully at everything they see, or have they learned to make quick judgments about what they see)? How might their actions be different if the visual environment were different (for example, ask them to imagine that magazines or television or Web pages contained no advertising, or that there were simply fewer constructed things to look at)? What changes would they like to make in this visual world to make it easier or smoother or to encourage different kinds of social behaviors?

When I do this activity with a class (as when I do the "Eye-witnessing" activity), I'm not trying to lead the class to definitive conclusions about sight. Instead, I hope this activity helps us see how much visual attentions are called upon in our day-to-day actions, and how the amount of attention asked of us shapes how we see as well as how then we act in the world—and that these conditions could be different.

EXPECTATIONS OF SEEING

For this activity, you need a number of picture postcards. (I have a motley collection that includes old black-and-white photographs of European cities, photographs of old movie stars, photographs of Amish children walking barefoot to school, photographs of Pablo Picasso in his sixties holding up his infant son, and so on. Students who have done this exercise send me postcards when they are on vacation or travels over summer or years later, so that the collection steadily grows.)

Divide the class into groups of 2 or 3, and give each group a postcard—but tell them not to look on the back.

Ask them to tell as much as they can about what is in the photograph on the postcard based just on what they see. When and where do they think the photograph was taken, and what can they say about who or what is in the photograph?

After about 5 minutes, ask them to share their postcards with the whole group and to say what they believe is going on in the photograph. Ask them also to say why they are making the guesses they are about the postcards. (Then they can turn over the postcard to see what information is there—it is often surprising how close they are, but it really doesn't matter, for this activity, whether they are right or wrong.)

After the everyone has shared their comments, and everyone has seen all the postcards, ask them if they are surprised by how much people were willing to say about the postcards, and if they were surprised by how much information there was in the photographs. (People will speculate about when the photographs were taken based on the quality of color or how people are dressed; they will speculate about where based on the kinds of cars or farm implements shown; they will speculate about relations between people based on ages and gender [for example, every student who has been given the Pablo Picasso postcard says that the child shown is a grandchild because Pablo Picasso looks to be in his sixties]; and so on: some people develop fairly elaborate narratives for the photographs, all based on the details of what they see.)

Ask students to take 5 minutes to write, for themselves, what they think is important to remember from this activity: How, for example, will they think about using photographs in the various texts that they are likely to make in the future? How might what they learned in this activity apply in the non-postcard world?

MATERIALITIES OF WRITING

TEACHER NOTES

GOALS

I use the various exercises of this activity because they encourage people to see the technologies we use for writing and how those technologies take part in shaping what we communicate. These exercises can help people to see how the designs of writing technologies not only encourage certain kinds of writing but that they also enfranchise some while disenfranchising others.

TIME

These exercises can be done as in-class work or as homework followed by in-class discussion.

LEVEL

I've used these activities with entering undergraduate students and with graduate students in classes where we are considering writing as a technological and more broadly material practice.

NOTE

These activities can be useful for beginning longer research explorations into the materialities of writing and/or seeing, because they can add concreteness to the explorations: when we see how something we had taken for granted as a simple tool has come to be designed in ways that disenfranchise some or that support only certain kinds of work, we tend to be more alert to how we use—and teach about—it.

EXERCISES

COLORFUL HANDWRITING...

Give students a short (1-2 page) writing assignment—and then ask them to turn in the assignment written in crayon (any color or colors) on any paper.

After they are finished, ask them what was different about the process of writing with crayon as opposed to pen or keyboard. What felt different as they wrote? Did they find themselves thinking differently? Did they come up with ideas they might not have had otherwise, or did they find themselves dropping out ideas because the actual writing was tedious or uncomfortable?

Ask them to look at all the pages made by all the different people in class. What adjectives do they apply to the way the various pages look? That is, do the pages look serious or refined or goofy or childish or unprofessional or creative? What qualities of the pages suggest the adjectives they name? How do they think they learned to have such responses to these texts?

Ask them to imagine a culture that had only crayons as writing implements. How do they think that culture would differ from ours? What do they think that culture would be most proud of, or would consider to be signs of intellectual prowess?

What general observations about writing implements and bodies do they want to venture, based on this? What general observations about writing implements and thinking do they want to venture?

SEEING (A PART OF) THE LITERATE WORLD

For everyone in class to see, hold up a typical print text used in your class: this could be a paper produced by someone in class or a book chapter or a journal article. Ask what someone needs to know in order to *read* the text, and have another person record the list. The list ought to end up longer than anyone expects: in addition to knowing the language the text is written in, and the various conventions of its genre, the list could include knowing what is right-side up for a page, how to turn pages, how not to expect print on the back of a page (in the case of a class paper), or what the page numbers indicate. You can prompt people by asking them to remember lessons on reading in their early years of schooling or to remember a time when they had to ask someone else to explain something they didn't understand about how to use a book. You can also ask them to imagine that they needed to help a visitor from another planet understand how to move through the text.

Then ask what someone needs to know to *produce* such a text. Again, keep a list.

Ask how they learned the things that are on the lists. In what were they given direct instruction? What did they pick up through personal observation? Why do they think their formal education only addressed some of the things they need to know in order to be able to read these texts?

Ask students to estimate how much time they've spent in their lives learning to read the kinds of texts you're discussing. Why do they think they have been encouraged to put so much effort into learning to read and write?

Ask students to imagine that they'd spent as much time learning to draw or to manipulate photographic images. What do they think their attitudes toward drawing or photographs would be? How might our texts be different?

REDESIGNING WRITING "TOOLS"

Divide the class into groups of 2-3, and give each group one of these prompts:

- Redesign the desktop computer as though no one on the Earth had eyes.
- Redesign the desktop computer as though everyone in the world used their eyes and noses and ears in the same way as cats and dogs do… (Choose either cats or dogs as a model.)
- Imagine you wake up one morning and find yourself—and everyone else in the world—with the body of a giant cockroach. Redesign the desktop computer so that everyone can use it with their new bodies.

They should sketch out their re-designs, and prepare to present their responses to others. (Their re-designs do not have to be fancy, but should indicate the most important changes they would make.)

After they present their re-designs to each other, ask students to consider what sight helps us know (things at a distance, for example) as opposed to senses like touch (which require closeness) or smell (which does not give us a sense of sharp boundaries between objects, as sight does). How do they think their relations with other people would be different if sight were not so emphasized in our communications?

The exercise can help them think about just how much computers—including monitors, keyboards, joysticks, and mice—have been designed to emphasize sight instead of other senses, and have been designed to fit individual bodies with hands and arms and backs that work in certain ways. The exercise can also help them think about how our general relations and ways of being with others depend on sight.

(If someone in your class does use adaptive technologies, and is willing to demonstrate them, this can be very striking for others: it is always surprising to realize how much we act as though the designs of our worlds can only be as they are, and how difficult it can be for people who have different kinds of bodies or senses to work within those designs.)

REDESIGNING TEXTS

This exercise can build off the previous exercise.

Ask students if they have ever tried to read the same essay or a book together with someone else, holding the book or journal together. How comfortable was the situation? What did they have to do differently than when they read alone (wait for the other person to finish reading a page before going to the next? push two chairs uncomfortably close together?)?

Ask students to take a paper they'd written earlier, of 3-5 pages (or longer), and (for homework) to reformat it so that it encouraged more than one person at a time to read.

In class, have them show their reformatted texts to each other. What redesign strategies most appeal to them, and why? How do the changes shape how they read and respond to the texts? Are there any formatting strategies that they can see using in other circumstances?

(You can also ask them to reformat texts to make them easier to read aloud. It's useful then to talk to people who present papers regularly at conferences, to see the range of strategies some people use [using larger typefaces, breaking the text up sentence by sentence, bolding the parts they want to be sure to emphasize as they speak, printing "remember to breathe!" in between sections so they will be less nervous, and so on].)

ACTIVITY 3

JUSTIFYING CHOICES

TEACHER NOTES

GOALS

In the course of this activity, students consider the range of rhetorical choices open to them in the materials they use for writing.

TIME

This is a homework activity in which students produce 2 short pieces of writing, followed by class discussion, followed by revision of one of the pieces of writing.

LEVEL

This assignment works equally well for undergraduate and graduate students who are accustomed to approaches to writing that do not ask them to consider the rhetorical potential of the materials/technologies they use. Students with experience in layout will benefit from seeing visual choices they might not have otherwise, and others will start to see the range of elements in writing that are open to visual attention.

NOTE

This assignment necessarily piggy-backs on some other short writing assignment. I use this assignment at the very beginning of courses in which the materials of writing figure in one way or another, courses that involve page layout to some degree, technical communication classes, or classes where theories of textual production come into play; it is also a useful assignment with first-year students, who generally can benefit from seeing that they can take rhetorical control over more aspects of their texts than they have often thought.

ACTIVITY

1 Ask students to do a short but formal piece of writing, i.e., 2-3 pages that need some attention to at least the minimal formatting of putting down their name, the date, and title on pages and choosing margins, etc. This writing can be about anything connected to class.

2 As homework in connection with that writing, ask students to write an analysis of their composition, as described in "Homework" below.

3 In class, ask students to compare their justifications, and to discuss questions like the following: How did they learn to format paragraphs as they did, and why? How did they learn to choose margins, and why? How many of these decisions did they make, and how many did they

leave to the default settings in the word-processing software they used? If they made a decision about formatting (margin sizes, for example, or where to put their names) based on what they were taught in earlier classes, were they given reasons in those classes for what they were taught? Why do they think they were told to place textual elements where they did?

4   After the discussion, ask students to revise (as homework) their first compositions. They needn't change any of their words, but ask them to make as many alert choices about formatting and visual presentation as possible.

5   In small groups in class, ask students to respond to each other's different versions of the writing. How do the changes affect how they perceive the writers? How do the changes affect how they read? What sorts of visual changes seem to encourage the largest changes in how others perceive the texts? Why do they think this is?

You can ask students then to write for 5 minutes, informally, to record what layout and formatting choices they would like to be more open to in texts they compose in the future.

HOMEWORK

Write a justification for the layout and visual presentation of the page (or pages) you are turning in. Why did you choose the typeface(s) you did? Why did you choose the kind and size of paper you did? Why did you use the margins that you did? Why did you put your name where you did? Why did you break paragraphs where you did—and why did you show paragraphs the way you did (that is, if you indented paragraphs or used two returns between them or used a large capital letter in front of each one—why did you make that choice)? Why did you use the color ink you did? Why did you use straight lines of type (if you did), and why are your words in blocks (if they are)? Please list and justify every single decision that is visible in the work you are turning in— whether you made the decision or it was apparently already made for you.

Anne Frances Wysocki

ACTIVITY 4

INTERACTIVITY

SCAVENGER HUNT

TEACHER NOTES

This activity works well toward the beginning of a class in which students will be developing Web pages or other kinds of digital texts in which they have different resources than with print for developing relations with their audiences. But this activity can also be highly useful for a class in which the production of print texts is the focus, for it can help people think about how they might vary the strategies they use in print for engaging their audiences.

GOALS

In the course of this activity, students observe a range of "interactivities" on Web sites in order to consider how different kinds of interactivity encourage different relations among a text's producer, the text, and the text's audience.

TIME

The first part of this activity asks students to look at Web sites for approximately an hour and then to do a short piece of writing, which can be done as homework or in class. Discussion about their work follows.

LEVEL

As with the preceding activities, this activity works equally well with first-year and advanced undergraduate students as well as with graduate students.

ACTIVITY

Make a Web page or print out a listing of a very wide range of Web sites that fit into categories that makes sense for your class: choose educational or health or nonprofit or political sites. The list should include at least 30 Web sites. (Feel free to use the motley listing I have at
<http://www.hu.mtu.edu/~ciwic/nmscavengerhunt/websites.html>.)
Give students the list or point them to the Web site, and ask them (alone or in groups of 2) to:

1   Look widely across the sites listed.

2   Choose 4 different sites from 4 different categories.

3   List everything on those 4 sites that you would consider to be a sample of "interactivity," and why.

After they have made their lists, ask them to work in groups of 2-3 to categorize the interactivities they listed according to the amount of engagement they think the kinds of interactivities ask of audiences.

After they have categorized the interactivities, ask them the kinds of relations with a text that the different interactivities ask of audiences. That is, did

32

some of the interactivities lead them to feel more or less respected by the makers of a text? Did some leave them feeling unengaged, and did some suck them in completely?

Encourage them to try to work out the conditions under which the different interactivities function as they do. That is, do they think that the kind of interactivity they see will function the same in a text about a different topic? What other conditions in a text contribute to how they responded to the interactivity?

Ask them to write for 5 minutes: what kinds of interactivities they saw today, and in what contexts, will help them build the kinds of relations they want with their audiences?

You might also ask them to think about how what they observed today could be applied in print texts that they produce.

ACTIVITY 5

MAPPING READINGS

TEACHER NOTES

This activity asks students to look back over a range of readings they have been doing on some topic and to "map" the concerns of the readings using materials they might not otherwise. When I've asked people to do this, they report that they believe they remember more about the readings as a result of the physical and visual construction they do than when they do such work in print: the objects they build give them structures onto which their memories of the texts can hang.

GOALS

In the course of this activity, students observe how using different materials and structures for "mapping" readings encourage different relations and levels of understanding with the readings.

TIME

This is an exercise for people to do at home, knowing that it can take 6-8 hours.

LEVEL

For this activity to work, it requires students to be reading a range of writers on a set of related topics—so it can work at any level where students are doing such reading.

ACTIVITY

(The steps below are those I used in a particular graduate class on theories of technology; I have kept the steps as they are to give you a concrete sense of how we approached this activity.)

1   Go back over the all the readings from the semester to pull out what you consider to be their key terms, concerns, motivations, and arguments.

Look also for how these writers address the following concerns/terms that have come up repeatedly across the readings and our discussions: human freedom, human ends, art, making/production, the totality/universality/autonomy of technology, desires/motivations/habits/structures of understanding that support technological approaches.

Finally, think also about how each writer addresses the 4 relationships we've been discussing in class, as they originally came out of our first discussions, of Morris and Marx. These are the relationships between:

worker/person and thing made

worker/person and others

worker/person and nature

worker/person and self

2 Using any materials, build a map for yourself in which you lay out the terms, concerns, motivations, and arguments you see adhering to each writer, and find some way of showing how those terms, concerns, motivations, and arguments overlap (or not) with the other writers.

Below are URLs for some graphic/conceptual kinds of maps (and, in one case, I do mean graphic; you'll be able to tell, I think, by the site name) that may give you ideas for starting:

http://www.cybergeography.org/atlas/shedroff_communications_large.gif

http://www.africaaction.org/bp/map.htm

http://mappa.mundi.net/maps/maps_010/johndec_map1.html

http://www.ala.org/alcts/organization/ccs/ccda/resmap.html

http://www.deviantdesires.com/map/mappics/map81002.gif

http://www.cybergeography.org/atlas/nw500_large.gif

http://www.socsci.mcmaster.ca/soc/courses/soc2r3/conmap1.htm

http://www.engin.umd.umich.edu/~charu/Theoretical/sld063.htm

http://www.thresholdofvisibility.com/Text/tovsitemap.html

http://ariel.adgrp.com/~ghb/talks/951016_BBN/map.html

As you are figuring out your map, figure out how to work yourself and your concerns into it. Any way you do this is fine, but just figure out how to show in your map your location or locations in the discussion. (You could do this most simply by drawing up a list of your concerns/key terms/motivations and appending it to what you make.)

3 Bring your map to class, and come also with at least 3 questions that come up for you as you make your map. These can be questions asking for clarification of a reading, or about matters that arise for you as you compare one writer's definition of technology with another's, or about how agency is shaped among these writers, or about how one could take on a Heideggerian perspective toward nature but still not end up with an atom bomb revealing itself… In class next week your questions will form the basis of our discussion.

Anne Frances Wysocki

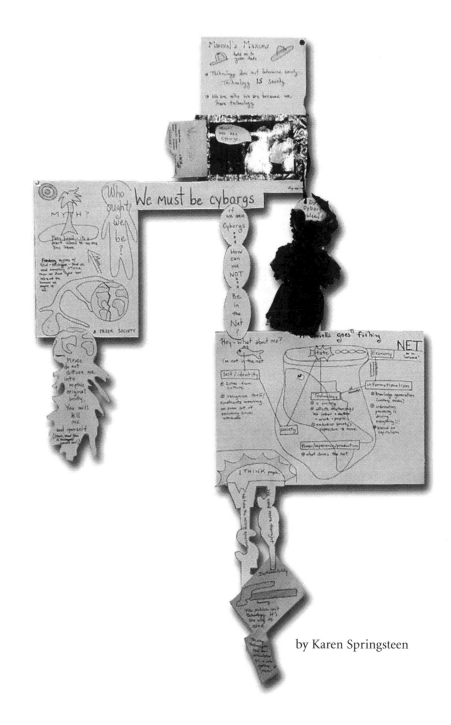

by Karen Springsteen

by Tom Henry

Anne Frances Wysocki

VISUAL ARGUMENTS

TEACHER NOTES

This activity is for a class that is either already considering "argument" as a form in print or that is considering the possibilities of visual texts.

GOALS

In the course of this activity, students:

- build visual arguments.
- consider how visual arguments differ from print-based arguments.

TIME

This activity has an initial homework assignment that should be given a week before the assignment is due, followed by in-class discussion, a reading (as homework), further in-class discussion, and finally, a revision of the original homework assignment (also discussed in class).

LEVEL

This assignment is useful in any level of class that is considering argument and/or visual texts—but be sure that the reading is at a level for which the class is ready.

ACTIVITY

1 Ask students to build, as homework, a visual argument.

Tell them that there are not (yet?) fixed definitions of what constitutes a "visual argument," so that they will have to work with what they understand "argument" and "the visual" to be—but also tell them that the visual argument they build has to stand on its own: others in class are going to respond to their arguments without an argument's composer being able to answer questions or explain.

If you are teaching a class on argument, students will have a working definition of "argument"; if they do not have such a working definition, ask them to write informally for a few minutes to define for themselves what they consider "argument" to be.

You can give them a topic around which to build their arguments if class work and discussion leads obviously to such topics. Or you can ask them to write in response to the following prompts to help them develop ideas for their arguments:

Brainstorming a visual argument

1 What are 3 (or more) concerns you have— political/economic/personal/cultural/educational/any other adjective—now?

2   List any visual images that come to mind when you look at what
    you listed in #1...

3   Which images from #2 seem most compelling to you? why?

4   What colors do you associate with what you listed in #1?

4a Why (do you think) do you associate the colors you listed in #4
    with what you listed in #1?

5   What associations might other people make with the images you've
    listed in #2?

5a What might you do with the images you listed in #2 to help other
    people make similar associations as you do? (and what sort of
    people do you want to understand your associations, anyway? that
    is, who is your audience for this imagery?)

So that they do not spend too much time constructing their
arguments—because the point is for them simply to get something
made to start discussion—you might want to limit what they build to
the size of a piece of posterboard or a single-computer screen,
depending on the media to which they have easy access. Tell them to
construct arguments that fit on a single screen or page—arguments
that use no words, only photographs or drawings.

The audiences for these arguments is the class.

2   When students bring their visual arguments to class, have them arrange
    them around the room, and put a sheet of paper (with their names at
    the top) next to what they have built.

    For approximately 30-45 minutes, ask the students to move around the
    room, looking at the visual arguments. On the sheets of paper next to
    the arguments, they should write down what they think the argument
    of the piece is, and why.

    After everyone has looked and responded, ask each person to read the
    responses to her argument, and to write her own observations, based
    on these questions: What did most people interpret the argument to
    be? What aspects of the presentation stood out most for people, and
    how did that shape how they interpreted the argument? What
    expectations did people bring to their looking, expectations that
    helped shape how they responded?

    If there is time, ask students to pair up and compare the responses they
    received. Do they see any general patterns in the expectations?

3   For homework, ask students to read the following article, which you
    will have to make available to them through the reserve systems
    available to you:

    Blair, J. Anthony. "The Possibility and Actuality of Visual
    Arguments." *Argumentation and Advocacy* 33 (Summer 1996): 23-
    39.

In this article, Blair defines "argument" formally and in a way very much dependent on the conventions of print. Because of how he defines "argument," Blair says that he is unable to find any instances of visual argument within a range of examples he examines, although he does not rule out that visual arguments might exist.

Ask them to bring their visual arguments, as well as the written responses they received about their arguments, to the class in which you discuss the article.

4   After they have read the article, use whatever strategies you usually do to help the class come to a general consensus over the arguments of the reading, and then encourage discussion around the following questions (and ask them to use their visual arguments as examples to support their responses, when appropriate):

- Does the class think Blair's definition of "argument" is the only possible definition?

- If they think that some of his examples are or do contain arguments, how does Blair's definition of argument have to be modified so as to include these examples?

- Does Blair's definition preclude the possibility of visual argument? (That is, *can* a visual argument have premises?)

- What might a visual premise look like? Are premises only possible when a text builds over time? Would a visual argument then necessarily have to have multiple screens or pages?

5   Ask students to write informally. Are they persuaded by Blair's arguments, such that visual arguments need to take the form of argument as Blair defines it, or do they think that other forms of argument are possible, such that there can be different kinds of visual argument?

6   Tell students that for homework they are to revise the visual arguments they made. They can revise their arguments to try to make them fit into the form of argument Blair defines, or they can revise them to fit other definitions that have developed in class.

Ask them to write for just a few minutes, informally: first, they should state their intended argument, and then they should write about any changes in the visual argument that might help them better achieve their ends, based on their responses to Blair's article.

7   Ask them to work in pairs: have each member of the pair describe what she intends to argue; then the pair should look at the feedback each received from classmates and discuss revisions that would help make the intended argument as visible and persuasive as possible.

8   When students bring their revised arguments to class, repeat step 2 for feedback.

After all feedback has been given, ask students to write individually in response to the feedback. What had they hoped others would understand about their arguments? How much success did they have in conveying their positions? What would they change, were they to revise again?

Then: Do they think visual arguments are possible? Why or why not? Do they think our notions of argument and persuasion need to be shifted or changed when we shift to considering non-alphabetic texts?

STUDENTS WHO TEACH US

A Case Study of A New Media Text Designer

Cynthia L. Selfe

Why have increasing numbers of English composition teachers turned their attention to new media texts in recent years? What is it about these texts—and the literacies associated with their creation and exchange—that keep us paying attention to them? And what is it that prevents many of us from using them systematically in the composition classroom?

In using the term "new media texts," I mean to refer to texts created primarily in digital environments, composed in multiple media (e.g., film, video, audio, among others), and designed for presentation and exchange in digital venues. These texts generally place a heavy emphasis on visual elements (both still and moving photography, images, graphics, drawings, renderings, animations) and sound, and they often involve some level of interactivity. Although such texts often include some alphabetic features, they also typically resist containment by alphabetic systems, demanding the multiple literacies of seeing and listening and manipulating, as well as those of writing and reading. Because new media texts often resist conventions of traditional fiction or nonfiction genres, they may appear unfamiliar to those of us raised on print texts and invested in the cultural systems of print literacy. Typical of such texts— especially those that locate themselves in the general area of experimental communicative arts—is an exploratory focus on aesthetics, design, and innovative visual presentation that spans prose/poem/performance (e.g., "The most painful distance in the world" at the *eneriwoman* site <http://www.eneri.net/>; "The Modern Era" featured in the experimental section of the online magazine *Artistica* <http://www.artistica.org/> or the texts in the Exploratives section of *Netdiver* <http://www.netdiver.net>).

1 Teachers of English composition are becoming increasingly interested in such texts, in part, because they see more of them given the growing presence of information technologies in so many areas of our live. We now encounter new media texts in online magazines and salons; in educational Web sites and home gaming contexts; on multimedia CDs and in online museums. And the topics of such texts also appeal to increasing numbers of teachers: new media texts now exist on William Blake, the Salem Witch trials, hip hop, the architectural history of Rome, women's suffrage, WWI, and the Harlem Renaissance, among many other topics. Our personal and professional interest in these texts may also be increasing because they have physical/material/aesthetic characteristics that people find appealing: they are often richly textured with combinations of visual elements, sound, and words; they are interactive and often hypertextual, and they can be aesthetically pleasing in ways that other texts are not.

2 It is also true, in a practical sense, that our interest in new media texts is increasing because more teachers of English composition now have access to the means of both viewing/reading/interacting with such texts and composing/designing/authoring them. (I will use combinations of these terms throughout this chapter to refer to both the consumption and production of new media texts.) Many schools—and even some home libraries—now include software that allows for multimedia authoring; digital photography and photographic manipulation; sound capture and digital sound manipulation; rendering of landscapes, objects, and human forms; painting and drawing, animation, movie production and editing; word processing, graphic design, and so on.

3 But perhaps more than any other reason, teachers of composition may be paying increased attention to new media texts because students are doing so—and their enthusiasm about reading/viewing/interacting with and composing/designing/authoring such imaginative texts percolates through the substrata of composition classrooms, in direct contrast to students' *laissez faire* attitudes toward more conventional texts. And given all of these converging factors, teachers can't help but notice new media texts—and worry about how or if such texts should be assuming a more prominent place in composition classrooms.

This chapter argues that we should be doing so, that teachers of composition should not only be interested in new media texts but should be using them systematically in their classrooms to teach about new literacies. This argument begins with a story about a student, David Damon. David is one of those smart, talented, and insightful individuals who, every once in a while, manages to help teachers glimpse the importance of different literacy values and practices—in this particular case, those literacies associated with new media texts. David's case, I believe, can help us understand how such texts are changing our understanding of what it means to be literate in the twenty-first century and help us understand our own role in relation to change.

At the end of this narrative, I try to articulate some of the lessons it suggests to me about the changing nature of literacy and about what this means for composition pedagogy. The last section of the chapter presents some activities for teachers who recognize the increasingly important role that emerging literacy values and new media practices have assumed in our culture at the beginning of the 21st century, but who may currently lack—as I do—the skills or the background training to address a full range of new media texts. **I believe in starting slowly, but starting nonetheless.**

Readers should know, up front, that I do not claim to have provided a full—or even a satisfactory—rendering of David's life, his talents, his concerns, his literacy in the following pages. My own position as a white, female academic; as one of David's former teachers, and as middle class and middle American precludes such an accomplishment. My goal is much smaller and more personal—I want to tell other teachers what I think David taught me about literacy and about the composition of new media texts.

DAVID JOHN DAMON [1]

David John Damon's story begins on December 15th, 1978, when he was born in a Detroit hospital—just about the time the first fully-assembled microcomputers went into commercial production in the United States. David was Black, and in Detroit, in the United States of America, in 1978, in stories about literacy, this matters.

In an interview conducted in the Spring of 2000, David reported his religious denomination as "reality" and his family's economic status as "broke." David never knew his father. His mother, a high school graduate, moved the family to Florida when David was two and began classes in what David called "beauty school" before she succumbed to a drug habit that eventually scattered the family. As David said, his mother

> couldn't care for me as she should have at first, uh, when I lived in Florida, I moved with my neighbors and they were OK people but they were order people and then I moved back with my mom then I moved with some lady, I haven't the slightest idea what the lady's name is and she was a nice person. Then I was able to move back with my mom and then we moved back to Michigan and I bounced from house to house since.

But Detroit, Michigan proved no better for the family than Florida, and David's life for the next few years was turbulent:

> Now between nine and ten, I moved from Detroit to Toledo, back to Detroit, back to Toledo, then back to Detroit. I stayed in Detroit from that point on until I was eleven, uh, got incarcerated, by, when I was 13... no, 12... moved to California. I had moved to California once before to but I can't remember the exact dates of that.

[1] This case is part of a larger study on digital literacy in the United States. This study has been generously supported by the National Council of Teachers of English; the Society for Technical Communication; the University of Illinois, Urbana–Champaign; Michigan Technological University; and Clemson University. Part of this chapter appears in *Literate Lives in the Information Age: Stories from the United States*, eds. Cynthia L. Selfe and Gail Hawisher, Lawrence Erlbaum, forthcoming.

[…] I moved back to Michigan three weeks before my mom passed, then my mom passed, then me and my sister's situation got rocky and they put me in a foster home… So I stayed there until I graduated high school.

Despite his ongoing family troubles, however, David enjoyed school and often found himself motivated best by individual teachers whom he remembered as upholding high standards. In elementary school, for instance, David recalled,

Uh, I started [to read] when… I was living in Pensacola, Florida… I still believe that their school systems are beyond the Michigan school systems… I had a teacher… she was a second-grade teacher that was turned into a kindergarten teacher… And at first, I thought, "Why is she teaching kindergarten?" But she had us so excelled, I mean we got computers in our classroom, uh, I learned to count to 100 within like the first week.

I didn't read too much before school, but, I mean, we were in our class and it was like everybody is dying to catch up and then probably about, uh, midway through that year it was, everybody was just excited to go to school. I've never seen that many people, I mean my whole class was just happy to be there.

David was also influenced by his mother's habit of reading. As he remembered,

there was never a lack of… books at the house… , she was a novel reader, that's all she read was novels… stuff like what John Grisham writes now. Uh, she wasn't too much into the romance novels nor mystery. […S]he just read all the time… Her and my sister are just alike. […I]f they get engrossed in a book then they'll sit there and they will read it all day and I can't do that…

[I]t was a habit. My whole family has picked up on it. I don't know if it started with my great-grandmother, my grandmother, but my whole family does it, my brothers will sit up and he'll read all day… I'm in college now… but, uh, I used to, uh, when I did learn how to read, *Encyclopedia Brown*, oh, I sat there and read *Encyclopedia Brown* all day. […]

I lived on Barcelona Street in Pensacola and about four or five blocks down was the library… Uh, I'd read them at the library, grab and bring them home. It didn't matter. I have them in school, on the bus on the way home since it takes me about a half hour to get to where I stay, so wherever I can read, I was there.

His love of language, David recollected, was also connected directly to a growing interest in music,

since I was about probably seven or eight, I was not necessarily dealing with music but just picking up on words that people are using in music and I started trying to use [them] myself and more and more I just started, uh, getting into the English thing. I was like, well, I know all these big words and you see that I know it so I just want to use them in sentences and use them in paragraphs and my papers are coming out great. I'm like, oh, it fits. I'd come out of class and I'd be struggling and I was like, why do I have to take all the English for? And… I guess that was the main attraction.

By high school, however, his unsettled family life had taken its toll on David's school performance:

I had a 1.5 [grade point average] when I started high school... um, my cousin told me, well my cousin and his friends, since we all lived in the neighborhood in the projects, they said, "Well if you don't have a 3.0, you can't hang around us." And, they had all the ladies with them, so, I decided to pick it up and I said, "OK, well, OK." I got a 3.0, then it became addictive. [...U]h, I don't think Detroit public schools actually prepare you for college. I'm a strong believer in that.

I was like, "Why go to school? It ain't no fun!" But, they started showing me things about school, why not go to school? It's boring if you ain't in school all day and when you are there, I mean, you've got your friends there, you crack jokes, and they were showing me things where you can crack jokes in class, but as long as you are getting your work done, you are pretty much doing OK.

Although David first encountered computers in elementary school, he remembered using them only to play games when the regular work of the class was done. And in junior high school and high school, while computers were present, they were not central in his life, nor were they integrated into the curriculum of his school or the work of his classes:

Uh, from where I'm from, computers was not the big thing... Uh, no computer at home, uh, actually nobody I knew in the neighborhood had one.

After I came back from California [in ninth grade], uh, I had a business course and I had to write a ten-page paper so I don't like using typewriters so I had to sit, so I sat in there and, uh, did the majority of the stuff in the library on the computer. [...]

[In high school], uh, I had, I had one of the hardest teachers they thought they had for English, so I had her and, she was hard enough so I wasn't, uh, too knowledgeable about the computers or what not [...S]o I would just go [to the library] to use the computers... they did have them, my last year there... Uh, I got to use them once or something like that but I wasn't even sure what I was exactly using them for.

During his last year of high school, however, David took a computer literacy course, and, after that experience, he began to see technology in a different light:

Late in high school, uh, it was like, wow, computers are cool and that's where all the money is going to be so I want to do it... Uh, my counselor, she had a list on her, uh, her door of the, like, the top-paying jobs... I was like, "Wow, you know, computers, all the stuff with the computers is up at the top of the list!" Now that I've went back, I look on the back of the door [and say], "Yeah, that's one of the most stressful jobs in the world, too, ain't it?"

But it was an athletic scholarship, ultimately, and not his late-blooming interest in technology, that got David into college. After several false starts in Computer Engineering and Computer Science courses, which he didn't like because they contained too much math or programming, he settled on a course of study in Scientific and Technical Communication—not particularly because that major involved the use of computers. Rather, he chose the program because of its emphasis on communication skills and language play, which he saw as feeding into his love of rap music. David described his fascination with rap in the following terms:

> And, uh, listening to… some of the words… the word play and where it was placed and, uh, using, um, basically using things that normal people might not catch. Yeah, it was like, it is always an underlying meaning. Underlying meaning to, uh, everything… And I was like, "I like that!" So, it was like, OK, I need to stay… here so I can learn how to do that.

In 1999, after joining a Black fraternity on campus, David began spending more time on the Internet and, later, developed a strong interest in Web design.

> Uh, I learned a little bit about them [the fraternity] through the Internet first, but I already knew a little bit, but they are just the reason why I use the Internet so much because I just create everything for them. I just like to put out information and… I created a Chi Alpha Phi's [Web site], well, we are Omega Chi Beta Chapter as of Valentine's Day and, um, I created the Web site for this chapter. I've also created the Web site for the Society of African-American men on this campus.

> Um, I'm starting a Web site for Phi Beta Sigma Fraternity, Incorporated which I am not a part of, uh, on this campus, but a couple of my friends are, and they asked me if I would do it since one of their members isn't here to do it.

> Um, I'm also, uh, the Webmaster for the Kappa Alpha Fraternity, Incorporated alumni chapter near Detroit.

Like most students, David learned his Web design skills on his own, copying code from other Webpages and experimenting with it, altering it and studying how it was composed. These activities, which many students use to learn html coding, might be mistaken by many teachers for plagiarism.

> I was like, oh, this looks cools. I want to do this. And somebody told us [the fraternity] we had a Web site. I didn't know everyone actually had a Web site. So after I found out […they] had a Web site, it was like, well, so how do I create one like these?

> And someone told me that they couldn't teach me how to do it but they suggested that I take, I just steal someone's code, plant it into my page, and go back and just mess with stuff. And the more stuff that you mess with certain things will change and you go, "OK, I think I want to put that back" or "I think I want to delete this," or something like that. So that's, that's how I started with the Web, with the whole Web site there.

By March of 2000, David had taken courses in computer applications and Web design, and was planning to take two courses in multimedia. He had begun to communicate so much and so consistently through email that he turned off his telephone to save money and learned how to telnet so he could check his mail from remote sites.

At the time we had our interview in the Spring term of 2000, David was confident in using several word-processing packages like Microsoft Word to compose documents; WebChat to speak with others synchronously on the World Wide Web; Poser, Bryce, and Photoshop to create various kinds of representations; and HTML, Java, and Shockwave to design Web documents. Most recently, he reported downloading and learning Flash. He was now getting paid for his Web work by the some of the Black fraternities and social organizations he served.

Despite these accomplishments, however, the year was not going well for David. Although his computer skills had improved by leaps and bounds, his skills in communicating in Standard English remained seriously underdeveloped—and his teachers in the English Department were very concerned about his ability to organize and write formal essays, his inattention to standard spelling, his inability to write sentences that were grammatically correct according to conventional standards, and his problems with development and logical argumentation.

As David continued devoting the majority of his days to online design work, spending weekends travelling to consult with his Web design fraternity clients, and writing and producing homemade rap CDs on departmental computers, he failed two of his more conventional communication classes—a move that dropped his GPA below the level allowed by the university. By the end of the year, he had failed out of the university—primarily because he couldn't produce a traditional essay organized according to the print-based literacy standards of linear propositional logic, Standard English, argumentative development, and standard spelling.

SOME LESSONS ABOUT LITERACY

David's story has a number of lessons to teach us, I believe, about inequitable patterns of literacy education in this country, and it has inspired me to write elsewhere about the intersections of race and class as these factors interact in powerful ways with the acquisition and development of electronic—or technological—literacies (Selfe and Hawisher).

Given the focus of this chapter, however, I would like to pay some specific attention to the lessons that David's case can help us learn about new media texts and the emerging forms of literacy evidenced in these texts.

LESSON 1

New forms of literacy don't simply accumulate. Rather, they have life spans. In different social contexts—different portions of the larger cultural ecology[2]—they emerge, accumulate, and sometimes compete with pre-existing forms of literacy... and they also sometimes fade or disappear. We need to understand the effects that such contested landscapes have on students working in specific English composition programs.

---

[2] By cultural ecology, I mean the "existing stock of social forces and ideas;" the current set of historic, political, and economic formations; and the communication environments that comprise a culture (Deibert, 31). These formations operate in many ways and at many levels—at the macro level of national and cultural trends, at the medial level of institutional and regional effects, and at the micro level of group and individual influences. I owe thanks for various parts of this term to the work of Marilyn Cooper; Ronald Deibert; and Bertram Bruce and Maureen Hogan.

David's story, I think—especially when it is viewed in the context of work done by contemporary scholars of literacy (Street; Gee; Graff; Brandt, "Sponsors" and "Literacy Learning")—reminds us that we can understand literacy as a set of practices and values only when we properly situate these elements in a particular historical period, cultural milieu, and or cluster of material conditions. Brandt ("Literacy Learning"), for instance, has noted that literacies—with the invention of computer-based communication technologies—have accumulated toward the end of the 20th century. Proliferating computer-based literacies, she added, have imparted a "complex flavor even to elementary acts of reading and writing [...] creating new and hybrid forms of literacy where once there might have been fewer and more circumscribed forms." This "rapid proliferation and diversification of literacy," Brandt continued, placed increasing pressure on individuals, whose ultimate success may be "best measured by a person's capacity to amalgamate new reading and writing practices in response to rapid social change" (651).

In such a context, David's intellectual curiosity, his skill at adapting to new situations, his unusual ability to self-sponsor and self-direct his own learning efforts, his love of language and communication, and his insight about the growing importance of new forms of communication functioned to his advantage as he taught himself new literacies—Web site composition, graphic design, animation, the use of sound—within the electronic environments he encountered in college. But, his story also suggests the contested nature of the literacy landscape David inhabited.

Literacies accumulate rapidly when a culture is undergoing a particularly dramatic or radical transition. And during such periods of rapid change, individuals are often expected to learn, value, and practice both past and present forms of literacy simultaneously and in different spheres of their lives.

David's case, I believe, highlights the contested nature of the literacy landscape he inhabited at the time he attended college. In 1999, David's literacy practices involved using several word-processing packages; several email and page layout programs; spreadsheet and database packages; rendering and animation software; the departmental and university networks and the World Wide Web; photomanipulation packages; Java, Shockwave, and Flash; and telnet. And I have probably missed a few. By 2000, David was doing many of his class projects, much of his peer-group communication, and much of his political networking online. And he had begun to earn money as a Web-design consultant, a creator of new media texts.

Clearly, there was a robust fit between David's newly acquired digital literacies—and the emerging literacy practices he acquired on a continuing basis as electronic communication systems underwent rapid change at the end of the 20th century. The formulation of online interest groups; America's dependence on electronic information services; the investment of David's educational institution in computer technology; and, at a larger level, the increasing influence of globalization and transnational finances-all of these factors and many, many more contributed to creating a milieu in which David's technological literacy practices were valued.

But the cultural ecology that David inhabited was not uniform in its predisposition to digital literacies. Although the institution David attended, for instance, valued computer-based literacies at some level and in some classes,[2] it also continued to value—especially in English classes and in most official assessments of communication ability—conventional, print literacy. Print literacy had, after all, been the major shaping force in the educational experiences of faculty members at David's school, and, thus, in the ongoing formulation of their official grading and evaluation standards. And the context of print literacy had also affected the hiring decisions of the university (especially in connection with tenure and promotion issues) and of the employers who hired its graduates (and expected them to be able to meet minimal standards of conventional print literacy). The culture of print literacy also shaped the expectations of many parents who enrolled children at the university, the degree requirements of the institution, and the historically defined literacy ideals of the larger society in which it existed and was expected to thrive.

This contested situation, in which print and computer-based literacies competed at many levels, may account for part of the reason that the English composition teachers who worked with David—raised and educated in a print culture, unsure of how to value and address new media literacies—failed to take advantage of, build on, and even to recognize, in some cases, the literacy strengths he did bring to the classroom and, therefore, missed important opportunities to link their instruction goals to his developing strengths.

LESSON 2

In a postmodern world, new media literacies may play an important role in identity formation, the exercise of power, and the negotiation of new social codes.

David's case can also help us understand that there may be a larger function new media texts serve for individuals composing in online environments.

Manuel Castells notes that the condition of postmodernism—the disturbing disappearance of familiar anchoring institutions such as nation states, the dizzying global expansion and rapid multiplication of micropolitical entities, the explosive growth of alienating forces like global crime and terrorism, the undermining of authoritative systems that insist on a

---

[2] David's institution prided itself on being a technological university with a heavy emphasis on engineering and sciences. Students are given ready access to computers, computer networks, and software; and they are expected to learn and be able to use such resources in most of their classes.

single version of Truth—has resulted, at least in part, from the rise of computer networks and the formulation of a networked society. The postmodern world in which this network plays such a part—as scholars like Baudrillard, Castells, and Jameson suggest—can be characterized by dramatic and significant changes in the ways that people understand the world, make meaning with language, and use language to form individual and group identities.

These transformations have taken place at multiple levels within an overdetermined system. Both Deibert and Castells, for instance, explain how the new electronic communication networks are linked to significant changes in how people learn about the world and learn about the many truths that matter to other humans on a global scale. High-speed global communication networks, for example, have been directly linked to the spread of multinational capitalism, and, thus, to the establishment of multiple and overlapping transnational authorities for economic and political affairs instead of the traditional sovereignty accorded to nation states. Such transnational patterns, in turn, supplant or undermine state-controlled economic regulatory systems and systems of political allegiance by establishing multiple and overlapping global authorities for economic and political affairs, as well as—importantly, for this chapter—by extending people's understanding of political, economic, and social roles beyond the physical borders of their home countries. As Marilyn Cooper explains,

> Postmodernism is, above all, a response to our increased awareness of the great diversity in human cultures, a diversity that calls into question the possibility of any "universal" or "privileged" perspective and that thus values the juxtaposition of different perspectives and different voices and the contemplation of connections rather than a subordinated structure of ideas that achieves a unified voice and a conclusive perspective. (142)

The rise of global information networks, Castells notes (I), has also been linked to additional changes attributed to postmodern society. Among these, for example, is the rise of global criminal and terrorist organizations that use networks not only to exchange information about the strategic movement of law enforcement troops and the best ways to construct home-made bombs, but also to share self-published hate manuals and to distribute news of their successful terrorist activities. Castells also links the rise of the networked society to the increased activities of fundamental religious and political systems. These groups construct increasingly defensive and communal identities to reinforce the boundaries of their belief systems when faced with the "destructuring" of familiar social organizations and "delegitimization of institutions" that has come to characterize increasingly globalization in a postmodern era (I: 3). The changing networked society and the process of globalization that characterizes it have also been linked to a complex process of economic polarization and the expansion of both poverty and "extreme poverty" (III: 133) that threaten to marginalize "whole countries and peoples" from information networks (I: cover) and mire them in a continuing cycle of misery, poverty, and crime.

What does this all have to do with new media literacy practices and composition instruction?

When power is "diffused in global networks of power, information, and images," disassociated with conventional centralized authorities like geographically determined nation states, social roles, political alliances, traditional systems of authoritative values, individuals may feel alienated, fragmented, confronted with a disturbing loss of traditional authorities or conventional certainties. But even as individuals and groups are confronted by such unstable and contradictory postmodern contexts, as Castells (II) points out, they are also coping strategically with them as social and political agents. Further, and paradoxically, this activity is happening, both within and in resistance to the very computer networks that contributed to the unstable conditions in the first place, primarily through a new kind of identity politics anchored around the powerful connections of race, gender, history, and common interests. The political identities formed around these nexus points are expressed through and within peoples' literacy practices in online exchanges and environments—and, I would argue, in various forms of new media texts.

As people exchange ideas and form interest groups and coalitions online, Castells adds, they are also involved in contesting, negotiating, and re-writing the new "social codes" under which "societies may be re-thought, and re-established" (II: 360). As Castells explains,

> This is why identities are so important, and ultimately, so powerful in this ever changing power structure—because they build interests, values, and projects, around experience, and refuse to dissolve by establishing a specific connection between nature, history, geography, and culture. (II: 360)

In the contested space of the networked society, Castells notes, "Identities anchor power" (II: 360).

And so we can learn another lesson from David's case. Although he attends a university that is more than 95% white and characterized by a solidly conservative political cast, he has established an active online identity—through his new media literacy practices—that links him to other Blacks who have created their own micropolitical organizations. These organizations—these social projects built around identity politics—are also represented and function partially online; are devoted to the support and success of their members; and are anchored, at least in part, in a system of racial identity and shared social values and codes.

And it is also true that David—at least in part because of his online identity and through his composition of new media texts—has voted on his literacy allegiances. David does not subscribe—at least in the same way that his teachers do—to the print literacy values and practices that many faculty at his university still hold up as standards; he has found them, frankly, of limited relevance in his life, in his attempts to get an education and to enter a sphere of economic success and personal fulfillment.

He has, in fact, resisted these standards or renegotiated their importance in his life. And, in doing so, he has reappropriated, at least in part, the currency of the academy—not to mention the material realities of a multi-million dollar university computing system—and applied this currency to his own project of identity politics composed, in part, through new media texts. And, I suspect that if forced to choose between the traditional authority associated with a college degree—based on the standards of and allegiance to print literacy—and an opportunity to make a living as a Web designer specializing in representing Black clients through new media texts, there would be little to sway him toward the degree.

LESSON 3

To make it possible for students to practice, value, and understand a full range of literacies—emerging, competing, and fading—English composition teachers have got to be willing to expand their own understanding of composing beyond conventional bounds of the alphabetic. And we have to do so quickly or risk having composition studies become increasingly irrelevant.

David's story suggests something about our own responsibilities toward competing literacies—especially at a time when the cultural ecology of literacy—and literacy forms themselves are changing so rapidly.

The rapid rise of computer networks and the linking of institutions, groups, and individuals through communication technologies over the last two decades has changed not only political and social structures that characterize our world, but also the ways in which people understand this world, make meaning, and formulate their own individual and group identities.

Transnational mass media and computer networks, for instance, have made it possible to send texts easily and quickly—across national borders, time zones, language groups, and geographic distances. Increasingly sophisticated computer software and hardware, in addition, have made it possible for authors/designers to employ video, audio, graphics, animation, and alphabetic elements to compose the texts they exchange.

The new media texts that grow out of these contexts differ so radically from those with which we are familiar, Gunther Kress notes, that a conventional "emphasis on language alone simply will no longer do" ("'English'," 67) for teaching about composing and designing texts:

> The focus on language alone has meant a neglect, an overlooking, even suppression of the potentials of representational and communicational modes in particular cultures; an often repressive and always systematic neglect of human potentials in many of these areas; and a neglect equally, as a consequence, of the development of theoretical understandings of such modes. Semiotic modes have different potentials, so that they afford different kinds of possibilities of human

expression and engagement with the world, and through this differential engagement with the world, make possible differential possibilities of development: bodily, cognitively, affectively. Or, to put it provocatively: the single, exclusive and intensive focus on written language has dampened the full development of all kinds of human potentials, through all the sensorial possibilities of human bodies, in all kinds of respects, cognitively and affectively, in two and three dimensional representation. (85)

This same case is made a slightly different way by The New London Group—a collection of scholars committed to an expanded understanding of literacy. These scholars note that the "realities of increasing local diversity and global connectedness" (64)—generated at least in part by the expansion of computer networks across traditional geo-political boundaries— have changed not only forms of communication that humans employ as part of their daily lived experiences, but also the nature of the workplaces they inhabit and the responsibilities they encounter as citizens.

These changes, members of The New London Group point out, necessitate the use of "new and emerging discourses"—including those associated with visual images, multimedia, and graphic design—that allow for "adaptation to constant change [...], innovation and creativity, technical and systems thinking, and learning how to learn" (67) and that allow individuals to design and redesign communications that work across traditional language barriers and national borders, that resist the limitations of one symbolic system and its attendant conventions. If educators hope to prepare citizens who can "participate fully" in new forms of "public, community, and economic life"—in other words—we must teach them to design communications using "modes of representation much broader than language alone" (64).

And so David's story also suggests that if we continue to define literacy in ways that ignore or exclude new media texts, we not only abdicate a professional responsibility to describe accurately and robustly how humans communicate, and how they compose and read in contemporary contexts, but we also run the risk of our curriculum holding declining relevance for students. Evidence of this fact is clear if we examine the increasing importance—for many citizens in our country and around the world—of being able to access and act on information presented online in new media texts as well as to produce such texts themselves (Gruber and Csomay; Romano, Field, and De Huergo; Kitalong and Kitalong; Hawisher and Sullivan).

Operating successfully in these contexts requires multimodal approaches to communication—the ability to create meaning both in alphabetic and in visual modes, and combinations of the two. Such multimodal skills—as The New London Group suggests—are now at a premium in not only in the globally situated software and hardware industries, but also in an increasing wide range of social, economic, and educational contexts as well.

If, however, English composition teachers recognize the insufficiency of maintaining a single-minded focus on conventional alphabetic texts—which generally comprise the officially sanctioned literacy in our contemporary society—and, indeed, have an increasing level of interest in such texts as they encounter them in their personal and professional lives, they do not necessarily know how to design a meaningful course of study for composition classrooms that accommodates a full range of literacies, especially those literacies associated with new media texts. Hence, few composition programs around the country have integrated systematic attention to—and instruction in the composition of—new media texts in their curricula at all levels of study. Those programs that have begun to recognize the importance of such texts often deal with the problems we have identified in this chapter by offering one or two courses focused on new media texts. Such courses, however, are frequently taught by new media experts on whom the rest of the composition faculty—unsure about their own expertise or responsibilities to new media—confer the departmental responsibility of dealing with emerging literacies.

And therein lies a major challenge for our profession, as well as the motivating purpose for this book.

WHERE DO WE GO FROM HERE?

SOME SPECIFIC STRATEGIES AND ACTIVITIES

The lessons suggested by David's case indicate that we need to integrate new media literacies, as well as alphabetic literacy, into a full range of composition classes if we want to do a responsible job of preparing students for the world they face outside the classroom; and if we want to do a responsible job, for ourselves, of understanding how meaning is being made in the new multimodal communication contexts (New London Group).

The specific strategies for proceeding with this project, however, depend on individual teachers: on their willingness to experiment with new media compositions, to take personal and intellectual risks as they learn to value the kinds of texts, to integrate attention to such texts into the curriculum, to engage in composing such works themselves; and on the computer resources, technical support, and professional development that they have available at their specific institutions. These resources, of course, are unevenly distributed, as David's case suggests, along the related axes of race and class (Selfe, *Technology and Literacy*).

I can, however, suggest for all teachers the wisdom of starting this effort by paying attention to the whole range of literacies that students bring to the classroom: literacies practiced in the home, the community, the church, and online; literacies dependent on oral, visual, and aural performance; literacies based in multiple languages, cultures, and contexts. Such an approach—as the work of Graff, Street, Gee, and Barton and Hamilton suggests—can serve as a much needed counterbalance for our overly narrow focus on official forms of literacy, often the only literacy acknowledged in schools. It might also help us avoid the violence attendant to labeling individuals as illiterate when they are perfectly capable of communicating, making meaning, and exchanging information within various systems and contexts.

I can also suggest that teachers start the effort of paying attention to new media texts and emerging literacies by learning from students. More than twenty years ago in *Culture and Commitment*, Margaret Mead argued some cultures change so fast—she termed them "prefigurative"—that they exist "without models and without precedent" (xx). In prefigurative cultures, change is so rapid that "neither parents nor teachers, lawyers, doctors, skilled workers, inventors, preachers, or prophets" (xx) can teach children what they need to know about the world. New media texts, I would argue, are an important part of a postmodern technological culture undergoing the same sort of rapid changes. They exist in electronic and technological environments that change so rapidly, few teachers of English composition are able to keep up. Students, in contrast—frequently immersed in new communication contexts—are often the first to experiment with new kinds of texts, to discover new literacy values and practices. They are also the first to understand the functions new media texts fulfill in their lives.

When teachers begin to pay some respectful attention to the new kinds of literacies students develop in these electronic contexts, composition classrooms might become better places in which to learn and teach. Such a move could not only help us expand our conception of literacy beyond that of single official version of reading and writing, but it may also help change the dynamic around literacy studies altogether, encouraging, as Freire described it,

> the teacher-of-the-students and the students-of-the-teacher cease to exist and a new term emerges: teacher-students with students-teachers [...] They become jointly responsible for a process in which all grow. (67)

ACTIVITY 1

TECHNOLOGICAL LITERACY

AUTOBIOGRAPHIES*

TEACHER'S NOTES

The purpose of this activity is to find out what literacy practices and values—both in new media and more conventional media—that students are bringing with them to composition classrooms.

Teachers should provide students the following questions as an early homework assignment, and ask them to respond as fully as possible with narratives from their own experience as literate individuals.

After the autobiographies are completed, have the class read at least 4-5 of them and reflect on their similarities and differences.

EARLY LITERACY DEVELOPMENT

- What stories did your parents tell you about their own efforts to learn to read and write? Speak and listen? Compose/view/interact with texts of various sorts?
- What kinds of values did they place on reading and writing, speaking and listening, viewing/interacting and composing in various settings?
- What specific kinds of reading and writing, speaking and listening, viewing/interacting and composing did your parents do? (Think about—but don't limit your response to—such things as the following: reading newspapers, magazines, books, or novels; writing poems, lists, plays, or letters; speaking in front of groups or to individuals; listening to speeches, sermons, or lectures; viewing television, movies, or plays; interacting with computer games, kiosks, or video games; composing posters, songs, rhymes, or Web sites.)
- What stories can you tell about your parents and or family and the kinds of reading and writing, speaking and listening, viewing/interacting and composing activities they did and encouraged you to do? (Consider—but don't limit yourself to—the kinds of activities done online, in print, and on television; at home, at school, among relatives and friends, at church, in the community)
- What stories can you tell about when, where, how you first came in contact with computers? (including mainframe computers, personal computers, computer games)
- What stories can you tell about when, where, how you first learned to use computers to read or write? To speak or listen to others? To

---

* This activity has been developed in various forms by Gail Hawisher and me, and by Dickie Selfe, Karla Kitalong, and Tracy Bridgeford. This particular version of the technological literacy autobiography is an amalgam of the work of these scholars.

view/interact with/compose texts? Where did this take place? Did anyone help or encourage you? Who helped? How did they help? How old were they, and how old were you? What kind of support did you have? How much access did you have to a computer per day/week/month? How often did you actually use the computer per day/week/month?

- When you were growing up, how did you feel about using computers to read or write? To speak or listen to others? To view/interact with/compose texts? At home? At school? Other places?

- When you were growing up, what determined how frequently you use the computer for reading and writing, speaking and listening, viewing/interacting and composing? Are there any stories/incidents that you can tell about this?

- When you were growing up, what did your family think about using computers for reading and writing, speaking and listening, viewing/interacting and composing? What values did they place on this activity? On your participation? On their role? Do you have any stories you can tell us that would illustrate their attitudes?

- When you were growing up, what did your friends think about using computers for reading and writing, speaking and listening, viewing/interacting and composing? What values did they place on this activity? On your participation? On their role? Do you have any stories you can tell us that would illustrate their attitudes?

- When you were growing up, what did your teacher think about using computers for reading and writing, speaking and listening, viewing/interacting and composing? What values did they place on this activity? On your participation? On their role? Do you have any stories you can tell us that would illustrate their attitudes?

CURRENT LITERACY

- Do you (or your family) own a computer(s) now? If so, please describe it (them).

- What specific kinds of reading and writing, speaking and listening, viewing/interacting and composing do you do now in computer environments at home? At school? Elsewhere? (Think about—but don't limit your response—to such things as, reading newspapers , e-zines, books, or email; doing research for school on the World Wide Web; writing/sending friends instant messages and writing in chat rooms, writing programs or papers, contributing to listservs or bulletin boards; speaking to friends and relatives; listening to CDs and sound files; viewing movies; interacting with computer games; composing Web sites, works of art, or interactive fiction.)

- What determines how frequently you use the computer for reading and writing, speaking and listening, viewing/interacting and composing? Are there any stories/incidents to tell about this?

- Now, what does your family think about using computers for reading and writing, speaking and listening, viewing/interacting and composing? Your parents? Sisters and brothers? Uncles and Aunts? Cousins? Grandparents? What values do they place on this activity? On your participation? On their role? Do you have any stories you can tell that would help illustrate their attitudes?

- Now, what do your friends think about using computers for reading and writing, speaking and listening, viewing/interacting and composing? What values do they place on this activity? On your participation? On their role? Do you have any stories you can tell us that would illustrate their attitudes?

- Now what does your teacher think about using computers for reading and writing, speaking and listening, viewing/interacting and composing? What values do they place on this activity? On your participation? On their role? Do you have any stories you can tell us that would illustrate their attitudes?

- Has your experience with composing texts for online environments taught you anything about "reading" or "writing" more conventional texts, texts that appear in print? Online texts? If so, please explain.

- What are your favorite kinds of projects/activities in online environments? Please explain.

- What kinds of literacies do you seem younger children acquiring today—both online and in print? Which are like your own? Different from your own? What do you think these younger people are learning from communicating online? From communicating in print?

- In the next ten years, what online literacy skills and understandings will be increasingly important for students to acquire? Why?

- If you were designing an online literacy curriculum (how to read and compose in online environments) for secondary students today, what kinds of things would you include? Why?

- If you were designing an online literacy curriculum (how to read and compose in online environments) for college students today, what kinds of things would you include? Why?

- What are your strengths and your weaknesses in reading/viewing/interacting with/listening to texts online? In print?

- What are your strengths and your weaknesses in composing/designing texts online? In print?

- List a few adjectives that you'd use to describe the work you do online.

- Fill in the blanks in the sentences below. For each item, elaborate by explaining why you answer as you do.

  A computer is like _____.

  Elaboration:

  A computer is a _____.

  Elaboration:

- Draw a picture of you and your relationship to computers (or to a particular computer).

STUDYING NEW MEDIA TEXTS

IDENTIFIED BY STUDENTS

TEACHER'S NOTES
This activity depends on teachers being willing to become students.

ACTIVITY
Ask students, for homework, to identify one or two different kinds of "new media texts" they have seen on the World Wide Web. Encourage students to select texts that seem different from conventional print-based documents—some combination of still photography, video, sound, animation, and/or alphabetic text—but that are effective and appealing as texts designed for digital environments and for specific audiences.

Ask students to consider the following questions in relation to the texts they choose:

- What makes this a new media text? How does it differ from a conventional print text?
- What particular elements make this text most effective for me as an audience? Why?
- What particular elements make this text least effective for me as an audience? Why?
- Who composed, designed the texts and why? What is the author's/designer's/ composer's purpose?
- Who is the audience for these texts? Who is not? How can you tell? (Be specific.)
- Can you tell what kinds of software and hardware were used to create this new media text?

In class, have students show the texts they have chosen. As a class, identify the collective characteristics of these new media texts, paying careful attention to how they are composed, organized, presented, viewed/read/interacted with in digital formats.

As a class, compile a class list of the characteristics that effective new media texts have and compare these characteristics to those of effective print texts. Also discuss ineffective new media texts and speculate on why they fail as communications.

ACTIVITY 3

ALLOWING FOR ALTERNATIVE
APPROACHES TO COMPOSING

ACTIVITY

Invite students who are familiar with new media software to do one or more of their papers for the term in an online environment, using different media to achieve their purpose. Or, for extra credit or a re-graded essay, let those students who have some facility with new media redesign a conventional print paper in a new media context.

Have students who take on such projects write, and hand in, a cover memo for the project that reflects on what they were able to do in the new media texts that they couldn't do in a more conventional print text or what they thought they could do in a print text that they were not able to do in a new media text.

Invite students who do not have access to—or facility with—new media to create a multiple media redesign of a paper they have written using images pasted on poster board, audio tapes, photographs, and/or video elements. Have students who take on such projects write and hand in a cover memo for the project that reflects on what they were able to do in the multiple media they used that they couldn't do in their original print text or what they thought they could do in a print text that they were not able to do in a new media text. Have these students present their texts in class.

CONSIDERING THE EFFECTS OF NEW MEDIA IN/ON A SPECIFIC GENRE

TEACHER'S NOTES

For this activity, you will need access to a computer network and to the World Wide Web.

ACTIVITY

Provide students 3 poems (in print form) that you have regularly used as part of your composition classes, either as general prompts for writing or as specific texts for analysis.

In small groups, ask students to looks at 3 of the following new media poems/performances:

- "The Modern Era," Artistica design Collaborative, Issue 5 of *Artistica*, Experimentals section at <http://www.artistica.org/>
- "Genius," Words:Thomas Swiss,/Design: Skye Giordano, Summer 2001 issue of *Poems that Go* at <http://www.poemsthatgo.com/textarchives.htm>
- "Strings," Dan Waber, Vispo at <http://www.vispo.com//guests/DanWaber/index.html>

Ask students to consider the following questions/tasks:

- What characteristics make a new media poem? Do such texts differ from print poems? If so, how?
- Pick 2 of the poems you read in print or online; choose your favorites. Make notes about the particular elements make this poem most effective for you as an audience.
- For each of the poems you choose, write for five minutes on the following question: *What does this poem say to me as a reader/viewer/interactor?*

In a large group, have students discuss their answers.

For students who have access to—and facility with—PowerPoint (or any other new media composing environment such as Dreamweaver, Premiere, Director), ask them to write a new media poem in that environment, focusing on one or more of the issues you have covered in class.

Students who have access to—and facility with—PowerPoint (or other new media environments) might also like to work with another student who does not have this literacy to collaboratively author a poem. In this case, require that the student without the new media expertise sit at the keyboard and work in the online environment. The student with new media expertise should direct the composition without touching the keyboard.

For students who do not have access to—or facility with—new media environments and do not want to collaborate, have them create a multiple media poem using images pasted on poster board, audio tapes, photographs, and/or video elements.

Have all students present their poems in class and reflect on what they learned in writing them.

TOWARD NEW MEDIA TEXTS
Taking Up the Challenges of Visual Literacy

Cynthia L. Selfe

How can teachers of composition *begin* working with new media texts—especially when they feel less than prepared to do so? One productive route of approach, I suggest in this chapter, is through visual literacy.

It is not unusual for faculty raised on alphabetic literacy and educated to teach composition before the advent of image-capturing software, multimedia texts, and the World Wide Web to feel inadequate to the task of teaching students about new media texts and the emerging literacies associated with these texts. Many have used computers extensively in the composition instruction they offer students, but most, if not all, of the assignments they favor regularly depend on the alphabetic, demand it as a primary focus, have—in most cases—been limited to it.

In part, faculty may limit their teaching in this way because they lack familiarity with a range of new media texts that they consider appropriate for study in composition classrooms. Given their educational backgrounds and expertise, after all, most faculty remain book readers, primarily. Further, although they may have encountered some new media texts, and may even enjoy these texts in many ways, they may not be convinced that such texts are worth further study in the English composition classroom. In addition, faculty may feel that they lack the analytical skills they need to conduct serious study of these texts, an effective vocabulary and set of strategies for discussing the structure and composition of new media texts, or that they lack expertise with the software packages typically used to create such texts—Macromedia Director™ and Dreamweaver™, Adobe Photoshop™ and Premiere™, Corel Poser™ and Bryce™, among others.

2 Importantly, operating from these constraints, many English composition faculty realize that they can offer only limited help to students who read new media texts; and they cannot help students who want to compose such texts. And, as the work of scholars as diverse as Manuel Castells, Gail Hawisher, and The New London Group suggests, this illiteracy can be costly in terms of faculty's understanding of the ways in which communication is changing at the beginning of the 21st century. Perhaps more importantly, however, it may have a cost for the students in their classes—individuals who need to learn more about the new media literacies now being used to shape meaning and information as it is composed and exchanged.

3 To work toward a better understanding of new media texts—and to open composition classes to some of the expanded possibilities suggested by such texts—a good first step may involve focusing on visual literacy and on texts, both online and in print, that depend primarily on visual elements and materials.

My reasoning in suggesting this approach is simple, but then so, too, is my level of skill in this new area: one of the primary elements that make new media texts new for me—and at times difficult to discuss in a composition classroom—is their heavy dependence on visual communication. This is an area in which I, personally, feel less than confident as a teacher of English composition, given our profession's historical focus on alphabetic literacy and uncertainty about whether visual studies is an appropriate focus for composition classrooms (cf., George; Sean Williams). Therefore, like most of my colleagues, I have only limited ability to help students analyze the visual elements of text and even less in helping them create texts composed of such elements.

Given this context, I suspect if we can help teachers become more knowledgeable and comfortable in working with students to read, discuss, and compose texts that depend primarily on visual elements, they will also be increasingly willing and able to apply these understandings to the teaching of new media texts as well. For me, focusing on the visual in composition classrooms is a productive first step—albeit not the only route—toward the larger goal of focusing on new media texts in the same environment.

This chapter, then, seeks to provide a brief rationale and several specific strategies for integrating visual literacy into composition classrooms—both in terms of consumption and production.

Most teachers thinking about integrating visual literacy into composition classes need some definitional focus for their efforts. And although, as Diana George notes, the definitions of visual literacy—and the related terms of visual communication, visual rhetoric, and the visual—remain under formulation in our profession, it may be useful to pose a temporary working definition for some of the key terms in this chapter, while recognizing that the larger professional effort to settle on a formal acceptable definition will continue to go forward.

By visual literacy, then, I will refer to the ability to read, understand, value, and learn from visual materials (still photographs, videos, films, animations, still images, pictures, drawings, graphics)—especially as these are combined to create a text—as well as the ability to create, combine, and use visual elements (e.g., colors, forms, lines, images) and messages for the purposes of communicating (cf. Kress and van Leeuwven, *Reading Images*; Debes and Williams; *The On-line Visual Literacy Project*). And—although I understand some of the problems posed by using the lens of alphabetic literacy to understand visual literacy (Wysocki and Johnson-Eilola)—based on the work of scholars such as Brian Street, James Gee, Harvey Graff, Deborah Brandt ("Literacy Learning"), and David Barton and Mary Hamilton, for the purpose of this chapter, I will assume, further, that visual literacy (or literacies), like all literacies, are both historically and culturally situated, constructed, and valued.

By texts that depend primarily on visual elements, visual texts, and visual compositions, I will refer to communications (e.g., visual poems, visual essays, visual messages, visual arguments, collages, multimedia presentations, among other forms) that people compose/design (both online and in print environments) in which visual elements and materials assume the primary burden of communication.

I will also use the term **the visual**, to refer broadly to a focus on visual elements and materials of communication, and the term visual compositions to refer to the texts that individuals or groups design/compose, primarily of visual elements and materials, for the purposes of communicating.

Finally, I will use the term **composer/designer**, instead of "author" or "artist," for instance, to describe an individual who produces or creates a visual text and the term **design/compose** to describe the complex set of activities involved in such a creative and strategic task. To refer to the reader of visual texts, I will use the term **reader/viewer** and, for the complex set of activities associated with understanding and interpreting a visual text, I will use **reading/viewing**. Although I understand these terms have their own limitations, I believe they are suggestive of the richness of visual compositions and will provide teachers some help, even if on a temporary basis, in reading this chapter.

MORE ABOUT APPROACH AND AVOIDANCE

If focusing visual literacy may be a useful first step in approaching new media texts, it is, itself, not always an easy one for teachers of English composition.

Although we have always acknowledged, at some level, the visual appearance of alphabetic texts (their formatting, their appearance, the spatial presentation of information), both visual compositions and the new media texts on which this book focuses typically privilege such information—depend on and focus on visual images, photographs, animations, multimedia depictions in ways that print texts typically do not.

This emphasis on the visual presentation of information, as Gunther Kress ("'English'") has noted, is manifested broadly in our culture and represents an important "turn to the visual" (66). Alphabetic texts, Kress continues, are being challenged by texts that are more oriented toward visual elements:

> The visual is becoming more prominent in many domains of public communication. From a different perspective this is to realize that written language is being displaced from its hitherto unchallenged central position in the semiotic landscape, and that the visual is taking over many of the functions of written language. (68)

Acknowledging this turn toward the visual—which has occurred in print texts as well as new media texts—scholars have begun to re-examine the role of visual literacy and our understanding of the visual in composition studies. Wysocki and Johnson-Eilola, for instance, have pointed out the limitations of using alphabetic literacy as a lens for understanding the new—and often visually rich—compositions that students are encountering in computer-based communication environments. Geoffrey Sirc has argued that visual compositions may provide teachers a valuable "demographic" that they have, in the past, lacked, one which reveals the "form patterns"—born of poetic expression—that individuals "actually make in their lives" as they try to "live their desire" (11) in a postmodern culture. Diane Shoos and Diana George argue for much broader definition of literacy, composition, and reading, one that takes a critical, visual intertextuality into account, among other things, and that acknowledges the "relationship(s) of texts [visual ads of commercial magazines, film posters, documentaries, television fiction, essays among them] to one another and to their multiple contexts" (124). And this is only a small sampling of the recent work done in composition studies with an emphasis on the visual.

Despite this work, however, as Diana George has recently pointed out, many teachers continue to rely on impoverished approaches to teaching visual literacy in their composition classrooms, introducing visual texts as the less-important and less-intellectual sidekicks of alphabetic texts. Such approaches are deeply sedimented, not only in the cultural, linguistic, and historical practices that privilege alphabetic literacy (cf. Wysocki and Johnson-Eilola; Wysocki, "Impossibly Distinct"; Jay; Kress, "'English'"), but also in the practices and approaches of our profession. As George reminds us, when English composition teachers have thought to bring visual forms into their classes—a practice which they have carried on for at least forty years—they have typically presented them as second-class texts: either as "dumbed down" (32) communications that serve as "stimuli for writing but [...] no substitute for the complexity of language" (22) or as texts related to, but certainly not on an equal footing with, the "'real' work of the course" (28).

English composition teachers have continued to privilege alphabetic texts over texts that depend on visual elements, I believe, because such texts present familiar forms, forms with which we have developed a comfortable, stable intellectual relationship. We know, for instance—from lots of previous experiences—how to approach a book or a non-fiction essay; we have developed many strategies for reading and understanding such texts, for analyzing and interpreting them, for talking about them. Indeed, we feel confident about teaching students how to compose alphabetic texts primarily because we are so familiar with those forms. Relatively few English teachers, however, feel as comfortable in approaching a visual text unless they have some training in art or design. Given this context, we remain unsure how to approach visual texts, how to explore them, how to understand them, and how to teach them. And we also feel less than competent about composing visual texts ourselves.

Part of the reason this feeling has persisted, of course, has to do with the material conditions of teaching and learning in the United States and the relations of such conditions to technologies of production and composition. Many of us, for instance, had our last art class in elementary school and have learned since that time to pin our hopes for academic and professional success on alphabetic texts. As a result, we have also learned to use and value technologies—pens, pencils, typewriters, ditto machines, books, journals, and, more recently, computers and word-processing packages—for the ease they afford us in creating alphabetic texts. It is only recently—in conjunction with the cultural turn to the visual, I believe—that increasing numbers of composition teachers have had some access to technologies which allow for the production of texts highly dependent on visual elements (color photocopiers, digital scanners; computers that contain page-layout, photo-manipulation, animation, multimedia software, etc.). Many of these technologies, however, are still expensive—and, thus unevenly distributed in schools along the axis of material resources—as well as relatively difficult to access and learn.

Finally, I would suggest, many English composition teachers have downplayed the importance of visual literacy and texts that depend primarily on visual elements because they confront us with the prospect of updating our literacies at the expense of considerable work, precious time, and a certain amount of status. Teachers continue to privilege alphabetic literacy over visual literacy, in other words, because they have already invested so heavily in writing, writing instruction and writing programs—and because we have achieved some status as practitioners and specialists of writing. Undertaking the study of literacies based in visual studies, learning to analyze and talk about and compose these texts—especially with a high degree of technological sophistication will take time and effort—may also force us to acknowledge gaps in our own literacy sets.

Recently, however, our single-minded focus on alphabetic texts in composition classes has come to seem outdated, even obdurate, in the face of practical realities. Global communications, for example—exchanged via increasingly complicated computer networks that stretch across traditional geographic and political borders and that include people from different cultures who speak different languages—increasingly involve texts that depend heavily, even primarily, on visual elements (New London Group). Moreover, with the ongoing expansion of global markets, political systems, and communication networks, such an emphasis is sure to continue, if not increase.

Given the pace and scope of changes accruing from this set of circumstances, if our profession continues to focus solely on teaching alphabetic composition—either online or in print—we run the risk of making composition studies increasingly irrelevant to students engaging in contemporary practices of communicating. Students already, as Diana George reminds us, have a "much richer imagination for what we might accomplish with the visual" than we ourselves have (12).

By continuing a single-minded focus on alphabetic literacy—and failing to give adequate attention to visual literacy—as Sean Williams points out, we not only unnecessarily limit the scope of composition studies, both intellectually and practically:

> Restricting composition to verbal media and reproducing the verbal bias in our classrooms is perilous [...] because it contradicts the critical thinking skills that we as composition teachers strive to teach. [...I]f composition's role is to help students acquire skills to lead a critically engaged life—that is to identify problems, to solve them, and to communicate with others about them—then we need to expand our view of writing instruction to include the diverse media forms that actually represent and shape the discursive reality of students. The verbal bias, then, reveals two closely interwoven perils;
>
> - a political one that reinscribes a conclusion-based rationality, and
>
> - a rhetorical one that ignores the possibility that different media function more or less effectively in different contexts. (25)

As Kress and van Leeuwen (*Reading Images*) put the case, then, it may be time to rethink what 'literacy' ought to include, and what should be taught under the heading of 'writing' in schools (32).

By adding a focus on visual literacy to our existing focus on alphabetic literacy, we may not only learn to pay more serious attention to the ways in which students are now ordering and making sense of the world through the production and consumption of visual images, but we may also extend the usefulness of composition studies in a changing world.

Individual teachers and programs, surely, will differ widely in their willingness to experiment with the challenges of visual composition, to take personal and intellectual risks as they learn to value visually-oriented texts, and to engage in composing texts that combine the visual as well as the alphabetic.

The following pages provide examples of assignments designed to provide teachers a range of approaches to visual texts, even when instructors have no formal coursework or professional preparation in this area.

1 The assignments connect what is—at least for some teachers—the less-familiar realm of visual composition with the more-familiar realm of alphabetic composition.

2 Most of the assignments deal at some level with a combination of both visual and alphabetic literacies. Most—following the lead of scholars such as Susan Hilligoss, Sean Williams, Clay Spinuzzi—use a rhetorical approach to analyzing the audience, purpose, and messages conveyed by a visual text—employing questions that many instructors already use in teaching students how to compose more conventional alphabetic texts.

3 And most of the assignments do not require teachers or students to use sophisticated computer environments as contexts for visual assignments—three of the four assignments, for example, suggest that students might want to create visual compositions on poster boards; and only the last assignment requires that students know how to create a Web page.

4 Importantly, I would add that most of the assignments involve teachers and students as co-learners in the project of paying increased attention to visual texts. As a result, they do not require teachers to begin with a great deal of information or background on visual literacy. Through the completion of the assignments, both teachers and students will acquire some basic conceptual vocabulary that they can use to discuss the reading/viewing and composing/designing of texts that rely primarily on visual elements. For those colleagues who feel more comfortable approaching such assignments with some background reading under their belts, I can suggest Kress and van Leeuwen's *Reading Images: The Grammar of Visual Design*.

The topics of the following assignments are far less important than their focus on the visual, and so teachers are also encouraged to revise them to fit specific courses. For example, the first assignment is currently designed for an undergraduate course on literacy issues. It asks students to create a visual essay that describes their general development as readers and writers over the course of their lifetimes. However, in another course focused on the American novel, the same assignment could be revised to ask students to trace a more specific line:

focusing on their family's history in America. Similarly, the second assignment—currently designed for a first-year English course focused on the relationship between humans and robots/cyborgs—asks students to make a visual argument about what this relationship will look like in 2050. In a course focusing on issues of race, this same assignment could be revised to ask students to make a visual argument based on their stance toward affirmative-action programs.

Ultimately, the goal set for these assignments is both modest (in that the general process will be familiar to most teachers of composition) and exceedingly challenging (in the attempt to focus primarily—although not exclusively—on the visual), and one I hope many teachers of composition can embrace: to help students and ourselves better understand the communicative power and complexity of visual texts by reading and looking at them, by thinking seriously about these texts and analyzing their components, by talking to other people about our interpretations of them, by composing visual texts ourselves, by sharing our efforts at composing with other author/designers, and by reflecting on the compositions we create and exchange with others as complex symbolic instantiations of the human need to communicate.

ACTIVITY 1

A VISUAL ESSAY

TEACHER NOTES

GOALS

- To involve students in reflecting on and representing
  - the range of the literacies they have developed in their lifetimes (both online and in-print).
  - the development of these literacies.
  - their feelings about/values toward various forms of literacy.
- To help students understand how much tacit knowledge they have about visual composition.
- To provide students some basic vocabulary they can use in talking about and analyzing visual compositions.

TIME REQUIRED

- one homework assignment to compose visual essay (1 week for out-of-class work).
- 30 minutes in class for viewing and reflecting on visual essays
- 30 minutes in class for discussion of successful strategies for:
  - creating overall visual coherence
  - visually identifying 2-4 of the essay's most important points
  - visually indicating pattern(s) of organization
- one homework assignment focused on comparing author/designers' reflections and audience/viewers' reflections

SEQUENCE

1. **Creating a visual essay.**

   As a homework assignment, each student creates a visual essay on the range of literacies (both on and off computers) they have developed over their lifetimes and their feelings toward literacy.

2. **Viewing and Reflection Session**

   In class, students form teams of three for a 30 minute *Viewing and Reflection Session*. During this session, teams do three rounds of reflection. During each round, the team views a visual essay for 10 minutes and reflects on a series of questions. Composer/designers reflect on what they tried to accomplish; readers/viewers write about what the visual essay communicates to them.

3. **Discussion**

   In class, the teacher asks students to point out the successful strategies that authors/designers used in their essays to:

1 impart visual impact

2 create an overall sense of coherence

3 indicate the importance of 1-4 major points

4 create pattern(s) of organization

4 Comparing Author/Designers' Reflections with Audience/Viewers' Reflections

As a homework assignment, each composer/designer compares his/her own answers on the reflection questions to those provided by the audience viewers. Each author/designer will summarize areas of agreement and disagreement.

USEFUL VOCABULARY

from Kress and van Leeuwan's *Reading Images: The Grammar of Visual Design*

- **Visual impact**: The overall effect and appeal that a visual composition has on an audience.

- **Visual coherence**: The extent to which visual elements of a composition are tied together with color, shape, image, lines of sight, theme, etc.

- **Visual salience**: Importance or prominence of a visual element.

- **Visual organization**: Pattern of arrangement that relates the elements of the visual essay to one another in a way that makes them easier for readers/viewers to comprehend

VISUAL ESSAY
HOMEWORK

ASSIGNMENT (HOMEWORK)

OBJECTIVES

- To reflect on the entire range of literacies (both on-line and print) you have developed over your life; the practices, understandings, and values that make up your literacies; where these practices, understandings, and values came from; how you have developed them; and who has helped you become literate.
- To represent this information as richly as possible in a visual essay.
- To provide you practice in documenting images.

TASK

- Compose a visual essay that represents and reflects on
  1. the range of different literacy practices, values, and understandings you have developed over your lifetime (from birth to now)
  2. how you have developed these literacies (where, how, who helped)
  3. your feelings about these literacies
- The audience for this essay is other students in the class. The purpose is to show the range and extent of your own personal set of literacies, their development over time, and your feelings toward literacy at various points of your life.
- For the purposes of this essay, we will define literacy broadly—not only as your reading and writing skills but also the values and understandings that go along with these skills. For instance, you might (but don't have to) include, such activities as reading and writing in print contexts (books and magazines, writing stories and plays), on computers (designing Web sites, reading gaming situations, writing in chat rooms), on television (reading the texts of television programs), in church (reading the Bible, writing for your church bulletin), at home (writing letters, reading directions); in school (reading lab reports, collaborating with a group to compose a report).
- The essays should demonstrate a high degree of visual impact.
- The essay should demonstrate an overall coherence (elements of the essay should be linked by color, shape, theme, arrangement, etc.).
- The essay should identify 2-4 major points as particularly important (using strategies to make these points prominent and stand out from other elements: size, color, contrast, placement, etc.).
- Use some pattern of organization to help viewers to comprehend your essay (arrange elements along a timeline, a path, a trail, or some other metaphor that represents your life; separate your computer and your book-based literacies or connect them if they are related).

FORMAT

- Your essay can take any number of forms. Be creative in your thinking and representation: create your own literacy path or trail, a diagram of human development annotated with images of your literacy activities, a scrapbook with "snapshots" of your literacy development; a map of your literacy landscape; a literacy game board; a literacy Web.

- Compose this essay either on a Web page that you create online or on a poster board that you purchase at the college book store.

- If you create a Web page, compose your essay from images that you find or create online. Before you download an image from another Web site, carefully check to make sure the Web site does not prohibit the copying of images.

- If you use poster board, create your collage from images you cut out of magazines or from family photographs.

- Include at least 15 images in this essay.

- Document the source of each image using the formats below.

WEB ESSAYS & DOCUMENTING IMAGES FROM AN ONLINE SOURCE

- Create a Web page for your essay.

- Create a separate Web page for each image's bibliographic citation.

- Link each image in your essay to the appropriate Web page containing its bibliographic entry. Here is a model, with an example:

  Artist (if given). Title of file. <Web site from which image was taken> (date on which you accessed Web site).

  Example: Doe, Jane. SpottedPig.jpg. <http://www.spottedanimal/pigs/#22> (Accessed 22 June, 2002).

POSTER BOARD ESSAYS & DOCUMENTING IMAGES FROM PRINT/PHOTOGRAPHIC SOURCES

- Create your essay. Number each image.

- Create a bibliography page. List entries in numerical order, numbering each entry to correspond to an image: [15] "Drink Milk." Time 20 September 2002: 15.

- Attach this page to the back of your essay.

  Artist (if given). "Title of image" (if given). Magazine Title or Photograph Collection Day Month Year: page number (if applicable).

  Example from a magazine: [15] "Drink Milk." Time 20 September 2002: 15.

  Example from a photograph: [15] Doe, John. "Me and My Mother." Personal photograph collection. Taken 9 August 1978.

REFLECTION SHEET
(COMPOSER/DESIGNER)

Composer/designer   _____

OBJECTIVE

- To articulate and reflect on what you are trying to convey about your literacies, literacy development through/in your essay.
- To identify what parts of your essay worked well and what parts worked less well.
- To reflect on your attempt to create visual coherence, salience (prominence/importance), and organization in your essay.

TASK

Take 10 minutes to reflect on the first three questions that follow. For homework, reflect on the last four questions and hand in this page—along with the reader/viewers' Reflection sheets from your team—at the beginning of next class. *Do not speak about or explain your visual essay to your readers/viewers..*

DURING CLASS

- What were you trying to convey about your literacies/literacy development in this essay?
- What parts of this essay worked the best? Had the most effect impact? Why?
- What parts of this essay worked less well in your opinion? Had the least effective impact? Why?

FOR HOMEWORK

- What specific techniques did you use to establish visual coherence in your essay?
- What specific strategies did you use to identify each of the 2–4 major points you were trying to make in this essay and to lend them visual salience (make them prominent to the reader/viewer)?

VISUAL ESSAY
CLASSROOM WORK

REFLECTION SHEET (READER/VIEWER)

Essay composed/designed by _____

Essay read/viewed by _____

OBJECTIVE

- To articulate what the visual essay conveyed to you as a reader/viewer.

- To reflect on what parts of the essay worked well/had great impact for you and what parts worked less well/had low impact for you.

TASK

Take 10 minutes to reflect in writing on the following questions. Do not talk to the composer/designer.

- What did the essay convey to you about the composer/designer and his/her literacies? His/her development as a reader/viewer or composer/designer? List at least five impressions you got.

- What parts of the essay worked the best for you—had the highest impact?

- What parts of this essay worked least well for you—had the lowest impact?

- Below, please identify the 2-4 main points you think the composer/designer wanted to make in the essay.

VISUAL ESSAY

SAMPLE EVALUATION

Composer/designer _____

1: OVERALL EFFECT OF THE VISUAL ESSAY

Essay's overall impact is low & presentation is less than effective

Essay has moderate level of overall impact and presentation is moderately effective.

Essay has exceptional overall impact and presentation is highly effective.

Comments

2: COMPOSER/DESIGNER'S DEVELOPMENT/FEELINGS

Essay provides modest information about composer/designer's development/feelings.

Essay provides adequate information about composer/designer's development/feelings.

Essay provides exceptional information about composer/ designer's development/feelings.

Comments:

3: VISUAL COHERENCE

Essay needs more visual coherence.

Essay is visually coherent.

Essay demonstrates exceptional visual coherence

Comments:

4: VISUAL SALIENCE

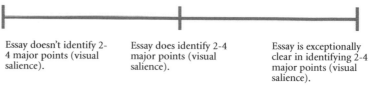

Essay doesn't identify 2-4 major points (visual salience).

Essay does identify 2-4 major points (visual salience).

Essay is exceptionally clear in identifying 2-4 major points (visual salience).

Comments:

5: ORGANIZATION OF THE ESSAY

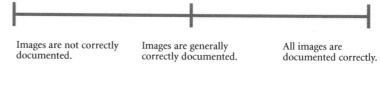

Essay's organization is unclear or confusing.

Essay's organization is helpful and clear.

Essay's organization contributes in exceptional ways to its overall effects.

Comments:

6: DOCUMENTATION OF IMAGES

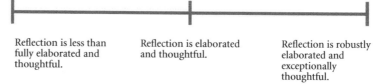

Images are not correctly documented.

Images are generally correctly documented.

All images are documented correctly.

Comments:

7: REFLECTION

Reflection is less than fully elaborated and thoughtful.

Reflection is elaborated and thoughtful.

Reflection is robustly elaborated and exceptionally thoughtful.

Comments:

V I S U A L   E S S A Y
C L A S S R O O M   W O R K

SAMPLE EVALUATION (a model)

Composer/designer   Michelle Sarinen

1: OVERALL EFFECT OF THE VISUAL ESSAY

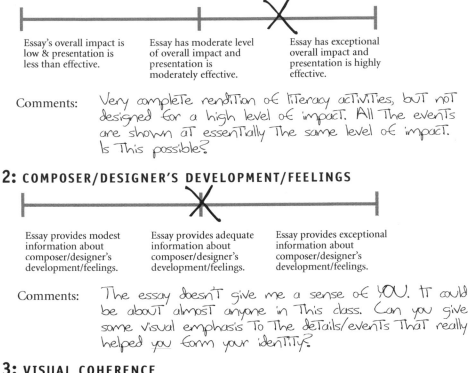

Essay's overall impact is low & presentation is less than effective.

Essay has moderate level of overall impact and presentation is moderately effective.

Essay has exceptional overall impact and presentation is highly effective.

Comments: Very complete rendition of literacy activities, but not designed for a high level of impact. All the events are shown at essentially the same level of impact. Is this possible?

2: COMPOSER/DESIGNER'S DEVELOPMENT/FEELINGS

Essay provides modest information about composer/designer's development/feelings.

Essay provides adequate information about composer/designer's development/feelings.

Essay provides exceptional information about composer/designer's development/feelings.

Comments: The essay doesn't give me a sense of YOU. It could be about almost anyone in this class. Can you give some visual emphasis to the details/events that really helped you form your identity?

3: VISUAL COHERENCE

Essay needs more visual coherence.

Essay is visually coherent.

Essay demonstrates exceptional visual coherence

Comments: I think you could make more effective use of color and line to make your points and get your essay to hang together. For instance, why not color-code the print-based events in your childhood to differentiate them from the computer-based events in your adolescence?

4: VISUAL SALIENCE

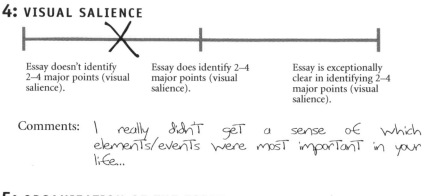

Essay doesn't identify 2–4 major points (visual salience).

Essay does identify 2–4 major points (visual salience).

Essay is exceptionally clear in identifying 2–4 major points (visual salience).

Comments: I really didn't get a sense of which elements/events were most important in your life...

5: ORGANIZATION OF THE ESSAY

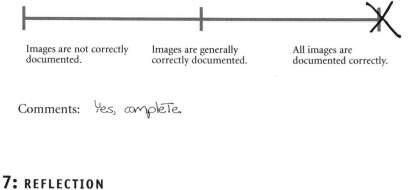

Essay's organization is unclear or confusing.

Essay's organization is helpful and clear.

Essay's organization contributes in exceptional ways to its overall effects.

Comments: Yes—The organization is clear: It's chronological

6: DOCUMENTATION OF IMAGES

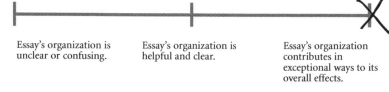

Images are not correctly documented.

Images are generally correctly documented.

All images are documented correctly.

Comments: Yes, complete.

7: REFLECTION

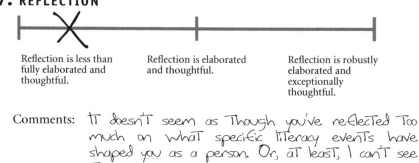

Reflection is less than fully elaborated and thoughtful.

Reflection is elaborated and thoughtful.

Reflection is robustly elaborated and exceptionally thoughtful.

Comments: It doesn't seem as though you've reflected too much on what specific literacy events have shaped you as a person. Or, at least, I can't see it...

ACTIVITY 2

VISUAL ARGUMENT

ASSIGNMENT *

TEACHERS' NOTES

GOALS

- Involve students in identifying effective strategies composers/designers have used in their arguments to establish visual impact, coherence, salience, and organization.
- Introduce some new vocabulary for discussing the concepts of visual impact, coherence, salience, and organization.

Below, we list some of the possible strategies that students may identify for establishing visual impact, coherence, salience, and organization. However, such strategies work differently in combination and within the context of specific arguments. Encourage students to identify unusual strategies that generate innovative and surprising effects—especially if those effects succeed.

DISCUSSION QUESTIONS

After students have completed the assignment on the following pages, look together at all the arguments they've made. Get the class talking by asking the following questions. The questions are set up around the vocabulary from the previous assignment.

questions about **VISUAL IMPACT**

VISUAL IMPACT is the overall effect and appeal that a visual composition has on an audience.

- *Which arguments that you looked at exhibited the highest overall impact/effect? Why?*

Ask the team members to identify the strategies they think the particular author/designer employed to establish visual coherence. Ask students on other teams to identify additional arguments that succeed in establishing overall coherence. Encourage students to identify strategies that are unusual, unexpected; that generate surprising (and yet successful) effects; that are innovative.

Students might mention these strategies for creating visual impact:

- author/designer employed an overall concept

---

* I am indebted to Dr. Diana George for the concept of visual arguments. She describes several such arguments created by students at Michigan Technological University in her article "From Analysis to Visual Design."

- author/designer used images that were especially effective
- author/designer used lots of details
- author/designer used color effectively
- author/designer composed an especially creative visual design
- author/designer used elements that the audience could relate to

questions about V I S U A L   C O H E R E N C E

VISUAL COHERENCE is the extent to which the various elements of a visual composition are tied together, represent a unified whole.

- *Which essays demonstrated an effective sense of visual coherence? Why?*

  Ask the team members to identify the strategies they think the particular composer/designer employed to establish visual coherence. Ask students on other teams to identify additional essays that succeed in establishing overall coherence. Encourage students to identify strategies that are unusual, unexpected; that generate surprising (and yet successful) effects; that are innovative.

  Students might mention these strategies for creating visual coherence:

  - composer/designer linked elements by using patterns or color
  - composer/designer linked elements through similar shapes
  - composer/designer created coherence with unifying pictorial graphics (lines, arrows, paths, etc.)
  - composer/designer tied elements together using proximity, overlapping, or juxtaposition
  - composer/designer tied elements together using a shared visual theme (images of books, pens, or computers)
  - composer /designer balanced major elements to create cohesion

questions about V I S U A L   S A L I E N C E

VISUAL SALIENCE is the relative prominence of an element within a visual composition. Salient elements catch viewers' eye; they are conspicuous.

- *Which arguments demonstrated an effective sense of visual salience?*

  Ask the team members to identify the strategies they think the particular composer/designer employed to establish visual salience. Ask students on other teams to identify additional arguments that succeed in establishing salience. Encourage students to identify strategies that are unusual, unexpected; that generate surprising (and yet successful) effects; that are innovative.

  Students might mention these strategies for creating visual salience:

  - composers/designers increased the size of major elements
  - composers/designers sharpened the focus for major elements
  - composers/designers increased the contrast (darker, lighter, more saturated colors) of major elements
  - composers/designers positioned major elements in the center

- composers/designers positioned major elements in the foreground
- composers/designers highlighted major elements with color
- composers/designers used pictorial graphics (lines, arrows, etc.) to point toward major elements
- composers/designers used/angled other elements to direct the viewer's eye toward a major element

questions about **VISUAL ORGANIZATION**

VISUAL ORGANIZATION is the pattern of arrangement that relates the elements of the visual essay to one another so that they are easier for readers/viewers to comprehend.

- *Which arguments demonstrated an effective sense of visual organization?* Ask the team members to identify the strategies they think the particular author/designer employed to establish effective patterns of visual organization. Ask students on other teams to identify additional arguments that succeed in establishing effective patterns of visual organization. Encourage students to identify strategies that are unusual, unexpected; that generate surprising (and yet successful) effects; that are innovative.

Students might mention these strategies for creating visual organization:

- composer/designer linked elements by using patterns of color
- composer/designer linked elements through similar shapes
- composer/designer created coherence with unifying pictorial graphics (lines, arrows, paths, etc.)
- composer/designer tied elements together using proximity, overlapping, or juxtaposition
- composer/designer tied elements together using a shared visual theme (images of books, pens, or computers)
- composer/designer balanced major elements to create cohesion

VISUAL ARGUMENT
HOMEWORK

CREATING A VISUAL ARGUMENT

OBJECTIVES

- To engage students in reflecting on the relationship between humans/robots/cyborgs and constructing this relationship actively through visual representation.
- To provide students practice in identifying and visually representing a line of argument.
- To provide students practice in analyzing visual arguments and evaluating their effectiveness.
- To provide students practice in documenting images

TASK

During this term, we have read Karel Capek's play *R.U.R*, and Isaac Asimov's *I Robot*, and we have watched Ridley Scott's *Bladerunner*. In discussing these works, we have asked the following questions, among others:

Are humans already cyborgs?

Can robots have a soul?

Why do humans guard intelligence so jealously?

Why do humans craft robots in their own image?

Why do humans fear robots?

With these readings and questions in mind, create a visual argument on the following topic:

By the year 2050, I think humans and robots will become more alike, become increasingly different, or should establish the following relationship: _____.

- You may want your argument to address questions like these: *Will robots have a soul? Should robots have emotions? Should robots/cyborgs be able to love/marry/inherit property/become a citizen/raise children? Will most humans become cyborgs? Should humans respect robots as living beings? Will humans be able to download their brains into robots? Should such robots be considered cyborgs?*
- Your audience is a group of ordinary citizens, one of whom will be selected (by lottery) to sit on a national panel of robot/cyborg ethics that will make decisions on the kind of robot/cyborg research that can/should go on in this country. Your purpose is to persuade these individuals to adopt the most productive possible understanding of the human/robot/cyborg relationship.

- In your essay, make sure you identify the premise(s) of the argument and provide adequate evidence for the position you are representing. Choose evidence that will be persuasive to your audience.

FORMAT

- Compose your essay either on a web page that you create online or on a poster board that you purchase at the college book store.
- If you create a web page, compose your essay from images that you find or create online. Before you download an image from another web site, carefully check to make sure the web site does not prohibit the copying of images.
- If you use poster board, create your essay from images you cut out of magazines.
- Include at least 15 images in this essay.
- Document the source of each image using the formats below.

WEB ESSAYS & DOCUMENTING IMAGES FROM AN ONLINE SOURCE

- Create a web page for your essay.
- Create a separate web page for each image's bibliographic citation.
- Link each image in your essay to the appropriate web page containing its bibliographic entry. Here are a model and a sample:

  Artist (if given). Title of file. <Web site from which image was taken> (date on which you accessed web site).

  Example: Doe, Jane. SpottedPig.jpg. <http://www.spottedanimal/pigs/#22> (Accessed 22 July, 2002).

POSTER BOARD ESSAYS & DOCUMENTING IMAGES FROM PRINT/PHOTOGRAPHIC SOURCES

- Create your essay. Number each image.
- Create a bibliography page. List entries in numerical order, numbering each entry to correspond to an image: [15] "Drink Milk." Time 20 September 2002: 15.
- Attach this page to the back of your essay.

  Artist (if given). "Title of image" (if given). Magazine Title or Photograph Collection Day Month Year: page number (if applicable).

  Example from a magazine: [15] "Drink Milk." Time 20 September 2002: 15.

  Example from a photograph: [15] Doe, John. "Me and My Mother." Personal photograph collection. Taken 9 August 1978.

VISUAL ARGUMENT
INCLASS WORK

REVIEW AND REFLECTION (REVIEWERS' SHEET)

Composer/designer_____

Reviewer_____

OBJECTIVES
- To give you practice in analyzing visual arguments and evaluating their effectiveness.

TASK
Form Review teams of three people. For each essay in your group (two essays per person), take 10 minutes to reflect in writing on the questions that follow. *Do not ask the composers/designers to explain their essays.*

- Provide a title for this essay that speaks to the argument and the position it represents.

- In one sentence, identify the premise(s) of this essay.

- Identify the evidence that the composer/designer provides for this argument.

- Does this argument depend primarily on logos? Pathos? Ethos? Explain your answer.

- Rate the visual impact/effectiveness of this essay from 1 (least effective) to 5 (most effective). Explain the reasons for your rating with specific reference to parts of the visual essay/strategies that the author used in composing the argument.

REVIEW AND REFLECTION (COMPOSER/DESIGNER'S SHEET)

Author/designer _____

OBJECTIVE

- To involve composer/designers in reflecting on their success in presenting an argument.
- To provide students practice in analyzing visual arguments and evaluating their effectiveness.

TASK

For your own essay, take 10 minutes to reflect in writing on the first 5 questions that follow. *Do not explain your essay to reviewers.* For homework, answer the last two questions. Hand in both the reviewers' comments on your essay and your own reflections at the beginning of the next class period.

IN CLASS

- Provide a title for this essay that speaks to the argument and the position it represents for you.
- In one sentence, identify the premise(s) of this essay.
- Identify the evidence that you provide for this argument.
- Does your argument depend primarily on logos? Pathos? Ethos? Explain your answer.
- Rate the effectiveness of your essay from 1 (least effective) to 5 (most effective). Explain the reasons for your rating with specific reference to parts of the visual essay.

FOR HOMEWORK

- What are the most effective parts of your argument? Why?
- What are the least effective parts of your argument? Why?

VISUAL ARGUMENT
IN CLASS WORK
EVALUATION

Composer/designer _____

1: OVERALL EFFECT OF THE VISUAL ARGUMENT

Argument's overall impact is low & presentation is less than effective.

Argument has moderate level of overall impact and presentation is moderately effective.

Argument has exceptional overall impact and presentation is highly effective.

Comments:

2: THE PREMISE OF THE VISUAL ARGUMENT

The premise of the argument is not clearly identified.

The premise of the argument is identified.

The premise of the argument is clearly identified.

Comments:

3: SUPPORTING EVIDENCE FOR THE ARGUMENT

The supporting evidence is less than persuasive.

The supporting evidence is persuasive.

The supporting evidence is highly persuasive.

Comments:

4: REFLECTION

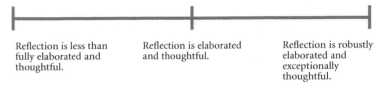

Reflection is less than
fully elaborated and
thoughtful.

Reflection is elaborated
and thoughtful.

Reflection is robustly
elaborated and
exceptionally
thoughtful.

Comments:

5: DOCUMENTATION OF IMAGES

Images are not correctly
documented.

Images are generally
correctly documented.

All images are
documented correctly.

Comments:

ACTIVITY 3

TRAVELING PHOTO EXHIBIT

TEACHER'S NOTES

GOALS

- To engage students in conceptualizing and composing a visual exhibition.
- To engage students in writing about exhibitions and images.
- To provide students practice in documenting photographs

TIME REQUIRED

- 1 homework assignment to visit photography websites, and to conceptualize and create a traveling exhibition (1-2 weeks).
- 1 class period to view and write about exhibition.
- 1 homework assignment to write a Curator's Commentary.

SEQUENCE OF ACTIVITIES

1 For homework, students will reflect on the most important/influential points of hatred/despair and points of hope they see as influencing contemporary American society and write informally about why each of these points seems to be a major influence on American society.

2 For homework, students will visit the AccuNet/AP Multimedia Archive <http://ap.accuweather.com/apphoto/index.htm> and select photographs that illustrate their vision of hatred/despair and hope in America to create a traveling art exhibit entitled: "College Students Envision the 21st Century: Hatred and Hope Construct America." Students will write an explanatory note for each image that explains 1) why this particular point/location is so important to/influential on American life and 2) how this point/location affects/shapes/structures American society.

3 In class, students form three-person Response teams and review each student's exhibit.

4 For homework, the exhibit designer will write an overall Curator's Commentary that ties together the images and the various points of social focus they represent. The purpose of this commentary is to indicate why these particular points/locations of hatred/despair and hope seem particularly important—as a coherent group of issues—to the designer/composer.

TRAVELING PHOTO EXHIBIT
HOMEWORK

MAKING A VISUAL EXHIBITION

GOALS

- To conceptualize, compose, and document a visual exhibition.
- To write about exhibitions and images.
- To provide you practice in documenting photographs.

TASK

- You have been asked to assemble a photography exhibit titled *College Students Envision the 21st Century: Hatred and Hope as They Construct America*. This exhibit will travel around the country and appear on various college campuses—usually in a setting like the student union.

- The goal of the exhibit is to portray what a typical college student (you!) sees as the 5–7 most important/influential points (locations) of hatred/despair and the 5–7 most important/influential points (locations) of hope that—collectively—structure the American experience in the first decade of the 21st century. The primary audience for the exhibition is college students—some of whom will see the world as you do and some of whom will not.

- **For Homework Task #1**, spend 10–15 minutes brainstorming about points (locations) of hatred/despair that you see affecting/structuring/influencing American culture (e.g., violence, war, hate crimes, prejudice, narrow mindedness)—and points (locations) of hope that you see affecting/structuring/influencing American culture (e.g., education, religion, family, friends, nature). List as many of these points (locations) as possible. Some points (locations)—like money—may structure the American experience from both the perspective of hatred/despair (e.g., poverty, the gap between the rich and the poor) and from the perspective of hope (e.g., upward mobility, security).

- **For Homework Task #2**, from your brainstormed list, choose the 5–7 most important/influential points (locations) of hatred/despair and the 5–7 most important/influential points of hope and do 5 minutes of informal written reflection about how each of these points/ locations structures/influences/shapes the larger American society. Your task is not to choose any 10–14 points (locations), but—rather—to choose the 10–14 most important/influential according to your own observations. Taken collectively, these points (locations) should serve as the major boundary conditions within which the American experience is constructed—and within which most Americans formulate their identity as they grow up.

- **For Homework Task #3**, go to

  Yahoo! Picture Gallery <http://gallery.yahoo.com>,

  Alta Vista ImageSearch <http://www.altavista.com/image>

  or

  the Electric Library site <http://www.elibrary.com> (sign up for the two-day trial)

  and find at least one photograph that provides a visual image of each point.

- **For Homework Task #4** create a traveling exhibit of 10–20 photographs that represents as a collection the most important/influential points (locations) of hatred/despair and the most important/influential of hope that American society faces in the first decade of the 21st century. Also write an explanatory card for each major point in the exhibit that explains why this particular point/location is so important to/influential on American life and how this point/location affects/shapes/structures American society.

- **Create your traveling exhibition on a web site or with paper.** This exhibition should demonstrate professionalism in organization and presentation. All images (online and offline) should be appropriately documented.

FORMAT

- Create this exhibition either on a web page or poster boards.
- If you create a web page, compose your essay from images that you find at the photography sites listed above.
- If you use poster boards, create your exhibition from works you have printed from the WWW.
- Include 10–20 images (and explanatory cards) in your exhibition.
- Document the source of each image using the formats that follow.

EXHIBIT ON THE WEB

- Create an opening splash page for your exhibition that contains its title and a link leading to each image and explanatory comment.
- Create a separate web page for every image. Beneath each work, identify the name of the photographer (if available), the date it appeared in print in a newspaper (day, month, and year), the title of the photograph (if available), the date the photograph was originally taken (if available), the newspaper in which it appeared (section and page—if available), and the address of the AccuNet/AP Multimedia Archive URL and date you accessed the site..

Example: Doe, Jane (14 February 1988). "Castle Edinburgh," taken on 2 February 1987. Gazette, D2, Accessed 14 April 2002 at <http://ap.accuweather.com/apphoto/index.htm>.

EXHIBIT ON POSTER BOARD

- Create a title page for your exhibition.
- Print copies of the images you select—one to a page.
- Beneath each work, identify the name of the photographer (if available), the date it appeared in print in a newspaper (day, month, and year), the title of the photograph (if available), the date the photograph was originally taken (if available), the newspaper in which it appeared (section and page—if available), and the URL at which you found the photograph.

  Example: Doe, Jane (14 February 1988). "Castle Edinburgh," taken on 2 February 1987. Gazette, D2, Accessed 14 April 2002 at <http://www.elibrary.com>.

RESPONSE AND REFLECTION (RESPONDERS' SHEET)

Composer/designer _____

Responder _____

OBJECTIVE

- To respond to a photography exhibit focused on a common theme.

TASK

Form Response Teams of three people. *View each exhbit in your group; write responses to the questions below. Do not ask composers/designers to explain their exhibits.*

- What points are particularly compelling in this exhibit? Why?

- What points are the weakest parts of this exhibit? Why?

- Choose one point for which the composer/designer does a particularly effective job of linking the explanatory card to the images. Explain why you think the card and the images work so well together.

- Choose one point for which the composer/designer does a less effective job of linking the explanatory card to the images. Explain why you think the card and the images do not work so well together.

- Reflect on the overall impact of the whole exhibit and the mood it creates. What message does the exhibit convey to you? How is this message/impact created (e.g., color, shape, focus, theme, subject, technique)? Employ specific references to images and explanations in the exhibit as well as to the exhibit as a whole.

RESPONSE AND REFLECTION (EXHIBIT DESIGNER'S SHEET)

Composer/designer _____

OBJECTIVE

- To involve students in writing about the exhibit they have created.

TASK

In class

Draft a two-page Curator's Commentary that introduces a college audience to the theme of this exhibit, reflects on that theme, and tells why you selected the points/locations and photographic images that you did. This Commentary should serve to bring together the different points/locations of hatred/despair and hope—to make a cohesive whole of the exhibit. The Curator's Commentary is the mortar between the bricks that compose the exhibit.

For homework

- Read the responses individuals had to your exhibit.
- Revise your Curator's Commentary.
- Hand in both the responses and the Curator's Commentary at the beginning of the next class period.

TRAVELLING PHOTO EXHIBIT
INCLASS WORK

SAMPLE EVALUATION

Curator _____

1: OVERALL IMPACT OF THE EXHIBIT

Exhibit's overall impact is weak & the presentation is neither effective nor creative.

Exhibit's overall impact is moderate & the presentation is somewhat effective and creative.

Exhibit is exceptionally strong and the presentation is effective and creative.

Comments:

2: CURATOR'S COMMENTARY

The Curator's Commentary isn't effective in making a cohesive whole of the exhibit.

The Curator's Commentary is effective in making a cohesive whole of the exhibit.

The Curator's Commentary is exceptionally effective in making a cohesive whole of the exhibit.

Comments:

3: EXPLANATORY CARDS

Explanatory Cards aren't successful in telling how & why points shape American society.

Explanatory Cards are successful in telling how & why points shape American society.

Cards are highly successful in telling how & why points shape American society.

Comments:

4: DOCUMENTATION OF PHOTOGRAPHS

The photographs are not correctly documented.

The photographs are generally correctly documented.

All the photographs are documented correctly.

Comments:

ACTIVITY 4

TEXT RE-DESIGN AND

RE-VISION

TEACHER'S NOTES

GOALS

- To engage students in re-designing and revising a print essay to make it more effective on the WWW.
- To involve students in assessing the effectiveness of their own and others' web designs.
- To engage students in exploring the possibilities of the WWW as an authoring/design medium.

NOTE

To accomplish this assignment, students must know how to create a WWW page. If there are some students in the class who do not know how to design a web page, schedule a class session (or a homework session) in which a knowledgeable student introduces a simple web editor such as Netscape's COMPOSER or Microsoft's FRONTPAGE. If no such students are available, have students access one or more of the web sites under Resources where they will find self-paced tutorials that they can use to accomplish their homework. If teachers do not know the rudiments of web design, they should do this assignment as well.

TIME REQUIREMENTS

- One in-class session during which groups review sample web essays and share findings.
- One in-class session or homework assignment in which students create a practice web site (2 days).
- Homework assignments in which students re-design and revise a print essay for the web (1–2 weeks).
- One in-class session or homework assignment during which student Review Teams advise on revision and re-design efforts.
- One homework assignment to reflect on revision and re-design effort.

ASSIGNMENT SEQUENCE

- In class, groups of 3–5 look at the following sites/essays and create a list of ways that author/designers can take advantage of the WWW to create essays that are more effective—visually and structurally—than they could be on paper. In class discussion, groups share findings:

<http://www.georgetown.edu/bassr/bishop/teenager.htm>
<http://www.georgetown.edu/bassr/bishop/dream1.htm>

<http://www.cwrl.utexas.edu/~daniel/hyperwriting/arguments/rodriguez/index.html>

<http://www.cwrl.utexas.edu/~daniel/hyperwriting/webarguments/barnhill/main.html>

<http://www.cwrl.utexas.edu/~daniel/hyperwriting/webarguments/fleishman/>

<http://www.cwrl.utexas.edu/~daniel/hyperwriting/webarguments/marcoux/index.html>

<http://www.cwrl.utexas.edu/~daniel/hyperwriting/webarguments/han/main.html>

<http://www.cwrl.utexas.edu/~daniel/hyperwriting/webarguments/gilbert/>

<http://www.cwrl.utexas.edu/~daniel/hyperwriting/webarguments/zumwalt/intro.html>

- In class or for homework, students use Netscape *Composer* or Microsoft *Frontpage* to create a practice web page with the following elements: a title, 2 imported graphic files, 3 links to other web pages (not created by the author designer), 3 links to web pages created by the author/designer (these can be dummy pages with minimal context), a cool background, some colored text, 2 appropriate navigation buttons.

- For homework, students will choose one print essay that they have written and had evaluated during the term. They will re-design and revise this essay to create a more effective essay on the WWW.

- In class or for homework, student Review Teams advise on revision and re-design efforts.

- For homework, composers/designers reflect on the effectiveness of their revision/redesign efforts.

- If possible, in all activities, encourage students to form and work in study groups that include at least 2 students who know the basics of web design.

RESOURCES & TUTORIALS FOR COMPOSING WEB SITES
Netscape Composer
<http://wp.netscape.com/browsers/using/newusers/composer/>

Microsoft FrontPage
<http://office.microsoft.com/downloads/2000/FPTutor.aspx>
<http://www.fgcu.edu/support/office2000/frontpage/>
<http://www.msubillings.edu/tool/fp/>

<http://www.kayetech.com/fp_intro.htm>

Both

<http://www.fluffbucket.com>

Best and Worst Examples of Web Pages (not student essays)

<http://www.coolhomepages.com/html/worstsites.html>

<http://www.coolhomepages.com/>

<http://botw.org/>

<http://www.killersites.com/2-sites/>

Design

<http://www.builder.com/Graphics/Design/ss2.html>

<http://www.webpagesthatsuck.com/>

Web Style (Advanced)

<http://info.med.yale.edu/caim/manual/graphics/graphics.html>

TEXT RE-DESIGN AND RE-VISION
HOMEWORK

REVISING FOR THE WEB

OBJECTIVES

- To involve you in expanding a text's effectiveness—in terms of organization, structure, presentation, scope, development, and visual information—by revising and re-designing it for the World Wide Web.
- To involve you in learning about the potential of the World Wide Web as an authoring/design medium.
- To involve you in learning—or learning more about—web authoring/design.

TASK

- In class, examine sample essays that take advantage of the World Wide Web as an authoring/design medium.
- For homework, choose a paper that you have already handed in and had graded this term—one that you would like to revise and one that you think could benefit from the expanded possibilities of the World Wide Web.
- Revise and re-design your paper to take advantage of the World Wide Web as an composing/design medium with expanded possibilities for information design, organization, enhancement, and presentation.
- Consider, among other options, that you might
  - revise the essay to present the information in a more effective way or to develop information more extensively or thoroughly (employing links and additional pages to accommodate the new presentation and information)
  - revise the essay by re-organizing it or adding to it (employing links and additional pages to accommodate the new organization and information)
  - revise the essay by adding links to related online resources that provide additional scope to the text
  - re-design the text to focus on its logical structures (representing the paper's organization in the 3-D space of the web)
  - revise the essay by adding appropriate visual elements (photographs, paintings, graphics, design elements, etc.) that expand and/or enhance its content
  - re-design the text to make use of color, layout, chunked text, spatial organization, etc.
- Make sure that your web essay represents a text that is both substantially revised and re-designed in comparison with the original print essay.

- Be sure to cite additional sources (including web sites and graphics) appropriately in the bibliography. Consult the following source for citation style: <http://www.apastyle.org/elecref.html>
- Your revised web essay should be creative (both in its visual and its alphabetic content), should contain information that is both robust and richly-textured, take advantage of the World Wide Web's potential, should be interesting and compelling for readers, and should be correct in terms of mechanics/grammar/documentation/bibliography.

TEXT RE-DESIGN AND RE-VISION
IN CLASS WORK

LOOKING AT SAMPLE WEB ESSAYS (IN-CLASS WORK)

OBJECTIVES

- To involve you in re-thinking the possibilities for a text presented on the WWW—considering possibilities for revision, information design, re-organization, enhancement, and presentation.
- To involve you in discovering and articulating the characteristics of effective web authoring/design.

TASK

- In class, in groups of 3–5, examine the essays represented at the following URLs:

    <http://www.georgetown.edu/bassr/bishop/teenager.htm>

    <http://www.georgetown.edu/bassr/bishop/dream1.htm>

    <http://www.cwrl.utexas.edu/~daniel/hyperwriting/arguments/rodriguez/index.html>

    <http://www.cwrl.utexas.edu/~daniel/hyperwriting/webarguments/barnhill/main.html>

    <http://www.cwrl.utexas.edu/~daniel/hyperwriting/webarguments/fleishman/>

    <http://www.cwrl.utexas.edu/~daniel/hyperwriting/webarguments/marcoux/index.html>

    <http://www.cwrl.utexas.edu/~daniel/hyperwriting/webarguments/han/main.html>

    <http://www.cwrl.utexas.edu/~daniel/hyperwriting/webarguments/gilbert/>

    <http://www.cwrl.utexas.edu/~daniel/hyperwriting/webarguments/zumwalt/intro.html>

- As a group, create a list of ways that these composers/designers take advantage of the WWW to create essays that are more effective—visually and structurally—than they could be on paper. Bookmark example texts for each item on your list.
- Be prepared to share your findings with other groups—showing and referring to example texts for support of your points.
- Take notes on the techniques that other groups identify that your group does not—these techniques will come in useful when you revise and re-design your own essay to take advantage of the WWW.

TEXT RE-DESIGN AND RE-VISION
INCLASS WORK

ESSAY REVIEW
(REVIEW TEAM)

Name of Review Team Member _____

PURPOSE

- To involve you in reviewing essays that have been revised and re-designed for the web and assessing their effectiveness.

TASK

In pairs, take 30 minutes to review your partner's web essay and comment on the following points in writing.

- What is the primary message you get from this web essay? What is its thesis?

- Rate the composer's/designer's overall success in revising and re-designing the essay to take advantage of the potential of the WWW on a scale from 1 (not much significant revision/re-design, not very successful) to 5 (significant revision/re-design, very successful). Explain your rating below.

- Rate the essay's interest level and impact level on a scale from 1 (not very interesting, low impact) to 5 (very interesting, high impact). Explain your rating below.

- Rate the texture and robustness of the information presented in the essay level on a scale from 1 (not very robust/thinly textured) to 5 (very robust/richly textured). Explain your rating below.

- Rate the essay's creativity on a scale from 1 (not very creative) to 5 (very creative). Explain your rating below.

- On the back of this sheet, provide the composer/designer with suggestions for further revision and re-design. Attach additional sheets if necessary. The composer/designer will attach all the Review Sheets to her/his Reflection Assignment and hand them into the teacher for grading.

TEXT RE-DESIGN AND RE-VISION
INCLASS WORK

REFLECTION MEMO
(COMPOSER/DESIGNER)

Composer/Designer _____

PURPOSE

- To engage you in reflecting on the Team Review commentaries for your essay and the assignment criteria with the purposes of determining its strengths and weaknesses and making a plan for the essay's revision.
- To provide you practice in writing an informative memorandum.

TASK

Write a memorandum to the teacher that informs him/her about the following points:

- The five matters that you consider most important to attend to in revising this essay.
- The order in which you are going to address these matters and an explanation of why you have chosen this plan of attack for your revision.

Attach this sheet and the Team Review commentaries to your memo and hand this packet of materials in at the beginning of the next class session.

SAMPLE EVALUATION

Composer/designer _____

1: USE OF WORLD WIDE WEB

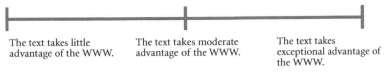

The text takes little
advantage of the WWW.

The text takes moderate
advantage of the WWW.

The text takes
exceptional advantage of
the WWW.

Comments:

2: OVERALL IMPACT OF THE TEXT

The text's overall impact
is low.

The text's overall impact
& interest are moderate.

The text's overall impact &
interest are high.

Comments:

3: CREATIVITY OF THE TEXT

The text is not very
creative.

The text is moderately
creative.

The text is exceptionally
creative.

Comments:

4: INFORMATION

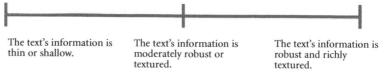

The text's information is
thin or shallow.

The text's information is
moderately robust or
textured.

The text's information is
robust and richly
textured.

Comments:

5: MECHANICS

The text is less than
correct in its grammar,
documentation, and/or
bibliography.

The text is generally
correct in its grammar,
documentation, and/or
bibliography.

The text is thoroughly
correct in its grammar,
documentation, and/or
bibliography.

Comments:

BOX-LOGIC

Geoffrey Sirc

Let me confess: it has been a frustrating last several years for me in my writing courses. The rapid advance of technology has meant a pedagogical dilemma for me: just what do I do in the classroom, what do I teach? Gail Hawisher and Cindy Selfe have written recently about this struggle, noting "the increasing change [in compositional media] and the increasing alienation that scholars are beginning to recognize as an outgrowth of such instability" (190). Is the essay still our central genre? Do our students do Web sites? Do we teach html? Email as a genre? Where do we go?

Well, where I wanted to go, what made the most sense to me personally, was Marcel Duchamp. Specifically, Duchamp's *Green Box* (1934), the collection of personal notes (reproduced above) he made to himself while working on his *Large Glass*.

Here's the more conventional textual form of the work, as published in Duchamp's selected writings:

> [1. MARGINAL NOTES]
>
> *The bride stripped bare by her bachelors even.*
> to separate the *mass-produced readymade* from the *readyfound*—The separation is an operation.
>
> Kind of Subtitle
> *Delay in Glass*
>
> Use "delay" instead of picture or painting; picture on glass becomes delay in glass—but delay in glass does not mean picture on glass—
>
> It's merely a way of succeeding in no longer thinking that the thing in question is a picture—to make a delay of it in the most general way possible, not so much in the different meanings in which delay can be taken, but rather in their indecisive reunion "delay"—/a delay in glass as you would say a poem in prose or a spittoon in silver
>
> l. 1912
> The machine with 5 hearts, the pure child, of nickel and platinum, must dominate the Jura-Paris road.
>
> On the one hand, the chief of the 5 nudes will be ahead of the 4 other nudes *towards* this Jura-Paris road. On the other hand, the headlight child will be the instrument conquering this Jura-Paris road
>
> This headlight child could, graphically, be a comet, which would have its tail in front, this tail being an appendage of the headlight child appendage which absorbs by crushing (gold dust, graphically) this Jura-Paris road.

It's the idea of the prose catalogue.

Text as a collection of interesting, powerful statements.

A kind of daybook or artist's notebook.

The way I myself work—jotting notes on the fly, sound-bite aperçus that sound good by themselves but can also become workable bits in a larger structure.

A basic compositional tool; a medium I feel my students (who are certainly capable of interesting stretches of prose) could work well within.

Jean Suquet has some relevant, deeply engaging commentary on Duchamp's amazing work:

> In Paris, in 1934, an edition of a hundred or a hundred and fifty copies of the Green Box was published—so named because of its green flocked cardboard cover and the assonance between "vert" [green], "verre" [glass], and "ouvert" [open]. Ninety-four scraps of paper bearing plans, drawings, hastily jotted notes, and freely drawn rough drafts were delivered in bulk. It was up to the reader to shuffle these cards as he or she pleased. There was no author's name on the cover; the work appeared anonymous and as if offered to the blowing winds. In light of this, I had not the least scruple, when opening it for the first time in 1949 at the request of André Breton, in making it speak (with Marcel Duchamp's consent) in my own voice; and out of its sparkling randomness, I began fishing words that resonated with something I felt deep inside me, something obscure yet promising illumination. If an interior journey goes deep enough, at some point it arrives where all roads meet. I was twenty. I dreamt—with due reverence—of taking up the journey where the previous traveler had left off. (86)

Suquet, then, had an encounter with Duchamp, a meeting, to which each of them brought their own experiences and searches, their own effort and commitment. He saw Marcel as a fellow-traveler, and their encounter changed Suquet's life, evoked in him a grand dream, a life-long project. His whole scholarly career became an extension or annotation of *The Green Box* and *The Large Glass*. Duchamp was able to effect this vocation in Suquet, perhaps, because the technology of composition he used was different, interesting, human-scaled, inter-active.

Formal requirements were left open, *ouvert*; the focus was on the idea behind the composition, the statement it made: "I considered painting as a means of expression," Marcel said in an interview, "not an end in itself [... P]ainting should not be exclusively retinal or visual; it should have to do with the gray matter, with our urge for understanding" (135-136). Duchamp, then, is concerned with the revelation contained in the text. His comment captures my own interest in technology— the means or media are not as important to me as the expressive or conceptual uses afforded by them. Especially uses that seem simpatico with my students' needs and skills. *The Green Box* is emblematic of how I want to use technology in my writing courses: as allowing students an easy entré into composition, a compelling medium and genre with which to re-arrange textual materials—both original and appropriated—in order to have those materials speak the student's own voice and concerns, allowing them to come up with something obscure, perhaps, yet promising illumination. It's difficult to define students' needs, of course. Elbow put the dilemma best, I think: life is long, college short; do we teach to life or college? I'm more and more persuaded to err on the side of life in my courses: both the public, cultural lives students live, as well as their own personal lives and expressions.

So I want a format or method suited to the long strange trip.

"Most of what we teach and what we do is wrong, out of date," Johndan Johnson-Eilola argued in his 2000 Watson conference address. **If we (finally) journey away from the linear norm of essayist prose, which the texts of the everyday world implore us to do, where do we go, especially in a composition classroom? What sorts of formal and material concerns guide a newly-mediated pedagogical practice?** This is where Duchamp, and others of his ilk, can help: ever since (at least) the *wunderkabinetten*, the box has provided a basic container or frame for storing and exhibiting one's most passionately cherished items. In terms of transcending essayist prose, then, and all its conventions/restrictions/impediments, the box offers a grammar which could prove useful in guiding our classroom practice in light of rapidly shifting compositional media: it allows both textual pleasure, as students archive their personal collections of text and imagery, and formal practice in learning the compositional skills that seem increasingly important in contemporary culture.

To tease out some notions of what **the logic of the box** has to offer composition pedagogy, I'd like to range between three specific scenes of historical boxes:

- Joseph Cornell, one of the true poets of American art, and one who made the box his artistic genre of choice.

- Walter Benjamin, unpacking the boxes of books that made up his personal library.

- George Maciunas, the founder of Fluxus, an international art movement that, among other things, relied on box technology to curate and disseminate creative work.

I'm going to give the most attention to Cornell because I'm most interested in composition that has an ultimate poetic effect.

Many critics have pointed to the city as a strong influence in the work of Cornell. In the 1920s, Cornell sold textiles throughout the lower Manhattan manufacturing districts, where he began to haunt secondhand stores and junk shops when he had time to kill. Those shops helped him refine his aesthetic, which included, like Benjamin's monumental attempt to interrogate the history of 19th-century Paris, an obsession for the historical-materialist European past, particularly the aesthetic realm circumscribed by the French writers he studied while a student at Phillips Academy and about which he remained passionate his entire life. That meant the world of poetry, music, theatre, and especially classical ballet. In Dore Ashton's words, he was a "thrall of the exquisite" (1). Also, he was particularly interested in early cinema, and was always excited to find prints of old films in junk shops. He was a pack rat by nature, and his house in Utopia Parkway became a repository for all the magical finds he made on his rounds. Influenced by the Surrealists who moved to America during the 1930s, especially Max Ernst and Marcel Duchamp, he began to make collages of his found objects. Soon, again influenced by Duchamp, he began to arrange his carefully chosen, highly associational objects into boxes. "I've never called myself an artist," Cornell said. "On voter registration, I call myself a designer. [...] I can't draw, paint, sculpt, [or] make lithographs" (qtd. in Ashton 4). Ashton felt what he did was create dream-texts, "captur[ing] the dream-thoughts clustered around a nodal point in the dream" (15). This especially makes sense when you consider the repetitive symbology Cornell used, and the deeply idiosyncratic associational logic he used to juxtapose his material symbols. As Freud noted, "the content of the dream merely says as it were: 'all these things have an element X in common'" (16). So **notions of articulate coherence, conventional organization, and extensive development seem irrelevant** to a box like Cornell's. Carter Ratcliff called Cornell "a virtuoso of fragments," and it's true—the way, in his hands, ready-made shards, invested with desire, can have such profound metonymic power: a "white dowel toward the front of [a] box, a toylike column, is an emblem of all of architecture" (43). Ashton nicely describes his compositional method: "Suggestive objects—that is, objects that are named and whose names bestir associations—are juxtaposed with elements provoking unnamed associations, such as glass fragments, mirrors, and astronomical charts. [... T]he Cornell box sojourns in a terra incognita between two art forms, the poetic and the plastic" (23). One might include the sonic, as well. Duchamp might have been the first to add sound to art, in his 1916 piece *With Hidden Noise,* but Cornell quickly appreciated the possibilities of extending his palette with noise: there are his sand boxes, those with rolling balls, or metal springs—even ones with music boxes in them. Almost immediately with Cornell, as a teacher, I get the possibility of student as passionate designer, with heart and soul as compositional factors that need as much attention as hand, eye, or brain.

The photos of Cornell's basement studio, shelves crammed with containers labeled "sea shells," "watch parts," or "owl cutouts," show the fruits of his obsession. Also amassed in his house were the immense files he kept, the notes and clippings he collected and which continued to grow to enormous proportions throughout his life; dossiers that became as massive as the ones Benjamin bound together in files called "convolutes" to organize his annotations on various aspects of daily life in 19th century Paris. Cornell, too, then, as the collector. Ashton speaks of "his trove of books, notes, and dossiers, which were his sustenance and inspiration" (1 2). For example, there is one of his most carefully tended dossiers, labeled "The Bay of Naples," "and its changing contents included, at various times, views of Vesuvius, photographs of windows, reproductions of works by Chirico, old Italian mezzotints that resembled Chiricos, and engravings of [Fanny] Cerrito" (Ashton 25). Cornell himself described his dossiers as

> a diary journal repository laboratory, picture gallery, museum, sanctuary, observatory, key [...] the core of a labyrinth, a clearinghouse for dreams and visions [...] childhood regained. (qtd. in Simic 35)

Our first aspect, then, to how we might use technology to achieve powerful ends with new media lies in aestheticizing the scene of composition in an idiosyncratic, obsessional way. It's the writer not only as selector (Duchamp) but as collector, where the choosing is suffused with desire. The personally associational becomes key criteria. A kind of idio-aesthetic or idio-connoisseurship. It's the mood of Benjamin, as he unpacks his library, namely, "anticipation": "join me," he invites his reader, "in the disorder of crates that have been wrenched open, the air saturated with the dust of wood, the floor covered with torn paper, [...] join me among piles of volumes that are seeing daylight again after two years of darkness" (59). **So, as readers, we might best take the anticipatory stance towards texts:** ready to enter an exhibit; students as curators, mounting another show of the ever-evolving permanent collection at their musées imaginaires. Text, then, as a collection of retrojective, idiosyncratic dream-moments, now electronically gathered, framed, and exhibited. Cornell, of course, was the ultimate curator, the ultimate collector. According to Kynaston McShine,

> Cornell's sensibility as a collector is an important element in his art. He treated the ephemeral object as if it were the rarest heirloom of a legendary prince or princess; one must respect the intensity of his vision and the magic with which he invested the ordinary with an eloquent and arresting presence. For Cornell, a necklace from Woolworth's had as much value as one from Fabergé, and it became the souvenir of a Romantic ballerina who danced for a highwayman on the snow while crossing the Steppes of Russia. (10-11)

Cornell loved his objects, "happy to possess [them], but careful not to[...] destroy [their] enigma" (O'Doherty 258). **The materially interesting, then, is what should guide acquisition.** Benjamin doesn't want to write about his textual collection in terms of its "history or even [its] usefulness to a writer" (59). Instead, just the buzz of collecting, the thrill, a feeling "more palpable," as he terms it (59), "the spring tide of memories which surges toward any collector as he contemplates his possessions" (60). So, finding those aspects of the real that are particularly suffused with fascination becomes a key part of box-oriented composition, putting the *wunder* into *wunderkabinette*. "The most profound enchantment for the collector," writes Benjamin,

Unless otherwise noted, quotations from Benjamin in this chapter are from "Unpacking My Library."

> is the locking of individual items within a magic circle in which they are fixed as the final thrill, the thrill of acquisition, passes over them. [...F]or a true collector the whole background of an item adds up to a magic encyclopedia whose quintessence is the fate of his object. [...] One has only to watch a collector handle the objects in his glass case. As he holds them in his hands, he seems to be seeing through them into their distant past as though inspired. (60-61)

So, text as box = author as collector,

as passionate re-fashioner of an idiosyncratic, metonymic world; students working to find their own personal symbologies. "Every passion borders on the chaotic," Benjamin writes, "but the collector's passion borders on the chaos of memories" (60). The challenge for the composer, then, is to capture that memory-laden thrill for the viewer, inventing a uniquely visionary world from carefully chosen fragments of the existing one. Even the backs of many of Cornell's boxes include items collaged into small collections: "he often included a line of poetry that interested him, occasionally a map, perhaps even noted the music he was listening to when the box or collage was being made" (McShine 12).

This presumes, of course, what another famous box artist, Fluxus founder George Maciunas, strove for: bringing an art consciousness to daily life. Maciunas claimed, "there was no need for art. We had merely to learn to take an 'art attitude'[…] towards all everyday phenomena" (Wijers 8-9). Harold Rosenberg writes that "when Cornell discovered a particularly brilliant chewing-gum machine in the Thirty-fourth Street station of the B.-M. T., he rushed around urging his friends to go see it" (75). Later, that same machine would provide Cornell with the template for his most famous box, his *Medici Slot Machine*. **A primary goal now in my writing classes: to show my students how their compositional future is assured if they can take an art stance to the everyday, suffusing the materiality of daily life with an aesthetic.** It's learning this possibly new, possibly foreign, reflexive art-attitude towards the stuff of their lives, "participating in the common life while holding [themselves] strictly apart from it" (Rosenberg 78). **In a composition class like mine, for example, centered on such treasured material as the texts of rap music, the student must step back, not looking at rap as *the bomb* (which would be popular writing, 'zine writing), but seeing rap as strange-d, made curious, something interesting to consider, an object of intellectual fascination as much as emotional possession. It's the writer not only as collector, but as dissatisfied collector, one impatiently seeking pleasure:** "Writers are really people who write books […] because they are dissatisfied with the books which they could buy but do not like" (Benjamin 61). So, composition as craving; teaching students to feel desire and lack. "Cornell [was always] drawn to popular art products, but only when they […] ceased to be popular; he [was] a devoted collector of old movie films, old phonograph records, old picture postcards" (Rosenberg 78). "[O]wnership," Benjamin felt, "is the most intimate relationship that one can have to objects. Not that they come alive in him; it is he who lives in them" (67). I want students, for example, to be as obsessed about rap, as interested in creating their boxed homages to it, as Cornell was about Fanny Cerrito. It's important, I think, to have students work with lived texts of desire (rather than, say, the middlebrow academia of a Jane Tompkins or Mary Louise Pratt) in order to develop a passional aesthetic like Cornell's and Benjamin's.

Materials are unoriginal, then, recycled, chosen on the basis of exoticism and strong interest, as well as availability. Work with a strong history to dwell in was key for Benjamin, too: "to renew the old world—that is the collector's deepest desire when he is driven to acquire new things, and that is why a collection of older books is closer to the wellsprings of collecting than the acquirer of luxury editions" (61). Involved here is an aesthetic of the found object, of interesting, quirky small-t truths one stumbles upon. The *objet trouvé* was used by modern artists as a way to protest the preciousness of art and reconnect us back to the reality of life. As German curator René Block sees it, such an endeavor "could be most concretely accomplished by using parts of the real world in art just as they were found. The *objet trouvé* became a quotation of reality" (n. pag.).

In 1912 Apollonaire spoke of a new source of inspiration:

> Prospectuses, catalogues, posters, advertisements of all sorts which contain the poetry of our age: The collage technique, that art of reassembling fragments of pre-existing images in such a way as to form a new image, is the most important innovation in the art of this century. Found objects, chance creations, [and] ready-mades[…] abolish the separation between art and life. The commonplace is miraculous if rightly seen, if recognized. (qtd. in Simic 18)

This genre very quickly suggested itself to Maciunas. Art historian Jon Hendricks notes

> The idea of producing Fluxus yearboxes of completely new, unpublished works by the most radical artists from many different countries was derived from La Monte Young's idea for *An Anthology*. Initially Maciunas thought of a magazine in an expanded format to promote the [Fluxus] movement. (120)

Maciunas soon changed genres from the magazine to the box, choosing for his Fluxus News-Policy-Letter of May 1962, "a flat box to contain the contents so as to permit inclusion of many loose items: records, films, 'poor man's films-flip books,' 'original art,' metal, plastic, wood objects, scraps of paper, clippings, junk, raggs [sic]. Any composition or work that cannot be reproduced in standard sheet form or cannot be reproduced at all" (Hendricks 120).

So box artists work amid their trove of personally meaningful detritus, which they know can yield poetry. O'Doherty referred to Cornell's Utopia Parkway house as "not just an abode, but an image of the artist's methods, dilemmas, and quests" (280). And Yoshi Wada provides a glimpse of Maciunas's methods and quests: "He had so many things—various collections of exotic items—spice, water, dirt, rocks, animal and bird shit, huge amounts of bags and containers, Fluxus boxes, archives—and it goes on and on. These were very well arranged on shelves" (Williams and Noël 134). René Block adds: "[Maciunas] was his whole life long on the lookout for 'good deals', special offers of all kinds, be it plastic boxes or groceries. His house was full of the most unlikely objects, acquired through special sales in large lots and bulk purchases" (Williams and Noël 158). Like Cornell and Benjamin, as well, it's the poignant mix of poverty and desire, laced with an aesthetic of the cool.

Cornell repeatedly wrote of his delight in finding things; he recalled lingering one day, before an appointment, in some second-hand shops:

> Found Jenny Lind song sheet, La Sonambula, and colored feathers in dime store. [...] Up to 59th St. windfall of Bibliotècque Rose to cover etuis, Souvenirs containing Gérard de Nerval (DeCampo), an original colored Deveria of a standing oriental woman musician—two heroic sized forest prints for owl boxes—unusual feeling of satisfaction and accomplishment, unexpected and more abiding than usual. (Simic 9)

These are artists whose material concerns are guided by their strong, visionary needs, their desires to recreate the deeply felt images that excited them. It wasn't a question of focusing on cutting-edge technology. Fluxus artist Dick Higgins' 1966 "Statement on Intermedia" holds true today and should make us cautious in theorizing new media pedagogies. Higgins asks,

> Having discovered tools with an immediate impact, for what are we going to use them? [... I]sn't it appropriate [...] to use what we really care about and love or hate as the new subject matter in our work? Could it be that the central problem of the next ten years or so, for all artists in all possible forms, is going to be less the still further discovery of new media and intermedia, but of the new discovery of ways to use what we care about? (173)

"[W]e are more impatient and more anxious," Higgins felt, "to go to the basic images" (172). The grammar of the box can keep us grounded in the basic image, in things we really care about. That homemade aesthetic history lovingly forged out of the materials of nineteenth century Europe, Ashton calls it Cornell's "other" tradition. As a compositionist, he was always working in two realities: both the actual world, and his own, personally-forged "other" tradition. The epigram for his prose piece *The Bel Canto Pet* (1955) reads, "the light of other days," and our charge to students, I think, is having them work in and perfect a broad-based textuality, lit by their own other days' light. What I'm hoping is that students, immersed in their material desire, might (as was said of Cornell's favorite poet, Nerval) "invite us to see things in a light in which we do not know them, but which turns out to be almost that one in which we have always hoped one day to see them bathed" (Ashton 111). The everyday transformed, then: Cornell's materials "are available to anyone," Rosenberg wrote, "but in his use of them they take on an entirely subjective character. Each object enters his imagination carrying a large cargo of associations—in the box, it is redefined so as to become a term of a unique metaphor" (78). His compositional goal, according to Rosenberg: "to unveil secret affinities [...] to pin down a state of being in the consciousness of things" (78-79). According to Charles Simic, "This is what Cornell is after[:] How to construct a vehicle of reverie, an object that would enrich the imagination of the viewer and keep him company forever" (44).

True connection with one's composition is when the work has a strong life in the writer, when it's part of an on-going project, which means it continues growing, appearing in variant versions. Thus, no draft is ever finished, especially in the arbitrary scope of an academic semester. For Cornell, "no 'work' could ever be really finished, for much of its meaning continued to mill in his imagination" (Ashton 2). The tops of his boxes, in fact, were often only screwed down, so he could re-open them and fiddle with their contents. Electronic composition has always tantalized with the potential for such open-ended text. Benjamin, unpacking his library, writes of his just unboxed books "not yet on the shelves, not yet touched by the mild boredom of order" (59). He speaks of his collection in terms of

> the chance, the fate, that suffuse the past before my eyes [...] conspicuously present in the accustomed confusion of these books. For what else is this collection but a disorder to which habit has accommodated itself to such an extent that it can appear as order? (60)

The raw, then, not the cooked. A loose, unthematized collection; the parts not necessarily inflecting each other as in a traditional essay. The mind will force an order on the resultant text (*the viewers make the pictures*, was Duchamp's famous pronouncement). The refusal to allow text as open-ended, un-screwed-down box, rushing instead to impose on it the mild boredom of order, is a concern I have with much computers and writing scholarship today. A recent chapter on using new information technologies in the classroom, for example, insists on speaking of students' Web work in terms of the well-wrought essay, demanding all "elements working together to make a unified statement," requiring "cohesion and thoughtful purpose [...] precision and clarity" (Gillette 3, 4, 9). Another writer sees as one of the "limitations" of new media work that "much of the information found on the Web does not meet the standards of text in print" (Applen 15). And another scholar who also uses Joseph Cornell to theorize students' new media works takes Cornell to task, giving one of his portfolios a mediocre grade, hallucinatorially finding that "its overall coherence could be enhanced by careful reconsideration and revision"—even suggesting a recent (i.e., non-thrilling) book on the subject Cornell could read to guide that more careful revision (Janangelo 38). Such formal quibbling is absurd: Cornell was the ultimate textual researcher; O'Doherty, for example, recalls that "Everyone who knew the younger Cornell remarks on the tenacity of his pursuit of information—or linkages—that he needed to furnish his mansion of European culture" (259). To second-guess him misses his aesthetic power. I'm more convinced by the work of a theorist like Greg Ulmer, who wants a brand of "learning [that] is much closer to invention than verification"; who sees the hypermedia composer as "construct[ing] an information environment [...] writ[ing] with paradigms (sets) not arguments"; and who believes that "the significant part of the narrative is not in the story but in the physical details of the scene" (xii, 38, 138). Benjamin speaks of the collector as having "a relationship to objects which does not emphasize their functional, utilitarian value—that is, their usefulness—but studies and loves them as the scene, the stage, of their fate" (60).

As genre, Maciunas felt "Fluxus art-amusement must be simple, amusing, unpretentious, concerned with insignificances, require no skill or countless rehearsals…" (Williams and Noël 144). *Poetic enactments, verbal bibelots,* and *static theater* were terms applied to Cornell's work (Ashton 4); Rosenberg called them *object poems.* The box, then, is the historically preferred format to archive our most treasured baubles. Johnson-Eilola wonders at the underuse of programs like StorySpace and Dreamweaver in composition classes. In a pedagogy of the box, their blank screens could act as a blank canvas or cartouche, a flatbed frame ready to be inscribed with the flotsam and jetsam of textual fragments from the real or virtual world, objects, images, sounds, along with sound-bite poetry or pensées. The simple frame-container as a reliquary for the personally valuable fragment. That was Cornell's way: always starting with the box as frame, then "drift[ing] into his procedure of association, putting in and taking out, much as a poet invests his poems with words that later may be changed or eliminated" (Ashton 58). **I want students—designers, now, not essayists—free for such associational drifts; entering things naively, without countless rehearsals; trying to capture a mood or vision.** The artist Mieko Shiomi gets a gift from Maciunas in 1976:

> It was a thin plastic box, which contained eleven small objects [one for each letter of my name], such as a dry strange mushroom, a sea shell, a key, a cigar, a thin glass tube filled with fine dry leaves, etc., and a blue card with this inscription: "MIEKO SHIOMI/Spell your name with these objects/Greetings from George Maciunas."
>
> This was the last thing I received from him. It continues to be one of the most precious objects in my collection. (qtd. in Williams and Noël 37)

Clearly, then, the element of play is important in box composition. Benjamin speaks of "the childlike element" (61) involved in collecting—namely, the ability to give new life to objects and, hence, **renewing existence.** To better appreciate this power to enchant, to see the elemental aesthetic of box-composition, bear in mind the other forms of wide-eyed renewal Benjamin cites: "the painting of objects, the cutting out of figures, the application of decals—the whole range of childlike modes of acquisition, from touching things to giving them names" (61). In an article Richard Selfe wrote in collaboration with his graduate students, they issue "a clear and useful warning to academic users and teachers of digital media! Don't suck the playful, exploratory spirit out of the digital media!" (334).

Think of the Vermeer paintings of rooms that were so influential for Cornell. Glass—whether opening onto room, box, or computer screen—as window into a private world, one jam-packed with personally selected matériel from one's wanderings. "The city is a huge image machine," Charles Simic remarks in his book on Cornell. **So, the student as cyber-flâneur in the virtual urban.** "My work was a natural outcome of love for the city," Cornell claimed (qtd. in Ashton 4). But "not the city as most of us experience it," Ashton noted, rather "a city of mysteries and hidden treasures" (4). In O'Doherty's words, it was "the city and its vernacular" (258). The subject matter of box artists is the small and possibly overlooked. Even Benjamin, whose topic was the nineteenth century, recreated it through its quotidian objects. About Cornell's films it was said:

> They deal with things very close to us, every day and everywhere. Small things, not the big things. Not wars, not stormy emotions, dramatic clashes or situations. His images are much simpler. Old people in the parks. A tree full of birds. A girl in a blue dress, looking around in the street, with plenty of time on her hands. Water dripping into [a] fountain ring. (Mekas 164)

Mainstream writing instruction too often prefers to put students into contact zones of heightened cultural import. But strong art, we see, can be created out of a collection of well-chosen interesting little bits of the everyday. In a box-oriented composition, I want to allow students immersion in their mediated desires, in order to refine their aesthetic; following whatever road of excess leads to their personal palace of wisdom. So **the two basic skills I focus my course around are practicing search strategies and annotating material**. My students engage in a *Rap Arcades Project*, reading and note-taking their way through the texts of hiphop as Benjamin did 19th-century Paris in his *P   a   s   s   a   g   e   n   w   e   r   k*. First we do intense study of search engines and strategies: various databases for articles, images, statistics, chat groups, and anything else they might like to wander through in their textual journeys. It's turning the internet into a virtual arcade, a city full of junk stores to cruise and study. I have even provided them with a Research Guide portal-site linked to my university's main library page, allowing students easy linkage to a wide variety of databases that I hope will serve as an immersive, interactive map to the infoscape's topography, providing the means for some interesting rambles. Watching students learn of Google's capacity for image searches, for example, finding they can call up a whole bunch of photos of Lil Kim, is to see Joseph Cornell's eyes light up as he walks through the door of a used bookstore specializing in 19th century ballerina memorabilia. And rather than essayist prose, we practice the art of annotation   and   note-taking.

Ashton reminds us that Cornell's "readings were so interwoven with his creative life that it is impossible to describe specifically the part they played in his work" (59). Selling students on the habit of notation will, I hope, help them bring an art consciousness to their world, having everyday life and their sound-bite commentary mesh and intertwine. **Arrangement of materials and notational jottings is a desperately important compositional skill.** Cornell's dossiers were archived in his house; they proved bulky and unmanageable at times, despite their crucial influence on his work. "At times he would ask friends to help him put his mass of notes and files in order ('This place is bulging with dossiers, something has got to be done')" (Ashton 2). Young visitors and assistants especially he begged to "make an arrangement of the materials to 'see what could be done with them'" (Ashton 77). Archiving such work in boxes on the internet would allow others to study and re-arrange our student's notational scribbles, in much the same way Suquet couldn't wait to get in and re-arrange Duchamp's scribbled notes from *The Green Box*. The ability to archive the mysterious wealth of the quotidian verbalscape is one of the things that initially intrigued many of us about the internet. The pedagogical potential of Cornell's dossier method was apparent to him. He spoke about his

Portfolios—*état brut*—explorations—as much potential as the boxes. The spectator can apply this to his own modus operandi. If domestic circumstances had been different, I'd have liked to get into teaching. The spectator can, if he likes it, go out and do his own picking [...] a kind of metaphysique of exploration. [... T]his kind of thing has potential for the young blood instead of the museum kind of thing. (O'Doherty 279)

There's something increasingly untenable about the integrated coherence of college essayist prose, in which the easy falseness of a unified resolution gets prized over the richer, more difficult, de facto text the world presents itself as. The box as dossier allows a credible collection of the variety of field-notes my students amass on their journey. It's interesting to share with my students examples of the notes Benjamin took for his Arcades Project. I genuinely believe those samples of scholarly glosses and poetic rêverie offer them new possibilities for verbal expression. I plan to teach even more strongly to such a genre, showing them, for example, the associationally suggestive, poetic box-grammar of the diary of Robert Schumann, one of Cornell's favorite composers. A typical entry in Schumann's diary reads, "Ave Maria... evening... the large garden... the dear child... the moon..." (qtd. in Ashton 21). This is the same logic at work in the diary entries of Cornell himself, as well as the notebook entries of Duchamp—both "liberally adorned with suggestive hiatuses" (Ashton 21-22). **Caesura—the stylistic device most absent in our curricula.**

Association as a conjoining logic is even more basic than juxtaposition. The objects of Cornell's boxes were like words from a personal vocabulary. He said he worked "in a rebus-like way" (Ashton 71). It is this associational logic of linkages that we need to develop in our classrooms, in order to help foster a personal aesthetic among our students. The logic of the box for writing instruction in an electronic environment would include a notion of textual form as short, amorphous, concrete, simply-structured; the importance of interestingly associational juxtapositions of word, image, and sound; a materiality in which desire is a key measure of quality; the unfinished nature of the "final" product, as representing perhaps the mere shimmer of an intention, rather than the result of Composition's endless perfectability-machine of revision. **A composition of underlying images; poetic concretism, object poems.** Not text as representation, but as trace or remainder, gesturing towards situations that once existed and were strongly felt, re-activatable with their concomitant quota of wonder. **Pulsion as a term we now need for evaluating composition.** A classroom practice that tries to resolve a key dichotomy in composition, that between craft and cool, what Benjamin named as "the struggle between builder and decorator, École Polytechnique and École des Beaux Arts" (*Charles Baudelaire* 158). **The expressive, substantially refined now, returned to prominence in our curriculum, ending the long reign of the strictly analytic.** "Cornell's objects express something," O'Doherty knew. "They are not subjects of inquiry, but immensely learned and allusive carriers of meaning. They support a vision" (283).

One of the most eagerly awaited events in popular music has been the publication of the diaries Kurt Cobain kept from his teenage years until just a few months before his death. The facsimile-page published version, a compositional box permeated with lived desire, went straight to the best-seller lists; no surprise—poring through Cobain's drawings, notations, unsent letters, drafts of lyrics and album covers, music video storyboards, impassioned rants, fake interviews, reminiscences, and endless reworking of his lists of favorite albums poignantly evokes a life. The possibilities of archiving such interesting, suggestive work, logically fitting into the open-ended, flatbed frame of the box, have me especially keen on teaching composition lately. In 1962, Fluxus artist Ben Vautier did *A Flux Suicide Kit*, catalogued as "Green cardboard and metal carrying case with handwriting containing rope, shotgun shells, razor blades, electrical plug and metal clamps" (Kellein 102). OK, that's kind of morbid, perhaps, but my students might do a Survival Kit: hypermedia with links, found objects, sampled sounds, and personal writing, containing all one would need, in their opinion (music, food, art, activities, etc) to get by. Or perhaps something after Maciunas's *Fluxpost (Smiles)* (1978)—a serial work, with textual overlay added: perhaps a series of people are asked a question like 'What's bugging you?' or 'What's worth buying?' Then digital photos of the respondents are image-mapped to activate their catalogued responses. I've already alluded to my Benjamin-derived genre of reading notes, students' engagement with texts they choose to help them think about a favorite topic, producing a record of **short fabulous textual realities, a kind of street-derived genre of drive-by criticism, blips of unfinished text** needing the reader as participant in the inquiry, to fill in the holes.

What I want, I guess, is to re-habilitate Thomas C. Buell's 1969 *CCC* piece called "Notes on Keeping a Journal." I want to choose a wide variety of textual possibilities (Buell suggests things like "Report on a local event," "Advertise a product for TV," "Destroy an enemy," "Transcribe a page from a book [...] which strongly appeals to you," even simply "copying down Beatles lyrics" [45]) to provide interesting, expressive contents for a journal. What a wonderful autobiographical box such a collection of genres would be. Others are moving in this direction. There's Byron Hawk's "Spring Break Assignment," asking students to produce a photographic essay, in text and images, documenting their life over Spring Break; Jeff Rice's assignment asking students to pick the date of their choice and research what was happening then in areas such as history, politics, literature, film, comics, music, art, business, or science, building a hypertext catalogue of the results (Rice, then, has unwittingly re-invented Maciunas's famous "Biography Boxes"); Jody Shipka's "A History of 'this' Space" assignment, in which each student must take a turn documenting the class in the medium of their choice (photography, fantasy narrative, interview, transcribed tape, personal ads, whatever), all results boxed together at the end of the class; and, in his chapter in this book, Johndan Johnson-Eilola's assignment in which students interrogate search engines and compare the results. I'm suggesting, then, a pedagogy of the curio cabinet, an aesthetic of the *objet trouvé*. One that rejects auratic craft as weird and obsessive, in favor of celebrating the basic image, seeing perception as a performative gesture. One whose contents mirror those desired by Maciunas for his early boxes: "'ready mades', 'found objects,' junk, records" (Hendricks 121). What is it that writers do, exactly, if not (as Katherine Stiles describes the Fluxus box artists) "point to things in the world and negotiate their meanings through symbolic productions" (67)? The new classroom activities to refine these elements let students use what they really care about and love (or hate) as the new subject matter in their work. Homepage as hommage; personal immersion in the stuff of one's other tradition as a writer's material composition. It's getting our students and ourselves back to the basic image. So the *ur*-assignment in our courses might be the one Charles Simic saw as underlying every one of Cornell's boxes:

> Somewhere in the city [...] there are four or five still-unknown objects that belong together. Once together they'll make a work of art. That's Cornell's premise, his metaphysics, and his religion [...] The city has an infinite number of interesting objects in an infinite number of unlikely places [...] America still waits to be discovered. (14-15)

IMPLICATIONS & ASSIGNMENTS

I don't expect students to produce a perfect Cornell (just as I don't expect them to write a perfect research paper). I do, though, want them to see the logic of the box as compositional grammar, what it implies about interesting research, selection, arrangement, and expression. The research can (of necessity) be definitively unfinished, closing only on a sense of the ultimate statement trying to be made (as well as any exciting bits along the way). It's the passion of appreciation and collection, combined with a sense of inquiry; a heartfelt concern mixed with intellectual problem-solving. Opening writing to new media affords us (really, demands) the opportunity to wipe the slate of classroom writing clean and ask, in true modernist fashion, "**What is essential to composition? What are the inescapable, minimal institutional constraints that must be considered?**" and, maybe better, in true postmodernist fashion, "**What are the inessential but desirable, interesting features of composition? What are the outermost institutional limits?**" And, since ours is a teaching discipline, "**What are the technologies and strategies both essential and desirable for students to perform and practice?**"

THE LOGIC OF THESE ASSIGNMENTS

To explain the logic for the assignments I've chosen, let me continue my art analogy a bit more: for most of my career as a composition instructor, I was uncomfortable with my status as academic gate-keeper. I bristled at that role of mine in an institution whose goals I saw as somberly conservative. But I've since learned to approach my role strategically. Take Hans Haacke, who creates highly-prized installations, exhibited in museums and galleries, which are deeply critical of the museum and its corporate-sponsored ability to fix form and content (not to mention its complicity in helping shape the larger cultural ambiance). When asked why he showed his work in museums, since he hated them so much, he answered:

> You have to be part of the system in order to participate in a public discourse.... As soon as you exhibit your work in galleries and museums, you are part of the system. I have always been part of the system. I am of the opinion that you cannot act outside the system, or be on your own, and participate in a discourse. ("School" 23)

As composition teachers, we mount exhibits, prize certain works, neglect others, and in so doing, lead our local patrons through a tour of form, content, and larger questions of cultural ambiance. **We are, indeed, curators**, but as such, we need to do our job well. SFMOMA's Bruce Weil feels his job as curator is to work actively against the museum's role as repository of the culture's finest, positioning the institution instead as a more neutral information-provider for people: art as ideas, data, rather than (overly determined) objects. As curators of academia, then, we can exploit the possibilities of our status, exposing students to a range of culturally valid forms as well as non-mainstream content;

in so doing, we provide our audience with a host of possibilities for worlds and forms to inhabit. What I see in many curricular projects these days, though, are a lot of weak, safe shows; shows with less-than-risky themes, all showing the same kind of middle-brow art. Most composition readers I see carry on some version of the traditional curatorial project, perpetually glossing the canon of our permanent collection, inviting students in to study the great works and contemplate "the way the text positions them in relationship to a history of writing" (Bartholomae 21). The titles of these shows (as reflected by the reader-textbooks so many teachers use to teach writing) all sound like the titles of those bland, corporate-sponsored traveling exhibits: *How We Live Now*, *Re-Reading America*, *Gender Images*, *Our Times*. I eagerly await textbooks with titles like *Pharmacy*, *Soap Bubble Set*, *Fluxkit*, *The Hotel Eden*, or *Medici Slot Machine*. Such courses are too much traditional Art Appreciation, re-charging the masterpieces for a student, re-enchanting them. It's pedagogy as docency. The "questions for further discussion" those reader-textbooks ask about their permanent-collection articles are designed to make the work come alive for students, to make them learn to savor it the way we in academia (supposedly) do, to make the work's discursive field viral, recombinant. We still have not learned from the work done by our field's historical avant-garde about the failure to see our composition classes in the larger world, particularly in terms of the student-imaginary. In one of his last textbooks, *Searching Writing*, Ken Macrorie locates his student not in the institution but on the street (in a camera shop, a fire station, a zoo): "Go to people," he urges his student-reader. "They're alive this year, up to date" (89).

Macrorie's idea of building a writing course on something as simple as the "deeply felt truth" (31) of experience has continued to resonate in my practice because it's the quality of my students' writing I like best, the aspect I think represents their strongest work. Take Greg White, a student for whom writing an essay is a tenuous process; he shows his true voice, his heart and insight, in short works, in in-class writings and in the email messages he sends me. Here, for example, in an email with the subject heading "been there, done that!," he reflects on the discussion we had earlier that day of some Tupac Shakur songs:

dear mr. sirc

i'm in class today were talking about 2pac and not so much disappointed, however the people in class don't understand 2pac the way i do. see my life is very different from what people think. it pissed me off to hear people in our class talk but not from experience. but from what they learne by the media. 2pac song "keep ya head up" is so true. how do i know? because everything he said i've been through remember when you said you can't listen to this song without having a tear come to your eye. well it did because it hurt for 2pac to be so much on point. the things this man said was so true for instance he said he blame his mother for turning brother into a crack baby. my mother had a child who is my brother who has down syndrome from my mother drinking. and then he goes on telling how he tries to find his friend but their blowing in the wind. when i went home i trie to find my friends the one's who i was hanging with when i was young they were around just always out of reach i understand when pac said he people use the ghetto as a scapegoat i love my ghetto i'm not just talking about the people i'm talking about the place. the people most of the people are good to me. the rest want to see my fell i have so many mixed feelings right now i can't stay focused on what i'm saying i guess that's another down fall us people from the "ghetto" have sometimes the feelings as pac fuck the world attitude and other times i say i'm going to show all these mother fuckers what i can do so many obstacles so little time makes me frustrated. so i can't focused i what i supposed to do.

I have many students like Greg, and my challenge, I feel, is to have these young people burnish not anthologized writers' essays but their own form of powerful *pensée*, while, certainly, at the same time learning some kind of basic prose styling to help them avoid verbal pitfalls in formal settings. It's a tough struggle, doubtless because it's the key tension in all fields throughout modernity with the idea of composition at their center: the tension between the academic and the avant-garde. **Box-logical composition focuses on the institutional space that enframes the human scene of written expression.** As such, it fits with what art theorist Hal Foster sees as the crucial difference between the historical and neo-avant-gardes: "the historical avant-garde focuses on the conventional, the neo-avant-garde concentrates on the institutional" (17). So Macrorie, Bill Coles, and the rest of Composition's historical avant-garde in the 1960s took as their focus the conventions of the texts students produced, opening them up to the passional possibilities of new forms like those generated by the Happenings; as William Lutz declared, "We must as teachers of writing concentrate first on the creative aspect of writing" (35). Our concern in the second wave of Composition's avant-garde is on academic spaces, and the traditional cachet that essayist prose doggedly enjoys there. We are not so fortunate, perhaps, to live in the heady times of the historical avant-garde. As Foster shows, those were times when the rhetoric was anarchistic. He cites the language of Daniel Buren's 1971 essay on "The Function of the Studio," calling for "total revolution" and "the extinction" of the studio (25). "Our present is bereft of this sense of imminent revolution," as Foster acknowledges; hence, contemporary artists engaged in the institutional critique of the neo-avant-garde "have moved from grand oppositions to subtle displacements" (25). So the goal becomes ways to pressure the academic context in firm but subtle ways. **The assignments I offer, then, are attempts at strategies to allow the voice and concerns of a Greg White to become a meaningful part of the academic verbalscape, to find credible genres for preserving such deeply felt truth.**

ACTIVITY 1

A BASIC BOX

TEACHER'S NOTES

A box-logic for composition instruction allows us to think of our work as teaching English Juxtaposition 101 (Lutz 36). The student becomes a mixer or DJ, practicing the key compositional arts of selection, arrangement, and expression. A simple but effective way to practice those arts is suggested in a work by Anne Carson. In one of her collections, Carson has a series of short poems entitled "Hopper: *Confessions*." In this series, the poems are all titled with the names of paintings by Edward Hopper; then, following each poem (in a kind of orchestrated colloquy), there is a quotation from the *Confessions of St. Augustine*, speaking to the emotions conjured by the amalgam of Hopper's image and Carson's reverie. So, for example, there is the poem "Office at Night":

Office at Night

Man woman windowcord paper fire stones.
Is
it
light
from
the
street streaming in unshaded
or
a
wind
of
autumn that pierces our bones?

Yes that one hour passeth away in flying particles.
(Augustine, *Confessions XI*)

55

Copyright 2000 Anne Carson. *Men in the Off Hours*. New York City: Alfred A. Knopf.

Carson doesn't reproduce the Hopper paintings, of course (counting on a contemporary poet's hyper-literate audience to be familiar with them), but it is worthwhile, as a way to think about students' initial work with new media, to literalize her composition a bit further.

Doing so, we might get something like the following:

Man woman windowcord paper fire stones.

Is

it

light

from

the

street streaming in unshaded

or

a wind

of

autumn that pierces our bones?

Yes that one hour passeth away in flying particles.
(Augustine, *Confessions IX*)

Edward Hopper, *Office at Night.* Collection Walker Art Center, Minneapolis
Gift of the T. B. Walker Foundation, Gilbert M. Walker Fund, 1948
Anne Carson, "Office at Night." Copyright Anne Carson 2000.

Speculating on how Carson came up with her work yields a process students might follow to develop a similar juxtapositional series. Surely, Carson might have thought of the Hopper pictures as powerful images. Somehow, the idea of using pithy quotes from Augustine to "read" and comment on those paintings (and the moods they called up in her) suggested itself. Her own poetic text captured the ideas or feelings generated by brushing those two information-sites against each other. This suggests the following lesson.

ACTIVITY

1 Students might (after being introduced to productive on-line or off-line search strategies, if that's needed) spend one or two class sessions searching for a similar body of interesting visual material. Entering the phrase "photo archives" into any major search engine will yield very interesting results, from high school sports photos to a photo-chronology of the life of Freud. (The canny instructor might prepare for this lesson by having a few interesting visual and verbal sites ready to show students, but the idea is for students to explore and find something personally meaningful.) And, of course, a search engine like Google

allows for image searching. Students should conference with each other on what they have or haven't found (if they like what they have, they can tell why; if some students haven't found anything yet, others can suggest ideas). On-line searching is the simplest, of course, but images might be scanned from books or come directly from digital photographs the students take (if those technologies are available and the instructor is comfortable using them). During the image conferences, students should also talk about the ideas evoked from the pictures, why they feel drawn to them, what message they hold for them (this will help guide the kind of verbal text they can juxtapose with those pictures).

2   Students look for their verbal (or aural, if they so desire) texts. Again, if students need tips on textual searching, those can be given (most composition handbooks contain fairly good surveys of print and electronic information indexes and sources to help students get started; but doubtless the instructor can supplement with sites tailored to students' specific needs). Again, conferences where students share their investigative results can help ensure good choices.

3   Students juxtapose quotes and images. If sophisticated graphic software is available and the instructor can easily introduce students to it, great, but words and text can be juxtaposed quite simply using text-editing programs, most of which currently allow both image-insertion as well as fairly interesting manipulation of text: for my version of Carson's "Office at Night" above, for example, I simply opened a Word document, inserted a simple table of two rows, put the Hopper image (which I found on-line, in a Web museum) in one box, and put the Augustine quote in the other; then I inserted a text box into the Hopper image (using the "no fill" and "no line" commands, so the text would simply be overwritten on the image) and typed the Carson poem into the text box. My experience with this assignment shows that students will be even more imaginative.

4   Once students have selected and arranged their juxtapositions, they can write their own expressive commentary, reflecting on what the juxtaposed texts mean to them (poetry is tough, so I would tell students prose is just fine), and artfully integrate it into the work. Again, students can add this element to their box any way they want (I had one student who figured out how to put his pithy, interpolative comments into the thin grey space below an internet browser window).

NOTES

This simple lesson in juxtaposition—found images **x** found text **x** student prose—is a powerful one to allow students to practice the basic skills of contemporary composition: search and selection, arrangement/juxtaposition/layout, and self-expression. They learn a little of the basic logic of academic, citational prose, as well: how one text is used to read or make sense of another text, with the writer's own work a triangulation among data-sites. Students get practice in using electronic technology (to both search and arrange), and they also get practice in writing as a way of being, of developing a stance and voice in the textual world. Mostly, though, they come up with cool virtual boxes. Hopefully, students will be as personally creative as possible: a skater, possibly, might take several digital photos of heavily pierced or tattooed friends in their skateboard gear; then he might search the National Archives site to find texts that comment on freedom, finding something like the one below, from the Eisenhower Library (Ike's letter to Nelson Rockefeller, filled with his musings on the "endeavor to insure each citizen the fullest possible opportunity to develop himself spiritually, socially and economically").

December 15, 1954

Dear Mr. Rockefeller:

An outstanding characteristic of our nation, I believe, is a constant endeavor to insure each citizen the fullest possible opportunity to develop himself spiritually, socially and economically. Faith in the individual, in his dignity and in his capacity for achievement is a basic principle of our system. The history of America is the story of men and women who came to these shores from all parts of the world and who have made full use of their opportunities, not only for themselves but in order that others might benefit. Of such is our strength.

It is my conviction that all the peoples of the world share the same human cravings for freedom and for opportunities to win economic and social advancement. In keeping with our heritage we seek to join with all peoples in a common effort to achieve and sustain the basic essentials of human dignity.

It is time for all of us to renew our faith in ourselves and in our fellow men. The whole world has been far too preoccupied with fears. It is time for people throughout the world to think again of hopes, of the progress that is within reach.

So that these matters may have the increased degree of attention they deserve, not only in the Departments and agencies but especially within my immediate staff, I hereby appoint you as Special Assistant to the President. I shall look to you for advice and assistance in the development of increased understanding and cooperation among all peoples. I shall also look to you for assistance in reviewing and developing methods and programs by

The student might juxtapose snippets of Eisenhower's rhetoric with the pictures of his friends, and next to each he might write reflections of times he and his friends were hassled for skateboarding.

Some of the results I've received: one student found a bunch of cityscape photos for her visual text, then chose street signs as her verbal component, interpolating them with some really nice poems she wrote. Another chose kooky photos of weddings he found online, overlaid them with snippets from Elizabeth Barrett Browning, and then added his own thoughts on marriage and romance in America.

EVALUATION

For an initial project like this, with a strong creative element, I would be very encouraging with grading. "A work needs only be interesting," was the single criteria Donald Judd put forward to judge contemporary art, and for student work here, I think any interesting effort—where some obvious care in choices has been taken in terms of finding images and text that produce, when juxtaposed, a frisson of drama or amusement—should be rewarded. Similarly, the instructor can doubtless judge the quality of a student's own written work. The instructor might also think about asking students to submit a reflective commentary with the work, to better estimate the quality of a student's effort in terms of the selection and arrangement goals targeted here.

RESOURCES

The Anne Carson book in which "Hopper: *Confessions*" appears is *Men in the Off Hours*. The only other resource needed, besides computers with Internet and text-editing capabilities—and possibly PowerPoint—(and a hand-out for how to create tables, insert text, and do simple design with the software), is possibly a list of search engines—or, a portal site like http://www.assignmenteditor.com, which includes links to all major search engines as well as to sites for newspapers (U.S., world, and tabloid), photo searches, politics, entertainment, money, and law enforcement, among many others.

RESEARCH BOX

TEACHER'S NOTES

As Cornell shows, a genre like the box can be an ideal vehicle to act as a compendium for students' research and inquiry. And just as Duchamp thought, investigated, and planned in writing, students, too, can think of their research box as a medium to store the textual results of their own inquiry-quests. This would be an ideal assignment to do collaboratively, students working in pairs or teams, depending on the complexity or depth of the inquiry desired. The topic might either be generated from students themselves or from the instructor; it can be tied into a central course reading or can simply be a stand-alone assignment.

What will result will be a very basic Web site of student writing and inquiry: rough notes/ideas/questions/sound-bites, along with more finished student text; interesting visual or verbal or aural items found off the Internet or in print-based media (if the technology is available) and reported on and/or sampled; and a catalog of any student interviews or surveys done.

When finished, the box will be a class research-page, either exploring the general course topic or helping to illuminate the central class reading—a compendium of cool enlightenment.

ACTIVITY

So, for example, students might get together (if they have the choice) and generate a class topic like clothing, why we wear what we wear. Then, various research teams would carve out the areas they will be responsible for: teams might explore their own ideas like a brief history of fashion, issues of clothing manufacture, a certain designer, regional differences in fashion, retailing and advertising, political issues (such as sweatshops or dress codes), even theorists of fashion. Then students search, read, interview/survey, and write through their inquiry, trying to amass and arrange as much interesting "objects" (textual or otherwise) as possible.

If the instructor chooses to link the research box to the course's central text, an equally interesting work can be done: say the students are all reading *The Autobiography of Malcolm X*—as they read, research teams will be finding information and collecting/writing/arranging it on topics like slavery, African-American religion, the Northern migration, Harlem nightlife, the Nation of Islam, Malcolm's speeches, Malcolm's media reception, the Islamic faith, and Malcolm's legacy today. An assignment like this (one very similar to digital storytelling) is both participatory and immersive, a good combination for education.

1 Present an overview of the assignment. If students are allowed to choose a topic, then that choice should be settled, but care must be given in a whole-class project like this to urge students to choose a topic that won't intellectually disenfranchise some class members; a topic like the clothing one I used as example above is good because everyone has a way into an issue like that. Once the topic is decided, students can suggest possible areas for research (instructor guidance and encouragement are obviously helpful here, as students might come up with a limited topic that will frustrate their research).

2 Once the teams are formed (2–3 per group seems right), then the instructor needs to explain the basics of research—on-line, as well as print- and community-based. I haven't met too many first-year students lately who were unfamiliar with search engines, but some explanation (even bringing in sites that seem especially fruitful) might be needed. It's been my experience that students are less familiar with print-based materials, so some care should be taken to familiarize students with those, especially the ones that will yield the most information (campus librarians might be contacted to either spend a day in class or to help with a guided tour of the library). Some good, basic techniques in interviewing/surveying should be given, too, if those are thought pertinent.

3 The class is turned loose to search, read, view, sample, scan audio/visual/verbal texts, take notes on them (be sure to introduce students to the kinds of note-taking you want them to do—I like a mix of summary, quotation, pithy analysis, and personal/reflective writing), and collect interesting sites to link to. All work should be saved electronically: this shouldn't be hard with verbal texts, but you might need to explain how to copy and save visual/aural texts.

4 As students are working (and such a project can be scheduled for anywhere from half-a-term to the full term), the class should begin to build a simple Web page. Most students and faculty I know find it easier to use an authoring program (such as Dreamweaver), which necessitates a minimum of prior knowledge. After explaining how to open a file, create tables, and make links (realizing your class will have the full range of familiarity with these styles), students can see how to enter text, insert images, and link internally and externally in the site. Students are very good at judging how little or much they need to know. They can simply choose images, write text about them (based on their research), and figure out what in that writing might best be linked to other data they've found in order to present an intriguing and informative view of the research they've discovered. Ping-ponging through that dynamic, they'll soon amass their site. Very basic features of text insertion, arrangement and linking are needed for this

assignment, as the goal is simply to provide a medium to capture what the students collect and write. Each team can do their own individual page(s), making whatever stylistic choices they want. The class might need a couple days to learn and practice the fundamentals here, and the instructor should provide a basic one- or two page handout the students can use for the actual page design. And I suggest you take time to let students explore a few simple but powerful digital stories on the Web (just search "digital story" to find a bunch) to see how well-chosen text and imagery can combine to form an interesting, informative, oftentimes delightful narrative. If your college or department has a technical support center, it might help if teams scheduled appointments for a little help, if they felt the need.

5   Most first-year composition classes require student practice in academic prose. Obviously the research box does not preclude such practice, and actually enhances it. Students will be much better prepared to write citational prose after engaging in their research (and reading each other's). The smaller bits of prose they generated for their Web page, and the insights they derived from their inquiry, have academic cachet and can serve as the seeds for a more polished, self-contained prose genre (an analysis, reflection, narrative, or some mixed genre), which can be a required component of the assignment.

EVALUATION

Following the box-artists discussed above, the important things emphasized here are voice, inquiry, atmosphere, selection, insight, and interesting materials. The actual Webwork should not be fetishized. Rather, measure process-traces:

- *How thoroughly did students range over resources for their task?*
- *What novel items/sources did they discover?*
- *How engaged was their original writing?*
- *Did they come up with interesting insights?*
- *Was a scene successfully re-created?*
- *If they did interviews and surveys, what sort of useful or creative information did they yield?*

Those are the criteria I would apply to this project.

RESOURCES

For background reading on the box as avant-garde genre, I'd suggest Brian O'Doherty's "Joseph Cornell: Outsider on the Left," from his work on several key contemporary artists, *American Masters: The Voice and the Myth* (Universe Books, 1988); Charles Simic's *Dime-Store Alchemy* (Ecco, 1992), though out of print, can be found in libraries and used-book stores, and gives a truly rapturous account of Cornell's art (if the project requires any short, reflective commentary by students, Simic's brief reveries on Cornell could be inspirational); there have been many books written on Fluxus recently, a good start is the exhibition catalogue *In the Spirit of Fluxus* (Walker Art Center, 1993); textual reproductions of Duchamp's boxes are found in his book *Salt Seller* (Oxford UP, 1973). Besides that background reading, the instructor would obviously need networked computers for students with a good browser, as well as a basic hypertext authoring program (either on the classroom computers or on machines students can access in the school's tech center). A hand-out for simple page-making commands is important. Also, the instructor should be prepared with some of the most interesting URL's to help students begin their research. If print-based material will be scanned, then access to appropriate hard/software will be needed.

D

[Boredom, Eternal Return]

Must the sun therefore murder all dreams,
the pale children of my pleasure grounds?
The days have grown so still and glowering,
Satisfaction lures me with nebulous visions,
while dread makes away with my salvation—
as though I were about to judge my God.

—Jakob van Hoddis[1]

Boredom waits for death.

—Johann Peter Hebel[2]

Waiting is life.

—Victor Hugo[3]

Child with its mother in the panorama. The panorama is presenting the Battle of Sedan. The child finds it all very lovely: "Only, it's too bad the sky is so dreary."—"That's what the weather is like in war," answers the mother. ▯ Dioramas ▯

Thus, the panoramas too are in fundamental complicity with this world of mist, this cloud-world: the light of their images breaks as through curtains of rain.

[D1,1]

"This Paris [of Baudelaire's] is very different from the Paris of Verlaine, which itself has already faded. The one is somber and rainy, like a Paris on which the image of Lyons has been superimposed; the other is whitish and dusty, like a pastel by Raphael. One is suffocating, whereas the other is airy, with new buildings scattered in a wasteland, and, not far away, a gate leading to withered arbors." François Porché, *La Vie douloureuse de Charles Baudelaire* (Paris, 1926), p. 119.

[D1,2]

The mere narcotizing effect which cosmic forces have on a shallow and brittle personality is attested in the relation of such a person to one of the highest and most genial manifestations of these forces: the weather. Nothing is more charac-

THE ARCADES

PROJECT

TEACHER'S NOTES

Duchamp's collection of notes on his *Large Glass* is a nice template to allow students to record *l'état brut* inquiry results; it's a good, open genre to allow them to think of research as an ongoing project of discovery. But advanced composition courses, as well as graduate seminars, could better use a template that meshes well with actual, engaged interest, one allowing sustained, focused, scholarly writing. For example, in the second course in my college's undergraduate composition sequence, I have found **rap music** to be a topic that students both live and love, one that allows them to see the logic in being engaged scholars. That email from Greg White was written in the basic writing class I center around **hip hop**. It's a course students have begged to get into for the past 6 years I've been running it, some even waiting an entire year to enroll. No surprise: hip hop is a rubric for some of the most exciting cultural media available to young people today, transcending perceived distinctions of age, gender, race, and ethnicity, and emphasizing rich verbal and visual style. My goal as academic curator in this case is to mount a hip hop exhibit that will satisfy my students' desire, as well as leave them with an intense formal, verbal, and conceptual experience, one that will give them cultural and discursive capital to do with as they see fit. Like most curators, I am a preservationist; and one of the curator's duties is to preserve for public consumption powerful but unknown works that might otherwise go unnoticed. I'm tired of seeing so many Greg Whites come and go in my courses and not have their heartfelt work archived in some culturally meaningful way.

To attempt such a trace-capturing in my class as a way to allow student desire to subtly pressure academic writing, I've been drawn to another box-theorist's catalogue of passionate inquiry, Walter Benjamin's record of his thirteen years of library research into the cultural preoccupations of nineteenth-century Paris, *Das Passagen-Werk* (The Arcades Project) (1927-1940, 1982). It is a work similar to both Cornell's and Duchamp's, a definitively unfinished project that one is intended to extend, "at best a 'torso,' a monumental fragment or ruin, and at worst a mere note-book, which the author supposedly intended to mine for more extended discursive applications" (Eiland & McLaughlin, x). According to the English translators of this work, the subject of the Arcades' quest was an idiosyncratic study of the residual objects left behind from the on-going performance piece called "Paris of the Nineteenth-Century":

> diverse material [from the literary and philosophical to the political, economic, and technological] under the general category of *Urgeschichte*, signifying the "primal history" of the nineteenth century. This was some-thing that could be realized only indirectly, through "cunning": it was not the great men and celebrated events of traditional historiography but rather the "refuse" and "detritus" of history, the half-concealed, varie-gated traces of the daily life of "the collective," that was to be the object of study, and with the aid of methods more akin—above all, in their dependence on chance—to the methods of the nineteenth-century collector of antiquities and curiosities, or indeed to the methods of the nineteenth-century ragpicker, than to those of the modern historian. Not conceptual analysis but something like dream interpretation was the model. The nineteenth century was the collective dream which we, its heirs, were obliged to reenter, as patiently and minutely as possible, in order to follow out its ramifications and, finally, awaken from it. (Eiland & McLaughlin ix)

teristic than that precisely this most intimate and mysterious affair, the working of the weather on humans, should have become the theme of their emptiest chatter. Nothing bores the ordinary man more than the cosmos. Hence, for him, the deepest connection between weather and boredom. How fine the ironic overcoming of this attitude in the story of the splenetic Englishman who wakes up one morning and shoots himself because it is raining. Or Goethe: how he managed to illuminate the weather in his meteorological studies, so that one is tempted to say he undertook this work solely in order to be able to integrate even the weather into his waking, creative life. [D1,3]

Baudelaire as the poet of *Spleen de Paris*: "One of the central motifs of this poetry is, in effect, boredom in the fog, ennui and indiscriminate haze (fog of the cities). In a word, it is spleen." François Porché, *La Vie douloureuse de Charles Baude-laire* (Paris, 1926), p. 184. [D1,4]

In 1903, in Paris, Emile Tardieu brought out a book entitled *L'Ennui*, in which all human activity is shown to be a vain attempt to escape from boredom, but in which, at the same time, everything that was, is, and will be appears as the inexhaustible nourishment of that feeling. To hear this, you might suppose the work to be a mighty monument of literature—a monument *aere perennius* in honor of the *taedium vitae* of the Romans. But it is only the self-satisfied shabby scholarship of a new Homais, who reduces all greatness, the heroism of heroes and the asceticism of saints, to documents of his own spiritually barren, petty-bourgeois discontent. [D1,5]

"When the French went into Italy to maintain the rights of the throne of France over the duchy of Milan and the kingdom of Naples, they returned home quite amazed at the precautions which Italian genius had taken against the excessive heat; and, in admiration of the arcaded galleries, they strove to imitate them. The rainy climate of Paris, with its celebrated mud and mire, suggested the pillars, which were a marvel in the old days. Here, much later on, was the impetus for the Place Royale. A strange thing! It was in keeping with the same motifs that, under Napoleon, the Rue de Rivoli, the Rue de Castiglione, and the famous Rue des Colonnes were constructed." The turban came out of Egypt in this manner as well. *Le Diable à Paris* (Paris, 1845), vol. 2, pp. 11–12 (Balzac, "Ce qui disparaît de Paris").
How many years separated the war mentioned above from the Napoleonic expe-dition to Italy? And where is the Rue des Colonnes located? [D1,6]

"Rainshowers have given birth to ‹many› adventures." Diminishing magical power of the rain. Mackintosh. [D1,7]

As dust, rain takes its revenge on the arcades.—Under Louis Philippe, dust settled even on the revolutions. When the young duc d'Orléans "married the princess of Mecklenburg, a great celebration was held at that famous ballroom where the

So we find entries such as the two, shown on these pages, from the convolute (or grouped sheaf of notes) on "[Boredom, Eternal Return]."

A vector analysis of these or any other pages from the *Passagen* gives an idea of the various genres in which Benjamin worked: quotation (of passages of varying lengths), summary, short critical reflection, more extended quotation and/or analysis, brief sound-bite snippets, notes to himself. In terms of the material content, it's more open, more lived than traditional text-based aca-demic inquiry—among the myriad topics covered are history, urbanism, desire, horror, shopping, pleasure, conspiracy, art, architecture, prostitution, gambling, engineering, even the simple transcription of names and signs (I like how the translators use the word torso because there is definitely a body moving in this space). He achieves, then, the true daybook for an engaged researcher, one whose method implies "how everything one is thinking at a specific moment in time must at all costs be incorporated into the project at hand" (Benjamin, *Arcades* 456). Finally we can note the pre-figurement of writing as hypertext: that entry above, for example, in the "[Boredom, Eternal Return]" convolute, with the "Dioramas" tag, anticipates readers who can click that selection, taking them to the "[Panorama]" convolute.

Why am I drawn to this method, and how do I advocate using it?

First, it's the idea of sustained inquiry, of the search as project—for me the most crucial part of the academic enterprise. Also, it's *form ouvert*, a minimalist building structure, that "slender but sturdy scaffolding" the historian erects "in order to draw the most vital aspects of the past into his net" (Benjamin, *Arcades* 459).

Currently, my students are involved in an *Arcades Project* trying to permeate the phantasmagoria of hip hop's drama because, as a curator, I want my gallery-space to be thought of as an important information-source for the student-audience. Each class member selects a convolute, based on desire (topics such as old school, cultural roots, the socio-political, gender, race, gangsta, 2Pac, Eminem, violence, the industry); some general theory and background are read and annotated; then, after discussion of sophisticated online and print-based searching, students do more specialized individual reading and note-taking as their contemplative, inquiry-based field work (they are Benjamins in their virtual Biblioteque Nationale). Audio and video are brought in as necessary. **It's a much more sustained and scholarly-focused version of the simple 'box' above, one requiring greater student prose effort. What they produce are a mass of brief snatches constellated together into the larger interactive project. This is writing that works minutely, from the inside out, to develop a statement.**

So Scot Rewerts, for example, begins his own Arcades Project on rap and politics by recording and reflecting on a text snippet concerning Malcolm X he found on a Web site dealing with *Rage Against the Machine* lyrics:

```
-El Hajj Malik El Shabazz aka Malcolm X was assassinated on
February 21 1965 but his connection to Hip Hop has been a long
and strangely eerie one. The man who once ran the streets of
Harlem, lived the fast life, and spent time in prison was a
bona fide Hip Hopper of sorts back in the days of his youth.
Malcolm went to all the latest shows, hung out with all the
coolest music cats. He was up on the latest happenings as they
were emerging from the streets. Back when he was a youth, the
Hip Hop of his day was known as Be-bop and Malcolm who was
always known for keeping it real was down with the whole scene.
(Davey D's Newsletter)

A direct correlation with one of the most powerful black men
that ever lived to hip hop, shows how truly political hip hop
is. In a Rage Against the Machine song Zach rap/rocks "Ya know
they    murdered    X    and    tried    to    blame    it    on    Islam!"
(http://www.musicfanclubs.org/rage/lyrics/wakeup.html)

--Background: 'Black nationalism'

'He may be a real contender for this position should he aban-
```

don his supposed obedience to white liberal doctrine of non-
violence…. and embrace black nationalism' 'Through counter-
intelligence it should be possible to pinpoint potential trou-
blemakers . . .and neutralize them' (http://www.musicfan-
clubs.org/rage/lyrics/wakeup.html

**--This is in the background to Rage's song "Wake up." This,
even though not really thought to be a hip hop genre of music,
is extremely political in reference to the Civil Rights movement.**

And here are some selections from Peter Prudden's convolute on the topic of
whiteness in rap music, responding to reading he did in Nelson George's Hip
Hop America:

"What had been proven in the 60's, particularly by Motown, was that R&B-
based music by black singers could easily be sold in massive quantities to
white teens, creating a lucrative commercial-cultural crossover" (3).

*- George brings up a very good point in this quote. I believe this is a fore-
shadow for the success of the rap industry. White teens indulge in gangsta rap
simply because it takes them from their middle-class suburban homes and into
the heart of the inner city. More importantly, it opens their imaginations to
drugs, sex, guns and violence, the very things they are sheltered from in their
daily lives.*

"The heroin invasion […] empowered a new vicious kind of black gangster.
Heroin emboldened the black criminal class. Hip hop would chronicle, cele-
brate, and be blamed for the next level of drug culture development"
(George 35)

*- From the words of Notorious B.I.G., "either your slingin crack rock or you gotta
wicked jump shot." Over time the African-American male has been notoriously
rocked with this assumption.*

"I can't leave the topic of rap and white folks without offering up this memory. It is summer 1995 and I am spending the long Labor Day weekend at a
house out on the tip of Long Island. To my surprise, in a local publication
I spot an ad for a Run-D.M.C. gig at the Bay Club in the Hamptons' town of
East Quogue. Along with two other old-school hip hop colleagues, Ann Carli
and Bill Stephney, I drive to the club, where we encounter a large drunken
crowd of college-age and young adult whites. The club is jam-packed and
the narrow stage swollen with equipment.

"When Run, D.M.C., and Jam Master Jay arrive onstage, the building rocks.
The 99.9 percent white audience knows the words to every song. "My
Adidas," "Rock Box," and "King of Rock" are not exotic to this crowd. It is
the music they grew up on. I flash back on Temptations-Four Tops concerts
that are '60s nostalgia lovefests. Well, for these twenty-somethings, Run-
D.M.C. is '80s nostalgia. They don't feel the music like a black kid from
Harlem might. No, they feel it like white people have always felt black
pop—it speaks to them in some deep, joyous sense as a sweet memory of

childhood fun. In a frenzy of rhymed words, familiar beats, and chanted hooks the suburban crowd drinks, laughs, and tongue kisses with their heads pressed against booming speakers. It may not be what many folks want hip hop to mean, but it is a true aspect of what hip hop has become." (74-75)

This quote [from Nelson George] depicts the classic stereotype of the white suburban teen seeking a revolutionary moment derived of independence, attitude, style, and tough guy mentality. I realize this image simply because I have fallen under these circumstances countless times. As a teenager living in a middle class society with rules and regulations operating in every arena the feeling of rebellion against the norm is consistently present. Others and I view rap as an escape to a world un-imaginable to our Abercrombie & Fitch lives, where the biggest thing we must decipher is whose house we will watch Dawson's Creek at. The fact is driving down the street with the windows down in the parent's expensive car with the latest track blaring and the bass bumpin' presents a bad boy thuggish image. The truth is we as adolescent white kids have absolutely no indication of what it means to live the life of the lyrics we feel associate with our lives. On how many occasions have you heard of a 14-year old white child shot to death for his Air Jordans? The reality is never, we dream and paint pictures in our minds of what life is like in the inner-city through these albums. I enjoy listening to rap music, but to say I can relate or I feel for those who lives are filled with drugs, guns, violence, poverty, and sex is completely asinine.

ACTIVITY

Students' writing in this genre can be entered onto Web pages the instructor has made beforehand or that the students work on themselves; additionally, weblogs could be used. À la Benjamin himself, as students write about topics that address the other convolutes, they can link appropriately. Text and visuals can be inserted where appropriate. The course my students do this work in is designed to culminate in a research paper, so students, in effect, are doing old-fashioned note cards for the term paper, only in a much more interesting format, one that is a genre in itself.

I feel good as a curator with this project because my students discover an already-enchanted space and wander through that (the classroom-museum now conceived of as populist, audience-responsive studio/data-site). In too many composition courses, especially those centered around *Ways of Reading*-type textbooks, students encounter high-toned, expansive, relatively empty spaces, far removed from their own world; they don't awaken from the dream of academic discourse, they learn to speak it and keep dreaming it. The *Passagen* is not the student's clever response to a docent-guided tour through the great works of literary culture, but simply a re-representation of the students' own self-guided tours through cultural detritus that fascinates, which maybe holds clues; as Macrorie termed these material searches, they are "stories of quests that counted for questers" ("Preface," n. pag.). Texts in such a curriculum become paratactic assemblage, with an intuitive structure based on association and implication, allowing the reader to fish out of them words that resonate with something felt deep inside (an escape to a world un-imaginable to our Abercrombie & Fitch lives). Writing *apassionato e con molto sentimento*. I really don't think it's up to me to teach students how to process that "serious writing, [...] the long and complicated texts" (Bartholomae and Petrosky iii) of the academy; if certain disciplines feel the need to use those texts, they're free to teach students their intricacies themselves. **A box-logical genre like this displaces such texts from the writing class, substituting a basic awareness of how to use language and information, a cool project, and a sense of poetry.** This, after all, is a highly respectable curatorial mission: "to reinvest art with a new humanism, using basic forms of symbolism, allegory, figuration, and language.... ask[ing] us to think about how we feel about the world we live in" (Auping 11).

1. The first thing you should do to mount an interactive exhibit like a Rap Arcades Project in your class is to look at Benjamin's text to determine if the flavor and format of the inquiry is one you find conducive. If it is, I urge you to begin planning where I did: working with reference librarians to design a Web-based research guide. Together, you can decide which sites/sources, both rap-oriented ones (or whatever subject your students will explore) as well as those pertaining to larger cultural contexts, will be key starting points for your students. At my school, the library's Web site has a section designed to get students started on intensive research paper assignments, so the page for my course (http://research.lib.umn.edu/results.asp?sid=439) easily fits into that site. We chose links to what seemed like the most useful scholarly indexes (ABI Inform, ComIndex, Expanded Academic Index, RILM Abstracts of Music Literature, and Sociological Abstracts), as well as some mainstream newspaper indexes (since so much of rap is reported on in the daily papers) and alternative press/ethnic sites. We chose a few of the richer hip hop sites, a rap dictionary, the best lyrics site, and an annotated list of some of the key scholarly texts in rap. We also included a few assignments students could work through: some to familiarize them with the differences between scholarly and popular sources, as well as one to help them judge the quality of some of those odd, unattributed sources that float across the Web.

2. Incorporate your best practices for introducing solid academic research writing (framing research questions and hypotheses; how to work with sources, and the distinction between primary, secondary, and tertiary; quotation, paraphrase, summary, and plagiarism; and documentation format).

3   Present students with the rationale and format for Arcades-style reading notes. I show a few examples from Benjamin and give students a hand-out articulating the various genres or styles of notes they'll be taking. I ask students to practice a page of notes for the next day's class, based on that night's reading assignment. Then we go over these together, so students have a sense of the range of notational strategies available to them.

4   As students begin working through the on-line sources, I require them to turn in 2 pages of Arcades-style notes per week. I have students turn them in on paper, so I can respond, question, and suggest leads/sources based on developing patterns of inquiry. But you could easily have students begin entering them on to a Web site or weblog immediately.

5   Then, it's just a matter of reading, responding, helping to guide inquiry, and suggesting links. I like to bring in different on-line and print-based resources every week to help them take their inquiry in interesting directions. These can be targeted to the whole-class and/or student-specific. So one week, if I see a lot of students trying to figure out how to make claims about fans, I would introduce them to the Usenet archives of rap discussion groups. If a student is trying to explore gender issues, she and I would spend some time figuring out the best sources for claims on domestic violence (or whatever the topic). Midway through the project we look at how books can help, as well as other print-based sources.

•   An individual conference with each student several weeks into the process of searching/reading/note-writing is a good idea, to see what problems/successes students are having and to help them think about a proposal for their research paper. The proposal should be due about 5 weeks before their final research paper is due; fleshing out a proposal will then shape the rest of their information-searching.

•   As time for the actual formal research paper moves closer, we talk about that as a text in itself, drawing on the Arcades-work done so far to show in detail the movement from notes to more specifically-styled formal prose (mapping, chunking, development, finished format).

EVALUATION

I evaluate my student's Arcades work, in part, on the basis of how thorough they have been in their investigation (most instructors can tell the difference between thin coverage and research that satisfies).

I also look for an engaged voice to appear in the work, the confident tone of a scholar immersed in a project, one who gives off a sense of control; a kind of perceptual growth, then (hopefully, with the kind of poetically expressed sentiments we saw in Peter Prudden's work). I'm also interested to see if they've discovered interesting, novel sites and sources I've never heard of (another sign of an engaged scholar). A two-pages-per-week requirement gives them a pace for their research; letting them see each other's work shows them what the more engaged students are doing (if they need to see that). It also allows me to respond to and maybe help shape their inquiry (excited comments for wonderful things they're finding, prompts to extend their search, caution when the work is getting too one-dimensional or the sources too similar). As above, I would not grade on the quality of any Web-work, but solely on the quality of the inquiry.

RESOURCES

Besides Benjamin's book *The Arcades Project*, if instructors desire to afford their students the opportunity to do a Rap Arcades Project, the instructor needs to be familiar with rap music. Davey D's Web site is a good place to start (www.daveyd.com); Davey's a Bay Area DJ with one of the best Web sites in hip hop (excellent archive and links), and he sends out a weekly newsletter over the internet (I have my students subscribe), informing readers of the current events and controversies in rap and publishing provocative commentary from both insiders and fans. There are a variety of books that serve as a general introduction to the topic (e.g., David Toop's *Rap Attack #3*, Serpent's Tail, 2000; Tricia Rose's *Black Noise*, Wesleyan UP, 1994; Nelson George's *Hip Hop America*, Penguin, 1998), as well as mainstream magazines like *The Source*. But the important thing is to listen to the music (find your city's best hip hop station or explore other cities' on Web radio; the BET cable is a good source for rap videos; and check out a few club shows). Spend some time surfing the net to find the hip hop sites you want your students to know about. And see your school's reference librarian to find out about a Web-based research guide to support your class.

MODIFICATION FOR A GRADUATE-LEVEL COURSE

An Arcades Project for a graduate seminar would be ideal, I think, as Benjamin was a sort of a model graduate student for the thirteen years he worked on his project. The topic for a graduate project would correspond to the seminar content; the students themselves could determine the convolutes they were interested in exploring. Early class sessions would be an ideal time to introduce students to the more arcane scholarly sites and sources they might still be unfamiliar with. Rather than providing them with a Web research guide, the students themselves could each generate a topic-specific one as a sort of review of on-line literature (if it was a graduate class in pedagogy, they could do a full-blown Research Quickstart-type page that they could use with their own students). The seminar would culminate in a publishable article based on their Arcades work, much like Benjamin wrote articles/chapters on Charles Baudelaire and 19th Century Paris based on his own Arcades work.

FINALLY...

My projects above are all attempts to use technology to infuse contemporary composition instruction with a spirit of the neo-avant-garde. The box-theorists provide a way to think about composition as an interactive amalgam, mixing video, graphic, and audio with the verbal; a medium in which students can both archive their desires as well as publish passionate writing on their social reality vis-à-vis the larger culture: the explorations, reflections, discoveries, and analyses regarding those desires. The result gives them a serviceable non-fiction prose, enchanted somewhat, I hope, with a sense of wonder about the world and an interest in making meaning about it. I don't want student voices to be changed, re-shaped, or made over; rather I focus on helping students with a better sense of awareness and language, voice and content, and an appreciation of information. Those are all good goals for life as well as good skills to take into another class.

It's the box-artist's goal: text rubbing against text, making an arrangement of materials to see what could be done with them. The open-ended forms and available materials permit an intimacy and intensity that more mediated genres make difficult; students see writing elementally, as a material encounter rather than commodified production.

And when provided with a rich range of materials, the result can be what Cornell strived to construct: a vehicle of reverie, an object that would enrich the imagination of the viewer. The model for college writing, then, becomes the contemporary DVD—a compendium of "finished" text, commentary, selected features, interviews, alternative versions, sections initially deleted (but now appended) from the main text, amusing bits, and other assorted items of interest, clickable as desired, rather than the traditional scholarly essay. Some of the most important rhetorical strategies are practiced, such as searching, selection, juxtaposition, and arrangement/layout, as well as the always-important ability to phrase important personal insights in as clear and memorable a way possible (what I call the heartfelt *pensée*).

The definitively unfinished nature (made more so if readers are urged to continue the work) captures the flux of contemporaneity, that direct experience of life, allowing us to participate in its unfolding. With the essay displaced, our new classroom genre might best be called a diary journal repository laboratory, picture gallery, museum, sanctuary, observatory, key... inviting us to see things in a light in which we do not know them, but which turns out to be almost that one in which we have always hoped one day to see them bathed.

THE STICKY EMBRACE OF
beauty

On some formal relations in teaching about the visual aspects of texts

Anne Frances Wysocki

The avant garde's response to the cognitive, ethical, and aesthetic is quite unequivocal. Truth is a lie; morality stinks; beauty is shit. And of course they are absolutely right. Truth is a White House communiqué; morality is the Moral Majority; beauty is a naked woman advertising perfume. Truth, morality, and beauty are too important to be handed over to the political enemy.

Terry Eagleton, *The Ideology of the Aesthetic*

One more "thought"—I have a conviction that the design, registered in the human face thro years of life and work, is more vital for purposes of permanent record, tho it is more subtle, perhaps, than the geometric patterns of lights and shadows that passes in the taking, and serves (so often) as mere photographic jazz.

Lewis Hine

My writing on these pages starts with two compositions.

The first composition is one you'll have to construct inside wherever you do your imaginative constructions, for it's a composition to take from words. My essay's title took shape for me as I was reading one of Carl Hiassen's novels about the political and cultural degradation of Florida's natural environment and beauty: in *Stormy Weather* Hiassen describes a minor (and unsavory) character's inability to escape the "sticky embrace of the BarcaLounger." I'd like for you to have that image of two (apparently) different orders of being—a heavy fleshy body and humanly constructed structure—uneasily and sweatily creased into each other as I shift your attentions to the second composition, one constructed of formed markings on paper:

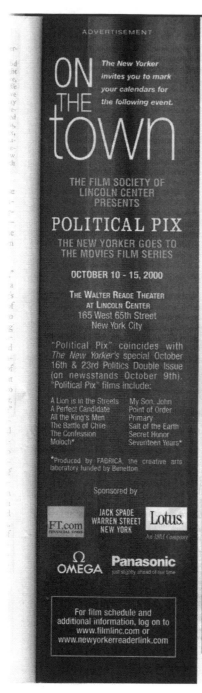
ciations of this kind were widespread among intellectuals in that fermenting period of Depression and the rise of Fascism in Europe. In Chicago, Saul Bellow and Isaac Rosenfeld were in an identical fever of radical world-upheaval. "Politics was everywhere," Rosenfeld recalled, looking back. "One ate and drank it." Trilling was quicker than most to fall away.

But when he advised the liberals of the forties to turn from "agencies, and bureaus, and technicians," and to cultivate instead a "lively sense of contingency and possibility," and when he was troubled by his complacent students of the fifties who glibly accepted antithetical ideas without resistance or perturbation—who were, in fact, bored by the subversive and the antisocial—how could he have foreseen the riotous campus demonstrations of 1968? In connecting politics with literature—"the politics of culture," he called it—he was unwittingly entering the vestibule of the politicization of literature, a commonplace in today's universities. Unwitting or not, Trilling was bemused to see how the impulse of unrestraint that inflamed the modern masters—Conrad, Mann, Lawrence, Kafka, Nietzsche—was beginning to infiltrate, and finally take over, popular thought and style. These writers, he pointed out, with all their relentless counterminings, asked "every question that is forbidden in polite society." By the nineteen-seventies, no question remained that was forbidden in polite society, and no answer, either; there was little left of the concept of polite society altogether. What was liberty for Lawrence became libertinism in the streets. The bold contrariness of the moderns had succeeded so well that Trilling starchily named its dominance in the country at large "the adversary culture." Babbitt and H. L. Mencken's booboisie were routed. Conrad's heart of darkness—the instinctual storm that had once been the esoteric province of modernist high art—had gone public. The Cossacks were astride the politics of culture.

Such were Trilling's ultimate convictions, hidden under the ornate historical scaffolding of "Sincerity and Authenticity," the Charles Eliot Norton Lectures he delivered at Harvard, in 1970. In language grown more and

To the left is a page out of the October 2, 2000 *New Yorker*, showing a column of text (which is working to bring Lionel Trilling back to life), and two advertisements. I'd like to draw your attentions (although I probably don't need to) to the advertisement on the right. When I received this *New Yorker*, I did what I usually do: I flipped through the pages to get a sense of what's going on, what I might want to read—and this page stopped me. I think this advertisement is a lovely piece of work, but it also angers me. When I experience pleasure and offense so mixed, I know I have a good opening into critical work—no matter where it leads me or how strange.

On the following pages I use resources from the fields of visual composition, graphic design, and visual communication to try to work out what gives rise to my seeing beauty and feeling angry. My inability to come to a satisfactory accounting leads me to consider how notions of beauty, developed in the late eighteenth century, have been used in attempts to hold together two different orders of being and—by our time—have failed. I do this not to raise issues of aesthetics for specific consideration, but rather to communicate what I've learned in trying to understand my responses to this layout: I'll be arguing that approaches many of us now use for teaching the visual aspects of texts are incomplete and, in fact, may work against helping students acquire critical and thoughtful agency with the visual, precisely because these approaches cannot account for a lot of what's going on in the Peek composition.

- What I came to understand when I turned to what's already published in the areas of visual composition, graphic design, and visual communication is that these approaches most often only partially explain my pleasure and none of my offense with the Peek composition: not only do these approaches assume a separation of form from content, but they emphasize form in such a way that "content" can be unremarkably disembodied—a very bad thing when the "content" is a particular body.

- Concurrently, by so emphasizing form, they propose that the work of shaping texts visually is to result in objects that stop and hold sight; I would rather that what we make when we shape the visual aspects of texts is *reciprocal communication*.

In my writing space here, then, I'm going to look at some present approaches to teaching the visual aspects of texts in order, grumpily, to argue the existence of the shortcomings I've just described. I will then turn back to eighteenth-century definitions of beauty and aesthetic judgment because they not only help me understand the shortcomings but because they also help me see grounds for shaping how we teach visual composition so that form does not override content, so that form is, in fact, understood as itself part of content, so that, finally, I better understand how to support students (and myself) be generously and questioningly reciprocal in our designings.

A FIRST FORMALITY

OVERLOOKING BODIES AND
HISTORY

If I were to turn to a very popular little guide for teaching about page arrangement (and one I do use in my teaching), *The Non-Designer's Design Book*, by Robin Williams, I'd find rules for explaining—and explaining pretty well—how my eyes travel through the Peek layout.

Williams offers four "design principles"—contrast, repetition, alignment, and proximity—for visual arrangement. By applying her rules, it is possible to say why (at least in part) my eye starts (or stops) here ▬ ▬ ▬ ▬ ▬ It is because of contrast: this is the lightest thing in this design and the only large round shape. The principle of repetition, meanwhile, says this design has harmony because the shapes of the text blocks repeat the shapes of the body; the size and proportions of the body repeat in the size of the ad itself, and the tones of grey repeat in photograph and typeface. As for alignment: the line of the body creates the line to which the other elements attach within the overall central alignment of the tall vertical shape of the layout. Proximity is at work here, following Williams' description, because similar words—the ordering information, for example—are all put close together.

Williams's principles allow for the creation of a clear visual hierarchy of elements in this layout, indicating what we are intended to see as most visually important in the layout. These principles do go a long way towards explaining why this layout seems "professional, organized, unified," the values Williams, in the first pages of her book (11), holds up for all layout along with, later, the value of "consistency."

The orderly—analytic and analyzable—arrangement of this layout must certainly contribute to the pleasure I take from it.

But Williams gives no grounds for the values she lists. Instead, those adjectives are simply and matter-of-factly stated, and so a reader could take from the book that those adjectives are not contingent, that they are neutral in their effects—that they have no effects other than the creation of organized layout—, that they should apply anywhere at all times, that they are not (that is) values.

Perhaps it is unreasonable for me to suggest that a thin, inexpensive, introductory handbook for visual composition should be self-critical. After all, the principles given in *The Non-Designer's Design Book* do allow me—and people in the classes I teach—to talk analytically about design; they do help us see how visual layout is not magic but is instead rationally organized and can be formally analyzed. But those principles, because they are presented without context or comment, also make it seem, as I have mentioned, that they are neutral and timeless.

Instead, the values that underlie Williams' principles have both history and consequences.

Johanna Drucker, for example, while describing how the field of graphic design took professional shape in the years and industrialization following World War I in the west, has argued that the values of organization and consistency inherent in most modern design are inseparable from ongoing pushes toward rationalization and standardization in industry, and thus inseparable from pushes toward shaping the standardized workforce necessary for industry to flourish. But rationalization and standardization became worthwhile in this process because something else is more essentially sought: that something else is efficiency—little wasted time or capital—in material production, but also efficiency in the production of workforces and of consumers for the material products. Graphic design, becoming a profession in this setting, gets shaped to be an efficient process for disseminating entwined information and desire. Implicit in Williams' principles and their underlying values, then, is the more essential goal that visual arrangement will make easy one's access to what is most important in a layout, that the arrangement will sieve out what is unnecessary or not to the point and will instead streamline the direction and speed of one's sight to hone in on... a woman's lovely in-soft-focus-so-as-to-almost-glow white ass, in this particular case.

We know from Joel Katz's writing about German memos from World War II some particulars of what can happen when efficiency is the value placed above—or used to mask—all others: it is possible for many people to forget or be unable to see, under such circumstances, that other people are having their lives horribly and finally shaped to destruction through and behind the finely-carved information passing over a desk. It is always a suspect rhetorical move to align one's arguments (especially when they are about such ephemera as a one-time advertisement on thin paper in a weekly magazine) with others that address the horrors of Nazism; I apologize for having made the alignment here, but it is hard not to think of Katz's arguments whenever efficiency is an unquestioned value at work in one's textual composition. I do believe that teaching Williams' principles "as is" can quietly encourage us to forget—they certainly do not ask us to see—that there is someone's body in this layout. At best, Williams' principles allow us to talk about this body (as I did above) as yet another—as only another—formal aspect of this layout.

When
form is treated as though
it is abstract—unconnected to time
and place—as it is in texts like *The Non-
Designer's Design Book*, then, bodies and history are not called to sight or to question. And what
is most valued, then, **is** form. Under such conditions, we are encouraged to look at the Peek layout as
something well arranged, something without time or
place, something therefore to contemplate: the layout is
an object on which we can place and move our eyes
pleasurably, with the pleasure that comes from
believing that our viewing is without
social or other consequences—without, also,
then, the consequences of us somehow
being shaped by the viewing.

We are not encouraged to ask about the woman in the ad as a woman,
only as a shape.

Although, as I have written, *The Non-Designer's Design Book* does give us help-ful vocabulary for analysis and composition of visual texts, it is—I am argu-ing—limited and limiting in what it gives us. Its approach does not help or encourage us to think about how we might have visual composition practices that helped us try out other, less abstract, forms, forms that support practices other than those of

> standardly efficient production and consumption.
> It does not help us think about pleasures
> other than those of isolated,
> private
> looking-at-objects.

A SECOND FORMALITY

OVERLOOKING STILL BODIES AND HISTORY

I incorporate other principles for understanding visual composition in my classes to try to flesh out the abstract formality of Williams' ungrounded prin-ciples; these additional principles do not allow me yet to explain fully my pleasure and anger with the Peek ad, but they do help me further articulate my concerns about how we help our students learn about the visual aspects of texts. These other approaches come out of the writings of Rudolf Arnheim, who does—almost literally—ground his ways of seeing: Arnheim uses our bodily experiences of moving over the earth to shape principles for analyzing and creating visual compositions. What Arnheim offers helps me talk, in class-es, about aspects of visual compositions that Williams' principles do not address; unfortunately, what Arnheim offers me—as with the Williams—only helps me consider part of the pleasures I take from the Peek advertisement.

In his book *The Power of the Center* Arnheim gives these grounds for prin-ciples of visual composition:

> When I look at the open landscape before me, my self reaches out to the horizon, which separates the lake from the sky. Turning around I see at a shorter distance the woods and the house, and even more close by the ground beneath my feet. All these sights are experienced as being seen from the seat of my self, and they group them-selves around it in all directions.
>
> [...]
>
> The foregoing is a distinctly egocentric way of experiencing the visual environment. It is, however, the primary way suggested spontaneously by what our eyes see. The world we see before our eyes exhibits a particular perspective, centered upon the self. It takes time and effort to learn to compensate for the onesidedness of the ego-centric view; and throughout a person's life there persists a tendency to reserve to the self the largest possible share of the power to organize the surroundings around itself at the center. (4-5)

Arnheim's principles of visual arrangement develop, then, out of this sense of a self in a body, a self both looking out from the body and experiencing the body as it is subject to the "cosmic" forces of the universe: "Physically, the world of our daily activities is pervaded by one dominant force, the force of gravity" (10). Arnheim uses these grounding observations to analyze how art—paintings and sculpture—makes meaning, primarily in the west. He thus writes, for examples, that

> To give tangible presence to the reference point of orientation facilitates the task of both draftsman and viewer. Elementary visual logic also dictates that the principal subject be placed in the middle. There it sits clearly, securely, powerfully. At a more advanced level, the central object is promoted to heading a hierarchy.
>
> Through the ages and in most cultures, the central position is used to give visual expression to the divine or some other exalted power. [...] In portrait painting, a pope or emperor is often presented in a central position. More generally, when the portrait of a man shows him in the middle of the framed area, we see him detached from the vicissitudes of his life's history, alone with his own being and his own thoughts. A sense of permanence goes with the central position.
>
> [...]
>
> Since the middle position is the place of greatest importance, the viewer attributes weight to whatever he finds in that position. (72-73)

Before I say more about how I apply Arnheim's observations to the Peek layout, let me add to his writing, by drawing on another book, by a different author, that grows out of a course in "picture structure" (xi) for children and adults as well as out of Arheim's groundings for "visual logic" (the book contains an introduction by Arnheim). Molly Bang's book *Picture This: Perception & Composition* steps a reader through building the story of Little Red Riding Hood by using abstract shapes—triangles, rectangles, circles—and then lays out for the reader "principles" of how we make meaning out of the shape and placement of objects on a flat surface. Bang's principles develop directly out of Arnheim's observations about our sense of body in a gravity-heavy world:

1. Smooth, flat, horizontal shapes give us a sense of stability and calm. [...]

2. Vertical shapes are more exciting and more active. Vertical shapes rebel against the earth's gravity. They imply energy and a reaching toward heights or the heavens. [...]

4. The upper half of a picture is a place of freedom, happiness, and triumph; objects placed in the top half often feel more "spiritual" [...]

The bottom half of a picture feels more threatened, heavier, sadder, or more constrained; objects placed in the bottom half also feel more "grounded."❖

[...]

7. We feel more scared looking at pointed shapes; we feel more secure or comforted looking at rounded shapes or curves. [...]

What do we know of that is formed from curves? Rolling hills and rolling seas, boulders, rivers—but our earliest and strongest association is with bodies, especially our mothers' bodies, and when we were babies there was no place more secure and full of comfort. (56; 58; 76-78; 98)

What Arnheim and Bang give us, then, are explanations for why elements placed in a visual composition can take on (some of) the meanings they do for us: we experience the world through the effects of directioned gravity on our bodies and so we call upon those experiences when we see them visually recreated on the two-dimensioned space of page (or screen). We can thus understand the black box at the bottom of the Peek ad as making solidly present the ground on which the layout—and the woman—stand. The woman's buttocks are given visual weight not only because of contrast (which is how the principles in *The Non-Designer's Design Book* allow us to talk of them) but also because they are at the center of the layout. The overall visual proportions of the layout, repeated in the upright stance of the woman, "imply energy and

---

❖ It is hard not to think here of what Kress and van Leeuwen say, in *Reading Images: The Grammar of Visual Design*, when they speak (for example) of the "information value of top and bottom":

If, in a visual composition, some of the constituent elements are placed in the upper part, and other different elements in the lower part of the picture space or the page, then what has been placed at the top is presented as the Ideal, what has been placed at the bottom is the Real. (193)

I was surprised when I first read this, for they offer no reasons for attaching these values to particular parts of visual compositions; instead, they analyze a number of examples along this line. I can only assume that their reasons for assigning the values they do align with what Bang and Arnheim argue about our sensational experience; Kress confirms this in his later book, *Literacy in the New Media Age*, when he writes that

In Western visual tradition, though perhaps much more widely, given our bodies' positioning in space ('feet on the ground,' 'head in the air') and the meanings which attach to that, the meaning-potential of 'bottom of the visual space' and 'top of the visual space' are broadly those of 'grounded,' 'of this earth,' 'the empirical'—meanings which might be characterized as 'real.' (69)

Kress and van Leeuwen do, however, acknowledge the limitations of (some of) these values they assign in the chapter of *Reading Images* in which they present this analysis:

Directionality as such [...] is a semiotic resource in all cultures. All cultures work with margin and center, left and right, top and bottom, even if they do not all accord the same meanings and values to these spatial dimensions. And the way they use them in their signifying systems will have relations of homology with other cultural systems, whether religious, philosophical, or pratctical. (199)

Even though Kress and van Leeuwen do not often remind their readers of the "other cultural systems" that underlie the terms they offer up as a "grammar" for visual design, their writing in this passage supports what I argue throughout this chapter, that it is always important to question—with our students—what systems we carry forward when we give our students any conceptual tools to use. It is crucial to keep in mind, with these value systems, that they are value systems—that directionality is always valued—as Shirley Ardener, in writing about "The Positionality of Space," reminds us as she examines anthropological recordings, such as this passage she takes from a 1909 text, *The Pre-eminence of the Right Hand*:

Society and the whole universe have a side which is sacred, noble and precious, and another which is profane and common; a male side, strong and active, and another, female, weak and passive; or, in two words, a right side and a left side. (115)

reaching toward heights"—they give the layout a vitality that would not be present were the woman laying down.

But how well do other of Arnheim's and Bang's observations apply?

For example, are we meant to see this layout aligned with the portraits of popes and men of power—and of men in general—that Arnheim discusses, so that we are to see the woman in the Peek ad "alone with [her] own being and [her] own thoughts"? Are we to see her, centered in the layout, as "detached from the vicissitudes of [her] life's history"? Such judgments are only possible if we pull in knowledge and experience that goes beyond how our bodies live with gravity. And given what we know about the articulations among women, sex, nudity, advertising, facial expressions, coffeetable books, and black thigh-high boots, I don't think any of us will judge the Peek ad as being about a woman alone with her own thoughts.

Another response to the possibility that we are meant to see this woman as alone with her thoughts comes from Bang, from her suggestion that I have the pleasure I do in seeing the curves of this woman's body because they are a sweet memory of maternal security and comfort. If we understand the body in the Peek layout through memories of losing ourselves into the curvy maternal body, then we are of course being given a body presented not as thinking or as even present to herself, in contrast to Arnheim's description of how we are likely to understand a centralized male figure. Instead, under this logic, this Peek body exists only for others, an unthinking natural being like the hills and rivers with which Bang associates it. Under this conception, how then can we understand the centrality of the body in the Peek layout as a formal presentation of a person "alone with [her] own being and [her] own thoughts"?

Even so, I do not think the woman in the Peek layout is being presented as an archetypal Mom, which is the only category offered in Bang that at all addresses the use of a gendered body in visual composition. I do not think that it is simply because Bang's book includes children in its audience that Bang does not discuss what is usually counterpointed to the perfect, unspeaking, warmly fleshed Mother, that is, the archetypal Prostitute, even though this latter figure can also be found being celebrated for its warm, generous, and curving comforts. To offer up this other figure would require acknowledging—among other cultural categories and structures with which the figure of the generalized Prostitute articulates—gender and gender relations, sexual orientation, the particularities of culture practice, relations and movements of capital and property, and so on. To offer up this other figure, in addition, with its complexities, would mean also necessarily bringing into this mix the complexities of the notion of Mother: when one body is acknowledged to be the result of multiple articulations, then all must be.

But that also means the body outside the layout, the viewing body on which these principles are based, must also be acknowledged in its complexity. In the passages I have quoted, Arnheim acknowledges that his approach is "egocentric"—and even though he writes that this ego-centeredness can be overcome, he does not describe in *The Power of the Center* what such an overcoming might entail or look like. Instead, the approaches laid out in that book—presented straightforwardly later as principles in the Bang book—reinforce a notion that anyone who regards the world visually (through a sight that is 'spontaneous') makes sense of the world and of human artifacts primarily by "reserv[ing] to the self the largest possible share of the power to organize the surroundings around itself at the center." And what sort of self is at that center? In the telling of Arnheim and Bang, it is an almost character-less self, looking out from a body whose actions are constrained only by gravity. This is a body without culture, race, class, gender, or age. This is a body with ten fingers and toes, able legs and arms, good strong posture, no genitalia; this is a body born to a mother remembered as nothing but soft and warm curves, a body that simply opens its eyes to see with unmediated understanding. This is the body that so many have written about since the latter part of the twentieth century, the body so many want to complicate and particularize, the body that exists nowhere but in abstraction, the body whose seeing—and understanding of what is seen—is now understood to be as constructed as any other cultural practice.★

A consequence of the generalized body being at the ground for what Arnheim and Bang write is that the pleasures of seeing—of looking at something like the Peek ad—are the pleasures of seeing one's apparently most essential self and experiences made visible. ~~In this telling,~~ **form** ~~comes from one's egocentric experiences and one takes pleasure in seeing those experiences comfortably inscribed in other objects.~~ I do not deny the physical necessity of gravity, and because, then, the elements of the Peek layout conform to my generalized experience of gravity, I can take some comfort in them: I can find pleasure in the layout's adherence and lack of resistance to a bottom-line physical, experiential, necessity that I experience daily. Following Arnheim and Bang, if I were to diagram my process of looking at the Peek layout, then, the diagram would show an arrow going in one direction: I look at the layout to see if its form matches what I know; the layout certainly does not look back at me, has no effect on me, my thinking, or my habits. I have argued that Williams' principles emphasize the layout as object, as container of abstract efficient form, as something to contemplate that has no effects on us as we contemplate; in parallel, I argue that Arnheim's and Bang's principles emphasize the layout equally as object, but now that object is a container of the form I experience as an abstracted body.

> In neither case is the designed object conceived as something made to establish relations between me and others; in neither case is the object conceived to exist in a circuit of social and cultural relations.

★ The number of books published within the last 20 years on how sight is contructed—and how it has functioned, in a particular configuration, as the shaping sense in the west—is large, so I will name only a few. For a historical/cultural overview, see Jay, or Brennan and Jay; for arguments that show other cultures using other senses to shape world-understanding, see Classen or Howes; for a cognitive perspective, see Hoffman; for a view that merges physiology and culture, see Elkins.

As with Williams' principles, Arnheim's and Bang's principles—based in a conception of the gravity of abstract bodies—*do* help me explain some of my pleasure in the Peek layout, as I have described. I do not, therefore, want to discard immediately the approaches of any of these writers—but it ought to be clear from my inability to use these approaches to speak with any complexity about my responses of pleasure (much less my anger) to the Peek ad, or about the specific body in the layout, or about any relationship between the body or the words printed over her, or about how this layout articulates to wider social and cultural practices, or about how this layout asks me to learn about women or suggests possible relations I have with others, that I am not at all comfortable in using these approaches as they come, by themselves, unchanged.

TURNING TO THE FORM OF BEAUTY...

If it were simply that the formal approaches to the visual I've described so far are neutral, that they don't discuss gender (or race or class or culture or economies or...) because they have nothing to do with the constructions of gender (or race or class or culture or economies or...), I could stop writing here. All I'd need do is recommend that we don't teach students formal vocabulary and principles for visual analysis and production unless we also consider the visual aspects of texts through the lenses of specifically gendered (and so on) material lives. That is, we could teach contrast and repetition and centering and other formal terms that show up in other texts about visual design and visual grammar, and then augment our teaching with texts that help students and us question how photographs (at least) teach us about gender and race and class and...There are certainly plenty of such texts available.✪

But the principles and guidelines that I've discussed for analyzing and giving visual form to texts are not neutral or universal, as I've started to argue in my initial discussions of them. They too arise out of and then in turn help shape our senses of who we are and what we are capable of doing (or not) in the world. They too need to be examined as choices, as actions that we take—when we produce texts that have any visual component—to build shaping relations with others and our selves. Several pages earlier I sketched out an argument about the development of graphic design in the twentieth century, for example, an argument that aligns the values behind many of the formal principles taught in the texts I've discussed (values such as unity, efficiency, and coherence) with the political and economic structures of industrialization, structures many of us find problematic. How, for example, do the evenly repeated—and endlessly repeated—regularly and rectangularly structured lines of the academic page function both to reflect and to teach us the visual pattern of (and so taste for) standardized linear order, such as we find on

---

✪ For teaching purposes, texts and readers in visual culture provide access to the cultural take on painted and photographic visual representations of race, gender, class, and other constructing categories. For an introductory text, see for example, Rose, or Sturken and Cartwright; for rich collections of articles that indicate the broad shape of this area, see Mirzoeff, or Bryson, Holly, and Moxey.

assembly lines, in parking lots, and in the rows of desks in classrooms? All these are sites for the production of regulated and disciplined workforces—sites to which I would then add the standard academic page.

I need to argue then that teaching about the visual aspects of texts in our classrooms can't be a simple matter of teaching about form (teaching the Williams or the Bang or the Arnheim, for example) supplemented by teaching about content (gendered and raced bodies, for example). Form is itself always a set of structuring principles, with different forms growing out of and reproducing different but specific values.

I want to make that last claim more specific now by turning to a point in our academic history when the separation of form from content was given a specific—and specifically gendered—inflection. I want—and need—now to turn back to the writings and judgments of Kant, to show how the separation of form from content can be, has been, gendered and abstracted. It is this particular way of constructing what form and content are, and how they relate, that leads particularly to my pleasure—and anger—in response to the beauty of the Peek ad but that also leads generally to recommendations I want to make for how we can teach carefully critical approaches to the analysis and production of visual texts of all kinds.

...A VERY FORMAL BEAUTY

KANT'S *CRITIQUE OF JUDGMENT*

I turn to Kant's aesthetics because his approach has been the dominant conceptual ground for the aesthetic conceptualizing of painters, designers, and other philosophers and theorists in the last two centuries; it has been the ground for understanding how our material bodily sensations entwine with our conceptual abilities, as in the sections I have quoted from Arnheim. I am not, obviously, going to do justice by Kant in these few pages (or in any number of pages or amount of hubris) but I turn to Kant because it is the structural—formal—nature of his analysis of knowledge, and so of beauty, that I believe has given rise, over the past two centuries, to the abstract approaches to visual composition, to the specific separation of form from content, about which I have been grumbling. But I also believe that Kant's analysis of what gives rise to judgments of beauty can be taken in other directions, directions that could give rise to alternative, less abstract and more socially-tied, understandings of the pleasures and complexities of visual compositions.

I will then, first lay out my understanding of the development of Kant's aesthetics   based primarily on the terminology and explanations in the *Critique of Judgment*—and then show the line of thought coming out of the form of the aesthetic that gives rise to what I've been discussing up to now in this chapter. Then I will lay out an alternative line of thought, in order to talk, finally, of different, more reflexive and reciprocal, approaches to visual composition.

Kant's aesthetics are integral to his understanding of the objects of philosophic inquiry, and so I need to sketch his understanding of the divisions of philosophy in order to show how aesthetic judgment serves an overarching function. Kant gives three divisions to the proper study of philosophy, corresponding to the three divisions—the cognitive, the ethical, and the aesthetic—used by Eagleton in the quotation that heads my essay: there are for Kant

> the study of nature

> the study of morals

> the study of taste or aesthetics

Kant's first major work, the *Critique of Pure Reason*, considers how we can know Nature—the first area of human inquiry for him—and Kant builds a three-part structure of explanation:

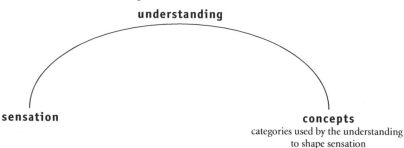

understanding

sensation

concepts
categories used by the understanding
to shape sensation

On the one side are the formless sensations we have from being bodies in Nature; think back, for example, to Arnheim's descriptions of our sensations of gravity. On the other side are the categories or concepts that provide shape from inside us to the formless sensations. It is the faculty of the understanding that brings the sensations and the formal categories together, allowing us to have thoughts about the world at all: sensations without concepts to shape them have no form, and hence cannot be discussed, considered, or even thought; to have concepts without sensations to apply them to is like having a pair of scissors but nothing that can be cut.

What is important for me to note here is the role of form: we cannot control having sensations—the having of sensations is simply a given, <u>necessary because humans are in Nature</u>—but for Kant we exercise what is most human in us when, as our faculty of understanding functions, we apply formal conceptual categories to the sensations so that they can have any meaning at all.

In the *Critique of Practical Reason*, Kant structures our <u>moral faculties</u> following the formal structure from the *Critique of Pure Reason*:

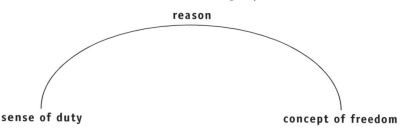

reason

sense of duty

concept of freedom

Here, in parallel to the bodily sensations that function in the understanding, Kant works with a sense of duty that he believes is inherent in us: when, for example, we see an older person struggling to cross a street, we (Kant believes) naturally sense that we might do something. But what gives shape to the observation—what allows us to form the sensation into a reasonable action— is for Kant the concept of freedom: in the same way that the concepts of the understanding are structures—such as causality or quantity—that shape inchoate sensation so that we can think about and act on what comes to us through our bodies, so the concept of freedom contains "morally practical precepts" (9) that allow us "to extend the sphere of the determination of the will" (7). As with the structures of understanding, what is most human for Kant within the structures of reason, and hence most important, is our ability to give reason-full shape to what comes to us necessarily out of our nature.

If you were to take the two diagrams I have used to lay out the formal structure the first two *Critiques*, and put them next to each other, I hope you can see how they repeat the structures of the individual critiques. In each of the *Critiques* what is given by nature is subordinated to what (for Kant) are universal concepts of human thought (through, first, understanding and, then, reason); the result, for Kant, is that in each of the two *Critiques* "nature is harmonized with our design" (23): in each of the *Critiques*, particular sensations are brought under the realm of universal thought. But the first *Critique* concerns, overall, "the realm of natural concepts" (15) whereas the second concerns, overall, human moral decision-making—so, again, there is Nature on the one hand and the forms of human intellectual work on the other. Kant thus needs, formally and conceptually, a <u>third</u> critique that can show how the natural focus of the first critique is brought in alignment with the free workings of reason in the second critique so that, once again and overall, nature is harmonized with human intellectual design. This is where judgment—taste, an appreciation of beauty—enters, to take on this general structure:

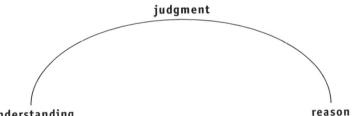

judgment

understanding   **reason**

In the third critique, then, the *Critique of Judgment*, Kant argues that, when we have a sense of pleasure, the faculty of judgment is what allows us to join the pleasure to the realm of universal design. This is not to say that we some how judge or reshape the pleasure to make it fit the design; instead, "the attainment of that design is bound up with the feeling of pleasure" (23): when we see what gives us pleasure, the pleasure, for Kant, comes when we recognize—judge—that the feeling is showing us how the particulars of our experience fit what is universal:

something in our judgments upon nature [...] makes us attentive to its purposiveness for our understanding—an endeavor to bring, wherever possible, its dissimilar laws under higher ones [...] —and thus, if successful, makes us feel pleasure in that harmony of these with our cognitive faculty... (24).

Let me put this another way, using the words of Ernst Cassirer, who places this movement on Kant's part—what may seem to us an odd move from reason and understanding to aesthetics—in the context of the "concrete historical origins of metaphysics" (275). Cassirer steps from Socrates to Plato to Aristotle to Plotinus, tracing through those thinkers morphing notions of relations between the particular to the universal, the real to the ideal, with the end result, in Neoplatonism, being that (if we consider this relation from the perspective of a working artist):

> the IDEA, which originally is encountered only as something mental and thus an indivisible unity, is extended into the material world; the mental archetype carried by the artist within himself commands matter and turns it into a reflection of the unity of the FORM. The more perfectly this is carried out, the more purely the appearance of the Beautiful is actualized. (278)

That is, under this telling, the Beautiful is (to quote Cassirer again) a "resonance of the whole in the particular and singular" (318), and the aesthetic is then "a type of contemplation that participates equally in the principle of empirical explanation of nature and in the principle of ethical judgment" (286). Aesthetic judgment is thus the awareness of a harmonious and interpenetrating relation between the parts of Kant's analysis, between the necessity of nature and the freedom of reason. For Kant, **nature and the laws by which we think and act are not separate, and when we see an object in which nature and law are harmonized, it is beautiful. When we see an object that is formed according to universal structures, then the particular and the universal are harmonized, and beauty is created.**

The faculty of judgment can thus, I think, be schematized more finely:

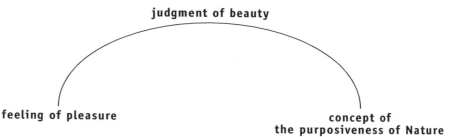

judgment of beauty

feeling of pleasure　　　　　　　　　　　　　　**concept of the purposiveness of Nature**

There are several aspects to such judgments of beauty that I want to emphasize here. Notice, first, that what gives rise to a judgment of beauty—whatever the object is (and Kant discusses people, buildings, music, animals, clothing, gardens, poetry)—is implied in this structure: a judgment of beauty starts with the object, but quickly moves to an appreciation of the formal relations suggested by the object.

Second, when (in Kant's view) we make judgments of beauty, they are not personal. Instead, judgments of beauty apply universally. Kant writes that

> it would be laughable if a man who imagined anything to his own taste thought to justify himself by saying: "This object (the house we see, the coat that person wears, the concert we hear, the poem submitted to our judgment) is beautiful *for me*." For he must not call it *beautiful* if it merely pleases him. Many things may have for him charm and pleasantness—no one troubles himself that—but if he gives out anything as beautiful, he supposes in others the same satisfaction; he judges not merely for himself, but for everyone, and speaks of beauty as if it were a property of things… (45, emphasis in the original)

Or, as Kant puts it later, "the *beautiful* is that which pleases universally" (54)—because, if a judgment of beauty is a judgment that finds universal design in a particular object, the quality recognized in the object must necessarily be universal. Eagleton describes Kant's position in this way:

> Given the nature of our immutable faculties, Kant holds, it is necessary that certain subjective judgments elicit the universal consent of others, since these judgments arise from the sheer formal workings of capacities we have in common. (96)

Because, that is, we all (for Kant) think in the same formal ways, we will find beautiful objects in which the forms of our thinking are made visible.

Finally, for similar reasons for Kant, anyone who makes a judgment of beauty must be disinterested in the judgment. Although the feeling one finds in a judgment of beauty brings what Kant calls "satisfaction," such satisfaction cannot make the judger lose himself in the object of the judgment. Instead, one must not care whether the beautiful object exists:

> We easily see that, in saying it is *beautiful* and in showing that I have taste, I am concerned, not with that in which I depend on the existence of the object, but with that which I make out of the representation in myself. Everyone must admit that a judgment about beauty, in which the least interest mingles, is very partial and is not a pure judgment of taste. (39, emphasis in the original)

A judgment of beauty for Kant, then, is a disinterested and universal judgment that finds universal form in the form of some particular object or person.

A FORMAL DISCONNECTION

Here is one way to summarize what I have just laid out about the structures of beauty in Kant's approaches to knowledge:

- For Kant, we are always to shape the particulars of emotion and bodily sensation according to universal principles.

- When we shape emotion and bodily sensation in accord with those principles, our motivations are not directed towards ourselves or others; instead, we are to act with disinterest, to act on judgments that could be (ought to be) made by everyone, everywhere.

• When we judge something to be beautiful, it is because beauty is formally inherent in the object.

In *Venus in Exile: The Rejection of Beauty in Twentieth-Century Art*, Wendy Steiner examines these statements within the context of Kant's time; she argues that Kant's approach to aesthetics has led us to conditions in our time that we might want to work against, conditions inseparable from the approaches to visual composition I have earlier described.

Steiner's arguments implicitly ask us to acknowledge that Kant's own philosophizing cannot be disinterested, in at least one way: from the beginning and throughout, Kant's philosophizing is gendered. That is, Kant's philosophizing—his certainty in the possibility of universal intellectual conditions—cannot be separated from how his sense of the world and its functioning grew out of his ability as a man of his time and place to look upon his experiences as being, necessarily, the experiences of all others. None of that, of course, enters Kant's *Critiques*. Steiner shows, however, how those conditions are stated explicitly by others: for example, she cites Arthur Schopenhauer stating that "Women are, and remain, thoroughgoing philistines, and quite incurable" (22). In Schopenhauer's thinking women are by nature incapable of true aesthetic feeling, just as they are incapable of the rigors of philosophic thought: because they are so tied to their bodies and emotion, they cannot approach the world intellectually, they cannot have the universal judgments Kant describes. Against such a cultural understanding of what a woman is and is capable of doing, it is not difficult to see Kant's philosophizing—the act of philosophizing as well as his philosophy's continual emphasis on formal abstract thought over what comes to us through our particular bodies—as a turn against aspects of life that have been and still often are culturally read as womanly.

Steiner quotes Mary Wollstonecraft's arguments that these womanly incapacities and inferiorities are not natural or inherent but rather the result of the limited lives, educations, actions, and positions that were (and are still) given to women; these inferiorities, Steiner writes, are what, "according to Mary Wollstonecraft, made women slaves to sensation" (23) because they had little or no access to the education that leads to abilities to perform (or a taste for) Kantian abstract intellectualizing. But precisely because Kant's philosophizing works continually to place and universalize understanding, reason, and judgment over bodily and other sensation, it abstracts body and sensation: body and sensation must be the same for all if thinking is to be the same—and so if someone appears incapable of thinking in the ways Kant has described thinking (as understanding, reasoning, and judging universally) it must because she is inherently incapable; there is no place in this structure for seeing, much less taking into consideration, how the particularities of one's material conditions shape one's structures of experience and thinking.

Against this background of necessary universals, Steiner delineates a reading of Mary Shelley's *Frankenstein* as a response to Kant's aesthetics. For Steiner, Shelley's writing—Frankenstein's monster and all that he wreaks—is a detailed teasing out of what happens when one acts with the disinterest required of the Kantian moral actor; the book is a way for Shelley to point out (according to Steiner) the "irony" in the aesthetics: "that in providing supposedly the most human of mental states, freedom, it utterly disregards love and family and pleasure, which have at least as much claim as freedom to define 'the human'" (13). But such disregard is never neutral; when we wish to indicate that something is not worthy of regard, when we diss what we regard, we make it so by making it not worthy of our sights. And so Steiner writes that

> If Kant wanted to detach aesthetic experience from self-concern, [Shelley] shows that this detachment leads to a devaluation and indeed dehumanization of the feminine and the domestic leading to the direst of consequences: war and political oppression. (14)

How are war and oppression—and all the deaths of women and children in *Frankenstein*—a result for Shelley of Kant's particular form of aesthetics? In a Kantian aesthetic judgment a particular sensation is brought under the form of the universal, and away from any truck with one's own self or body; one is thus distanced from the embodied object that gave rise to the judgment. Steiner thus writes that "the purity of Kantian beauty is a deprivation that inevitably evokes the enmity of the perceiver, who wants to punish it for its inaccessibility and distance," and so, "When woman is the embodiment of that beauty, she is at risk" (17).

Steiner carries her arguments out of *Frankenstein* and through late nineteenth and into twentieth century art and literary practices. She does this by quoting, for example, Leo Tolstoy's writing about the beauty of women as they live their lives, have children, and age—

> is this "beauty" real beauty? Of what use is it? [… T]hin and grizzled hair, toothless, wrinkles, tainted breath; even long before the end all becomes ugly and repellent; visible paint, sweat, foulness, hideousness. Where then is the god of my idolatry? Where is beauty? (36)

—to argue that Tolstoy found women "disastrous as symbols of artistic beauty, which must be universal, transcendent, safe from vicissitude and death" (36). She quotes Georges Braques saying, in 1910, that because he was incapable of depicting the full beauty of women he must

> create a new sort of beauty, the beauty that appears to me in terms of volume, of line, of mass, of weight, and through that beauty interpret my subjective impression. […] I want to expose the Absolute, and not merely the factitious woman. (44)

She quotes Apollinaire, who writes that "the modern school of painting"

> wants to visualize beauty disengaged from whatever charm woman has for man, and until now, no European artist has dared attempt this. The new artists demand an ideal beauty, which will be, not merely the proud expression of the species, but the expression of the universe, to the degree that it has been humanized by light. (48)

Steiner also quotes Pound, Mayakovsky, D.H. Lawrence, Marinetti, and Joyce, and she concludes that

As the avant-garde dodged the pathos of existence with their Promethean abstraction, they denounced sentiment and sensuality and stressed the purity of form and the self-containment of the aesthetic experience. (48)

[...]

In short, modernist artists turned the viewer's attention from subject matter to form, and symbolized this switch by subverting or eliminating the image of woman. In the process, they made the work a fetish, valuable in itself, compelling, a formal compensation for a problematic reality. (55)

Willem de Kooning, *Woman at Clearwater Beach.* Gift of Lee V. Eastman and John L. Eastman, Image copyright 2004 Board of Trustees, National Gallery of Art, Washington.

If we agree with Steiner's arguments—if they help us make sense of, for example, paintings of women by de Kooning or Picasso (two more of Steiner's many examples)—then we have this as one possible legacy of a Kantian notion of beauty:

we receive in our time a notion of form that considers itself timeless and universal and disinterested, inhering in objects for us to look at rather than placed there by our learned habits and tastes. We receive a notion that form is about pulling away from what is "factitious," what is particular, what is messy and domestic and emotional and bodily and coughs and sweats and bloats and wants to talk back and even sometimes touch. We receive a notion of form that not only allows to pull away from all that, but that expects us to pull away, that instructs us—visually, by what it emphasizes—that we are supposed to pull away, be distant, be in our selves away from others, from Others.

Pablo Picasso, *Woman with a Book.* The Norton Simon Foundation, Image copyright 2004 Estate of Pablo Picasso/ Artists Rights Society (ARS), New York.

What results, in this telling, are the two connected consequences I described earlier in response to Williams and to Bang and Arnheim.

- On the one hand, the object of art and design is formalized to abstraction, to the point where when I see it I can look at it as though it has no other qualities than the formal: beauty is contained in it, but only as form.

- On the other hand, my sense of my self is also reduced as I am separated from what gives me (formal) pleasure; in the telling of Arnheim, for example, a self is important here solely because its experience is guided by gravity, that most Newtonian and formal of forces.

Such a formal beauty has nothing to do with me
or with you.

YES, BUT... IT DOESN'T HAVE TO BE ART TO GIVE PLEASURE

But the Peek layout isn't art, you may say: that body has not been taken over by rough lines as in the de Kooning drawing; it has not been made into several circles hanging off a thin stem. But, well, hasn't it? Isn't the body on the Peek layout dissolving into abstract shape? The body is softly focused, fading into the background: we are not being shown this body so as to see any dry and flaking skin on its elbows or to see any monthly bloating or any scars. Instead, we see unblemished flat white skin abstractly rounded—as though the body were a blank page on which we can put what we want: the gloves and boots are like paper-doll or refrigerator-magnet-doll clothing, pieces to take on and off at whim. We see the body as shapes made to be in tune with the shapes of type and with the layout itself, as I wrote earlier when I applied the principles of Williams and Arnheim and Bang to the layout.

I want to argue that the body in the Peek layout <u>has</u> been made into form, has been departicularized: when we see this body, we are seeing a body only through the distant, universalized, formality that I have argued is well-seated in Kant's notion of aesthetic judgment and that we have inherited in much of our uncritical and uncriticized practices with and around the visual. And certainly my pleasure in looking at the body is, to some extent, formal, as I have written earlier: it must necessarily be so, because I have grown up into these formal approaches, I have been trained into—learned the vocabularies and the ways of seeing of (whether I can articulate them out loud or not)—this formal approach to beauty. I find pleasure in the Peek layout precisely because it is all abstracted, perfected, pulled out of the day-to-day, formalized.

And the anger that I feel, the anger I have been trying to understand since first seeing the layout, is inseparable from the pleasures I have been describing.

I've not spoken so far specifically of that anger, except to mention it at the beginning of this chapter, because I can only articulate it now, after having tried to understand my pleasure and how my pleasure is tied to Kant's formal aesthetics. It is easy to articulate a particular and well-known kind of anger about the Peek layout, about the layout being just one more in the endless pile of painted, photographed, and drawn representations of women shown as only sexual and also now used for selling, so that we all—men and women—are pushed to see women only as sexual objects, as objects serving as the means to the ends of others. **But what my analysis here shows me is that we should see this objectification—and the violence against women that can follow from it—as inseparable from the formal approaches we have learned for analyzing and making visual presentations of all kinds.**

The particular approach to form we have acquired through Kant asks us to think of form as separate from the content of the senses. It then asks, as we work with anything we wish to see or make as aesthetic, for form to take what is messy and particular and to abstract it and generalize it and universalize it. We have learned to <u>think</u> that form should do this, and we have learned to <u>expect</u> that form should do this, whether we are working with visual representations such as photographs or with the visualities of type on a page. When we see what is not so formally ordered, when we see what does not have beauty as an apparently inherent quality and that does not therefore live up to our formal expectations, we denigrate it, or try to lay (or force) perfect form upon it, or try to erase it.

And a result of this formal approach, then, is that women—like anyone else subject to this formalizing—are "at risk," as Steiner claims and as her quotations from artists demonstrate: first, when women and other Others are subjected to this aesthetic formalizing, they are made distant, objects to be observed, not people to live with; then, when we see them in all their particularities and compare them to aestheticized representations, they are judged as lacking of that form and so in need of being perfected (often through self-discipline—think anorexia or Michael Jackson) or of being taken out of the realms of formal judgment, sometimes violently.

My anger is that I see the Peek ad, and the woman in the Peek ad, as beautiful only because I cannot see the particularities of either. The Kantian formal conceptions of good form into which I—probably just like you—have grown up teach me to see in a way that doesn't value the particular and the messy. It isn't that I learn to objectify and simplify women simply because I see so many magazine covers or advertisements or movies or TV shows with abstractly perfected, airbrushed women; it is also that I have learned to believe that what is well-formed must be formally abstracted and perfected. **My very (learned) idea of what is beautiful, of what is well-formed, is dangerous for women and any**

aestheticized Others.

This desire for abstract formality we have learned—the Kantian universal formalism embodied in the layout of the Peek ad as well as in the vocabularies of Williams, Arnheim, and Bang—separate us from our histories and places, and hence from each other. If we believe that to be human is to be tied to place and time and messiness and complexity, then, by so abstracting us, this desire dehumanizes us and our work and how we see each other. This is dangerous.

We should look on these formal approaches with anger, and we should be working to change them.

STRETCHING TO FIND, THEREFORE,
PARTICULAR BEAUTY

If we want to change how we see women, then, or if we want to change how we see any group of people who are treated unfairly by our visual practices, it is therefore not enough to push for magazine covers and advertisements and catalogues and TV commercials that show (for example) women with fleshy and round and imperfect and aged flesh. We also have to to criticize and rethink the formal categories we have inherited for making the visual arrangements that we do; we need to try new and different formal relations in our layouts and we need to learn to appreciate formal arrangements and practices that do not abstract and universalize.

Steiner, for example, in response to the analysis I've summarized on earlier pages, writes that perhaps "our aesthetic socialization is a good thing, every touch with beauty amounting to an all too rare experience of community and shared values" (xvii), but this is possible only if we see beauty

> as a kind of communication. We often speak as if beauty were a property of objects: Some people or artworks "have it" and some do not. [… Instead,] Beauty is an unstable property because it is not a property at all. It is the name of a particular interaction between two beings, a "self" and an "Other": "I find an Other beautiful." (xx-xxi)⤙

And

> In our gratitude toward what moves us so, we attribute to it the *property* of beauty, but what we are actually experiencing is a special *relation* between it and ourselves. We discover it as valuable, meaningful, pleasurable *to us*. (xxiii, emphasis hers)

If we see beauty as a quality we build, rather than one we expect to discover, then we can potentially see beauty—and other aesthetic qualities like coherence or unity or balance—as shared values we can both celebrate and question. These are the values (and there could be others) that shape the material communication we build for each other and that thus shape how we see each other through what we build.

What if we were to build communications that, instead of seeking after the universal and abstract, sought after the particular? What if, instead of formal

---

⤙ Kaja Silverman argues for similar constructions of a loving approach to others, through sight, in *The Threshold of the Visible*.

distance from others, we worked to figure out what visual forms might embody generosity toward others, or patience, or pleasure in the particular, or …? What if, that is, we were to conceive as form as itself particular and temporal, tied to where and when and how we live, a set of structures for both representing and shaping how we see and experience each other?

ONE WAY TOWARD
A FORMAL RECONNECTION

How then might we develop a taste for the different—the particular—sense of beauty I've just suggested? How might we develop senses of beauty and pleasure that allow us to see that beauty is something we construct together, that it is a way we can reciprocally share with each other the pleasures of being with in the world together, of appreciating what is particular about our lives?

I am going to present here one approach that might help us understand judgments of beauty as the recognition of reciprocal relationship instead of as distancing; I am trying to build (and to test through my teaching) approaches that see form as this kind of recognition, tying us to others and to our times and places. To do that I am going to return, quickly, to Kant, in order to tell an alternate lineage for the aesthetic's ability to articulate the particular and the universal, necessity and freedom; I want to bring necessity and freedom more closely together than Kant's formal search for universals allowed, so that we see them necessarily entwined, not separable and separated. In order to do this, I need to move in my own way from Kant into the 20th century, as necessity becomes social and freedom gets strange.

I do not think I am limb-walking when I say that Kant's notion of the mediation of the senses gets socialized, in some lines of thinking, beginning in the late 19th and through the last century. For Kant, we have no immediate access to the real; there is instead always the mediation of the intellectual categories between us and our sensations—and those intellectual categories are, for Kant, as I've described, universal, the same categories for everyone everywhere. That is, with Kant, we are to understand our bodily responses and tastes as being the same as everyone else's because the categories we use for creating understanding out of sensation are not tied to time or place. But if we look at this structure of understanding through Bourdieu, for example, I think we can understand Bourdieu's notions of *habitus* and *taste* as giving social groundings to the categories of the understanding: that is, what is "necessary" in Kant's schematism of the aesthetic—in our time—becomes (through Bourdieu) what we have learned to take for granted by having grown up into our particular times and places and the shared values that Steiner argues we can see when we are moved by or attracted to a composition. When we experience gravity, that is, we can only experience it because we have a term "gravity," which carries with it whatever we have learned (or not) about Newton, the apple, and the solar system. When we experience weight, a result of gravity, we only experience it through the value-weighted forms gendered bodies can take in our time and place. In all those Kantian schema I laid out several pages ago, then, we can understand what Kant labels as necessary—our bodily sensations—as being social before we ever can experience them. The web of social and cultural practices in which we move give us the words and concepts, as well as the tastes, for understanding what we sense. This is the necessary—and necessarily social—grounding structure of the day-to-day, of all that we share as we move in our particular circles and lives.

How then might we learn to appreciate—see the beauty of, take rich pleasure in—the particularities of our experiences and those of others within this shared day-to-day? I believe that various particularities can be made at least temporarily special, can be made to stand out against but still (necessarily) within the background of the day-to-day. This is one way to consider how freedom could function in those Kantian schema I presented on earlier pages, if we look at freedom through the Russian formalists and Brecht, through their appeals to "strangeness"—or through Heidegger's naming of the *uncanny*: freedom could be manifest in that part of any aesthetic experience that encourages us, momentarily and pleasurably, to see and understand how the shared, necessary, quotidian rhythms of our lives are built out of numberless and necessary particularities. Victor Shklovsky, for example, argues that

art exists that one may recover the sensation of life; it exists to make one feel things, to make the stone *stony*. […] The technique of art is to make objects "unfamiliar." […] Art removes objects from the automatism of perception. (12-13; emphasis his)

There are problems with this approach, which can do exactly what Steiner describes by putting our attention not on the full particularity of what stands out aesthetically but by instead putting our attention on "strangeness" itself. If we learn to recognize, however, that what is strange can only be so within the context of the shared day-to-day, then the strange and the social stay linked; the social does not get forgotten so that the strange then seems to possess some inherent, universal property.

It is possible then to understand that the existence of the strange—our ability to make things strange so that they can stand out as worthy of thoughtful and respectful attention—both heightens our awareness of the necessity of the day-to-day as well as shows us the freedom we have relative to it: the one is not possible without the other. Something like this is at work in Sonja Foss's arguments about "the construction of visual appeal in images":

A novel technical aspect of the image violates viewers' expectations; the violation functions both to sustain interest in the image and to decontextualize it. Connotations commonly associated with the technical aspect then provide an unexpected but familiar context in which to interpret the image. (215)

For my purposes here it is not important to focus on Foss's use of "technical," but it is important for me to state that I think her arguments go beyond "images": what Foss describes—what Shklovsky describes—is a process by which we can change relations we build with each other through the communications we make for each other. If we think of beauty (which I have now made strange) as what can result when some expected day-to-day particular is made to stand out against the background of the larger realm of steady social practices, then we can develop not only strategies for teaching about it but also for how we might go about making change in the formal approaches to lives and detached bodies about which I have been—am—angry.

I flip Cassirer's explication of Kant here, a bit, because I'm speaking of the "resonance of the particular and singular in the whole" for this beautiful strangeness, but Kant's basic structure is still at work—although I have attached new words to the structure. Under what I am arguing, aesthetic experiences allow us to participate equally in the necessity of the social and in the freedom of pushing against—making strange—that social so that we can appreciate its particularities. We can create aesthetic experiences—visual compositions, for the purposes of my teaching—for each other where we use the expected social constructions of form just enough to hold onto what audiences expect, but where we can then also make visible the particularities of our own lives and experience and hence make visible the limitations of the forms we have been asked to grow into but, if we are to be safe and fully respected, cannot.

WHAT THEN IS NEEDED

If we think of the experience of beauty as coming out of the day-to-day necessities of our social existence—an "experience of community and shared values" to use Steiner's words—when particularities of that existence are made to stand out, then I think we can see direct strategies of approach for teaching. There is no question that there is a certain necessity to effective visual composition because a design must fit a viewer's expectations if it is to make sense… but if design is to have any sense of possibility—of freedom—to it, then it must also push against the conventions, the horizons, of those expectations.

I want people in my classes, then, to learn the social and temporal expectations of visual composition so that they can, eventually, perhaps, change some of the results of those expectations. I do not start my teaching with design principles, then, but rather by asking people in classes to collect and sort through and categorize compositions of all kinds, to try to pull "principles" out of those compositions and their experiences. One result is that, after looking closely at telephone book ads for lawyers, for example, they can see the limitations and contingencies of (for example) Williams's design principles: an accident-and-injury lawyer who wants to come across as strong and willing to do everything on your behalf does not do well presented through rules aimed at harmony, clarity, and restraint. But, also, when people in these classes then make their own visual compositions, they understand that there are principles and why they need to follow them (in order to fit with the learned expectations of their audiences, not because there are universal, neutral forms) but they are also then aware that they can—and often should—push against the principles. They see how the visual compositions they make embody particular aspects of themselves, that what they make are not objects for contemplation by others but rather reciprocal communications, shaping both composer and reader and establishing relationships among them.

But there is more to our discussions than how to make compositions for narrowly specific rhetorical situations: as students make their collections, we talk about how different compositional strategies shape us by asking us to view, read, and respond in the terms of the form on the page or screen. When students are the audiences of design, they see how designs work to shape and naturalize the necessity of their day-to-day worlds. When they produce their own compositions, they consider their visual strategies as having real and expansive effects—because they see their work as fitting into, reproducing but also trying to make strange, the necessary but contingent principles that underlie how we live with each other. They see the work as reciprocal, shaping themselves as well as those for whom the work is made. They also then see the stickiness of beauty as it—like any other value giving form to what they make—binds form and content, composer and audience, together.

We come to see visual composition as rhetorical, as a series of choices that have much broader consequences and articulations than visual principles (as I've argued here) suggest. After such a course of activities students see themselves able to compose effectively with the visual elements of different texts for different rhetorical circumstances… but I also hope that they see themselves capable of making change, of composing work that not only fits its circumstances but that also helps its audiences—and its makers—re-vision themselves and try out new and more thoughtful relations between each other.

Anne Frances Wysocki

1 The activities that follow tend to focus on students analyzing and composing texts on paper—but I use the same approaches (starting with collection exercises, asking students initially to pull design principles from what they see and from experience rather than from writing on design, and so on) when I teach about texts on screen. To make the exercises that follow work for onscreen texts, just replace "paper" with "onscreen" in the following pages—with one caveat.

In classes where we work along the lines of the exercises that follow, discussions about the (material and other) constraints of the communication technology we are using weave throughout our talk. With paper, for example, we discuss the economics of color reproduction and of page size; we discuss the different page-size standards in different areas of the world, the portability of paper, the technical issues with getting crisp contrast in a printed photograph to be xeroxed, and the ethics of getting others to notice your single-page flyer when it is up on the typical college wall with 3000 others. When we compose documents for the Web, on the other hand, we discuss the economics and access issues of standard monitor and browser window sizes, as well as of bandwidth and download times; we discuss how and why to compose using HTML or an editor and the different views that different editors ask you to take of what is possible online.

In either case, we start with intense and focused looking at as many examples of texts as possible made within the technological setting we are discussing, so that we see—we understand by seeing—how design principles (and our tastes) take shape, as well as how we might then work within and against and around those principles to achieve what we value, to achieve the visual relations we desire with others.

ACTIVITY 1

RHETORICAL OBSERVATIONS

TEACHER NOTES

DESCRIPTION

Students amass a collection of visual compositions, and through looking closely at similarities and differences in the collection, they draw up tentative principles for assigning the pieces to different categories of design, categories they name based on their observations. They use their principles for analyzing other layouts and for considering the uses—and strengths and shortcomings—of published design principles.

GOALS

In the course of this activity, students:

- Strengthen their abilities to pick out the varied details that are placed together to make a single composition.

- See how compositions designed for different audiences and purposes use different design principles.

- Gain confidence in talking about how visual compositions function.

TIME

This activity sequence is most effective when spread out over 6-8 class periods, if all the steps are followed.

LEVEL

I have used this activity sequence with first-year students and with graduate students: the activity is straightforward enough for the newer students but has many openings for graduate students to apply their theory-leanings. *What is required for this to work is that the students have little experience working with the visual aspects of texts.*

SEQUENCE

1   Students do the "Collecting Visual Designs" assignment described on the homework handout following this sequence description.

2   In class, students pair up to compare their collections. I ask them to spread their layouts out on the floor, and then to categorize their layouts (the shared set) following any scheme they can see. Some categories that students have used in the past include liquor ads, academic journal pages, pages with women who are smiling, pages that are supposed to make you frightened so that you will use the financial service being advertised, layouts with babies.

Once the groups of two have finished their categorizing, I ask each group to pair up with another, and to repeat the categorizing—but now they are working with the collections of four students.

3   As homework, students repeat the "Collecting Exercise"—so that they have a collection of 50 layouts. In class, they repeat step 2, with their larger collections: they see new and different categories, and how categories ebb and flow into each other.

When students have finished their categorizing a second time, we discuss why the categories might exist. This discussion brings up many issues: we talk about:

- *the prevalence of visual design in our culture, tied to advertising.*

- *how different categories of visual composition use different visual strategies to make different kinds of appeals: for example, layouts for nonprofit organizations often show a single person—and often with a full body—who looks directly at the viewer with a serious expression so as to evoke one-to-one connection and empathy, and these layouts frequently use little color; layouts for liquor very often have a large colorful photograph that bleeds off the page and that shows men and women at parties or moving happily on the street—and there is often a picture of the liquor bottle on the lower right of the page.*

- *how layouts in their various categories tend to simplify the audiences they address, focusing on one or two characteristics shared by the target audience.*

- *how what we see in all the layouts gives us a sense of—teaches us— what makes an exciting Friday night or a good body or appropriate behavior toward children.*

4   After this discussion, I ask students to write up their observations of the compositional strategies used in one of the categories they've identified. The "Comparing and Categorizing Designs" handout helps them do this, and that helps them start making explicit connections among compositional strategies, audiences, and design purposes.

5   In class, students compare their lists of strategies observed, so that their lists of strategies are as full as possible. This helps students continue to see the rich complexity of strategies they have available to them as they make their own work—and also gives them meat for discussing how and why other designers would make the strategic choices they do.

6   For homework, students apply their observations to compositions outside the categories they have looked at most closely: the "Design Analysis" handout for this asks them to analyze why a composer would make different design choices for different audiences.

7   Given the wealth of observation they have now accumulated, I now ask students to read an "official" set of design principles (such as I have

described earlier in this essay), and to see how well the principles hold up to their observations. There is a handout—"Other Categories for Design"—to help them do this. This leads to considerable class discussion about the functions of such guidelines, and about how they can make layouts that others will still judge as "professional-looking" even if they do not follow "official" guidelines. The emphasis of our discussions is on the rhetoricality of design—on learning about your audience and its (visual) expectations—and about how the choices a composer makes in constructing a visual layout cannot always follow "official" design guidelines if the layout is to work within its context.

RHETORICAL OBSERVATIONS
HOMEWORK
COLLECTING VISUAL DESIGNS

THE PURPOSE OF THIS ASSIGNMENT

This assignment will start you building a repertoire of the visual designs of others, so that you can start making observations about the kinds of designs— or design tastes—that are prevalent now, and so that you can start making decisions about the kinds of designs you want to make. This exercise helps you start to see the sorts of visual expectations held by the audiences for whom you'll be designing.

Such collecting is also a practice followed by many professional designers: their collections not only help designers develop a sense of what they need to do to work with an audience's expectations, but these collections are like idea-wells to which you can turn when you want a new strategy to try... or when you want to work against audience expectations.

WHAT TO DO

Collect 25 design samples. (And by "design," I mean here a mix of words and images on paper that you can tell was intended by the designer to stand alone, to serve some particular purpose. Do not bring in photographs or drawings that have no words. You can bring in designs that are made solely of words and have no photographs or drawings—but, please, no photographs or drawings without words.) (And do not think solely of advertising here, either, please...: look at the pages of your textbooks and the novels you read and the placemat under a fastfood breakfast...)

- Only collect designs that fit onto one, unfolded 8.5" x 11" page or smaller. (This is to make our task a little easier...)
- Make copies of the designs if you cannot bring in the original.
- To find these designs, look in the newspaper. Look in magazines in the library or in your bathroom. Look in the other places I suggested above.
- Bring the designs to class in a large envelope, so you have a way to hold onto them. Try not to fold them. Write your name on the back of each layout so you can hold onto your collection. (You'll be mixing your collections with others to make some observations, and then taking them back.)

COMPARING &
CATEGORIZING DESIGNS

THE PURPOSE OF THIS ASSIGNMENT

This assignment asks you to put into words many of the observations you have been making in class over the last several days.

By putting your observations into words on paper, you will be able to use them both to make and to critique other designs.

WHAT TO DO

Pick one of the categories of design you've been using over the last several days, and separate out all the designs you have that fit into that category.

Write down any design strategies you see the designs in this category sharing. (Not all the designs have to have the characteristics you note, only a majority in your collection.)

Anything you see that these designs have in common is worth noting, but here are some categories to help you get going:

- Are there kinds or amounts of colors or of typefaces that the designs have in common? Are placements of elements similar?
- Are the colors or uses of grey that these designs have in common? Are the same ranges of colors/greys used? Are colors used in the same places (in a photograph, say, or in type)?
- Do the designs use photographs or illustrations or drawings or...?
- Do the designs use similar kinds of photographs or illustrations?
- Do the designs use similar amounts of 'white space'? (And just because white space is called *white* space doesn't mean the space has to be white; rather, this term refers to *open space*, to space in the layout that has intentionally been left 'empty' so that your attentions can be directed to and focused on other parts of the layout.)
- When you look at the amount of space that is placed between elements (like between a photograph and a line of text, or between lines of text), does there seem to be a consistent kind of spacing across the different designs?
- Are similar kinds of words—that make similar kinds of promises or describe similar kinds of things—used?
- Is there a similar proportion of words to other elements?
- Are words treated graphically or not, across the designs?

These are certainly not all the questions you can ask, so any more you can address will be good. But these should start to give you an idea of the number of details to which designers are attentive.

Now, type up what you have done—being attentive to your own layout. (Format your layout in any way, using any typefaces, that you think encourages a reader to understand well your observations. If you want to scan and include a sample layout to represent your category, that would be fine.)

Be sure you carefully describe the category of design you observed, so that someone else who doesn't know you can easily understand what you are doing, and then add the list of observations you made about the category.

Finally, add a paragraph in which you speculate why this category of design has these particular set of design strategies in common. Is it because these layouts are trying to appeal to a specific audience, or create a certain emotion in an audience, or make the audience feel particularly smart (or poor or lacking)?

What you have typed up is a preliminary set of design guidelines for someone who would want to make a layout that fit into this category. (Start thinking about how you could make a layout that fit into this category but that nonetheless stood out in some way.)

Here are some categories others noted when they did this exercise in the past. See if you can add to this list:

If there are people in a layout:
- What is the facial expression?
- Where is the person looking?
- How many people?
- What sort of person: strong and tough looking, healthy, beautiful, no skin blemishes, tall, young?
- How much skin/hair/legs is/are shown?
- Is there some kind of innuendo in the layout or photo?
- What's the race of the person?

Other things to note:
- What is the quality of color: hard, soft, bright?
- What is the main visual focus of the layout?
- What kind of word choice is there?
- How much text is there?
- Is humor used?
- How much visual ambiguity is used in the layout or concerning the product? (Can you tell what the product is, in other words?)
- What kind of typeface is used?
- What's the background of the layout? A photo or illustration, or a color? Is the background realistic or unnatural or fantasy?
- Are metaphors used in the layout?
- Is there a headline? A slogan?
- Is the main textual information at the bottom?

RHETORICAL OBSERVATIONS
HOMEWORK

A DESIGN ANALYSIS, USING YOUR DESIGN GUIDELINES

THE PURPOSE OF THIS ASSIGNMENT

Now I want you to start applying the design guidelines you generated by using them to analyze other layouts. By applying your guidelines—through analyzing how the guidelines apply to different layouts—you'll be thinking about how and why visual designers make some of the design choices they do.

WHAT TO DO

Find 2 new layouts: the first is to be from the same category for which you have developed design guidelines; the second is to be from any other category.

Use the design guidelines that you wrote for the previous class to help you look closely at the two layouts. Your observations should be typed—try to use a page layout application (like InDesign or Quark), and be sure to think of your page(s) as a design.

For EACH layout, do the following in your writing:

- Describe, first, how the layout follows the guidelines you've written, and then describe how the layout deviates from those guidelines.

- Then speculate about the audience for whom the layout is intended. As you describe the kind of audience for whom you think the layout is intended, use the evidence of the layout to support your argument: that is, use not only the evidence of what is in the layout (the product being presented) but also the layout itself: *What kind of audience (for example) would be drawn by the kind of typefaces used in the layout?* or *What kind of audience would be drawn by the strong central (or curvy) alignment of the layout?* Whatever evidence you can see to support your contention for the audience for whom the layout is intended, write it up.

- After you have written about both layouts, write up some observations about why you think the one category of design uses certain visual strategies while the other doesn't. Is it because of different audiences, or different products, or attempting to evoke different relationships between audience and product...?

RHETORICAL OBSERVATIONS

HOMEWORK

OTHER CATEGORIES FOR DESIGN

THE PURPOSE OF THIS ASSIGNMENT

You've done a lot of looking at categories of layouts in the last couple of weeks. Now we'll look at someone else's categories to see what you think, what you can learn, what you can teach...

WHAT TO DO

[Here I ask students to read someone else's design principles: for example, this is where I would ask students to read the section of Robin Williams's and John Tollett's *Robin Williams Design Workbook* on categories of design.]

Please write approximately 500 words in response to the reading, using the following questions to guide your writing:

- *Do [this writer's] categories agree with what you have observed? Where are the agreements and disagreements? How do you explain the differences and agreements?*

- *How do the categories help you think (or not) about the design work you see yourself doing in the future?*

Please be sure your name is on your writing—and please be sure your writing doesn't have the default settings and lack-of-choice choices of usual academic writing; instead, please present your writing so that you cannot separate form from content. Thanks!

ACTIVITY 2

HOW DOES DESIGN WORK

ELSEWHERE?

TEACHER NOTES

GOALS

In the course of this activity, students:

- See how effective design strategies are tied to place and time.

- See how different design strategies encourage different values in the relations among audience, composition, and composer.

- Acquire a wider range of compositional strategies than were they to look only at designs from their immediate surroundings.

TIME

This activity can take 20-30 minutes for discussion of one example; there is then homework.

LEVEL

This is an activity I have used with first-year and with graduate students.

SEQUENCE

1   Pass around copies (or project or show on computer screens) a layout from the Victorian era or from Japan this year (or, depending on your class and purposes, from a very hip Web site or from an academic journal with which students are familiar—this latter instance often surprises students, since we have been taught not to think of academic pages as having visual aspects). There are some samples on the next pages.

2   Ask students to throw out adjectives that describe the overall tone of the layout. (To get discussion going, I will list adjectives that are drastically opposite to what we see: for example, when discussing a layout full of bright blues and pinks, I'll ask, "Is this depressing? Is this how you felt after your last thermodynamics exam?" This helps students say what may seem obvious, but it brings up an opening.

3   After students have given several adjectives, ask them "Why?" "Why [for example] does a layout seem cheery or serious or threatening?" They will often start with describing color, but encourage them to talk about how the objects in the composition are placed, what photographs are used, the use of photographs, and so on.

    As they describe what is going on in the composition, ask them also to describe why they think they link the compositional strategies they see with the meanings they take from the layout.

4   If you have worked through the Rhetorical Observation activity on the previous pages, ask students how the layout they are now seeing is different from what they have previously been observing.

Ask them to try to explain the differences: how, for example, does this layout ask an audience's eyes to move through the layout, as compared with what they have been observing. Does this layout use strategies that ask our eyes to linger or move slowly, or does it use strategies that ask us to be quick and brisk in our looking?

5   Ask students to write down any visual strategies they see that are new to them—and to write down how those strategies encourage different responses or meanings than they have previously observed. How might they use these strategies in the future? Could they use these strategies without modification for the audiences they know?

6   For homework, give students a visual composition from another place or time, and ask them to use similar visual strategies as are in the layout—but now to rework the strategies so that they support a line of thinking or acting connected to students' present lives.

I have included on the following pages examples of such reworkings off the Web (from the "Institute of Official Cheer" Web site, http://www.lileks.com/institute/instsplash/index.html; but also see the Adbusters Web site, http://www.adbusters.org/), examples that I think are particularly effective in pointing out how disruptive—strange and perhaps beautiful—it can be to see something familiar shown so differently: when we look at these layouts off the Web in class, students first look and say, oh yeah, that's from the thirties—but then they look again, and start laughing—and good discussion about why they laugh (and how they can bring on that laughter in others) results.

Looking at this work off the Web, or students' own compositions, is thus a direct opening into talking about the expectations we pick up from our day-to-day social movements and how those expectations can set us up not to look closely—or can set us up to look even more closely and question what we take for granted.

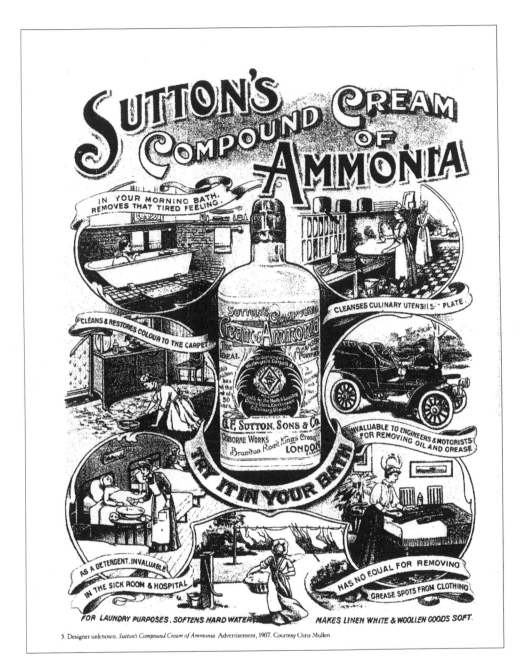

5. Designer unknown. *Sutton's Compound Cream of Ammonia.* Advertisement, 1907. Courtesy Chris Mullen

On this page and the next are three samples—an advertisement from 1907 and a web page and an ad for a computer monitor from Japan—to help students see how the values of visual composition vary over time and place.

The Sticky Embrace of Beauty: ACTIVITIES

185

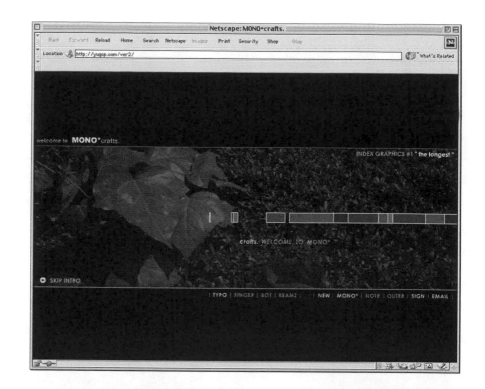

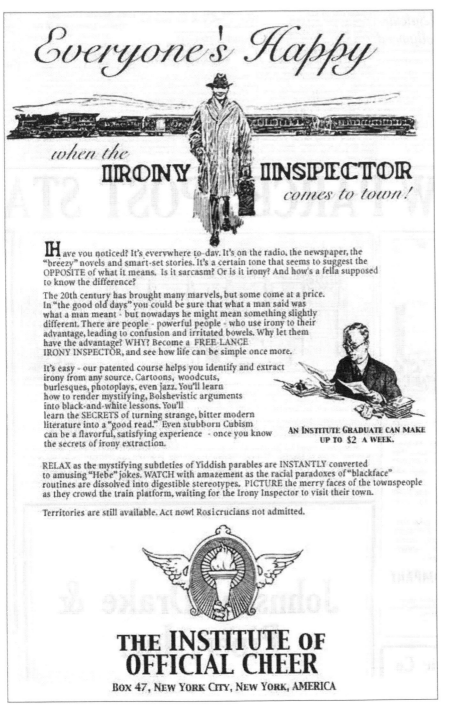

Everyone's Happy

when the IRONY INSPECTOR *comes to town!*

Have you noticed? It's everywhere to-day. It's on the radio, the newspaper, the "breezy" novels and smart-set stories. It's a certain tone that seems to suggest the OPPOSITE of what it means. Is it sarcasm? Or is it irony? And how's a fella supposed to know the difference?

The 20th century has brought many marvels, but some come at a price. In "the good old days" you could be sure that what a man said was what a man meant - but nowadays he might mean something slightly different. There are people - powerful people - who use irony to their advantage, leading to confusion and irritated bowels. Why let them have the advantage? WHY? Become a FREE-LANCE IRONY INSPECTOR, and see how life can be simple once more.

It's easy - our patented course helps you identify and extract irony from any source. Cartoons, woodcuts, burlesques, photoplays, even jazz. You'll learn how to render mystifying, Bolshevistic arguments into black-and-white lessons. You'll learn the SECRETS of turning strange, bitter modern literature into a "good read." Even stubborn Cubism can be a flavorful, satisfying experience - once you know the secrets of irony extraction.

An Institute Graduate can make up to $2 a week.

RELAX as the mystifying subtleties of Yiddish parables are INSTANTLY converted to amusing "Hebe" jokes. WATCH with amazement as the racial paradoxes of "blackface" routines are dissolved into digestible stereotypes. PICTURE the merry faces of the townspeople as they crowd the train platform, waiting for the Irony Inspector to visit their town.

Territories are still available. Act now! Rosicrucians not admitted.

THE INSTITUTE OF OFFICIAL CHEER

Box 47, New York City, New York, America

On this page and the next are two visual compositions (there are more) from the "Institute of Official Cheer" website—
http://www.lileks.com/institute/instsplash/index.html—
that show how putting present "content" into form from another place or time can help make present—and past—practices strange.

Anne Frances Wysocki

is irony

tearing your family apart?

Does your husband laugh with joyless derision when he pages through a magazine full of things he can't afford? Does your child laugh at Fred Allen's radio programs in a way unbecoming his age? Do YOU wonder why the happy pictures in your Hollywood magazines strike you as idiotic and false? Are your domestic "spats" laced with bitter, cutting remarks that have their roots in subtle, pervasive economic worries?

YOU could all be suffering from Irony-Rich Blood.

Only **IROLINE** is formulated to calm, soothe and relieve the dread of existential awareness. Rub it on - feel its healing warmth - *relax* as things start to look sunny again. Great as a cake frosting, too!

Available at fine non-Rosicrucian-staffed drugstores everywhere.

IROLINE

The Black & White Worldview in the Blue & White Tube

188

ACTIVITY 3

ANALYZING A COMPOSITION

TEACHER NOTES

GOALS
In the course of this activity, students analyze a visual composition of their own.

TIME
This is a homework activity.

LEVEL
The style of this assignment is aimed at undergraduates.

HOMEWORK

ANALYZING YOUR OWN COMPOSITION

THE PURPOSE OF THIS ASSIGNMENT
Competent, thoughtful designers—especially those whose work supports the values they consciously wish to spread in the world—are able to describe why they have made the design decisions they have. They are able to look at layouts and say why the layouts work and how they could be better. This requires practice, both practice in looking but also practice in using the vocabularies we have been developing together this semester and practice in thinking about how you build a relationship between your composition and its audience.

WHAT TO DO
From all the layouts you have made so far this semester, pick one you particularly like or think is particularly effective for the rhetorical situation in which it was designed.

Write a 750 word analysis of your layout. I want you, in this writing, to aim at describing as fully as possible how your set of chosen design strategies asks your particular audience to respond to your composition. You'll need to describe your audience and your compositional strategies in as much detail as possible. What kinds of looking or acting does your composition encourage in your audience, do you think?

You might start out by saying "I think this layout works well for [insert audience description here] because I believe such audiences would be drawn to clear, straightforward, and geometrically ordered pages. My layout asks them to see the elements of my layout in a slow, thoughtful, and orderly manner…" You would then give your reasons why you think the particular audience you describe should be drawn to such strategies, and then argue how the various elements of your layout come together to create the order you have described.

Use terms that we have discussed this semester: there's contrast and repetition, balance, and alignment, and there's descriptions of typefaces, but also think about visual hierarchy, the shapes that are made on a page, colors, the size of a page and its orientation, the emotional appeal that arrangements of elements create and why, the sense of the designer that you get from a layout and why, and so on—we have been discussing these issues (and their meaning-making all semester—pull out your notes). All these elements come together to create the effect a page has.

> *Consider your own layout of this writing, as you compose. I am not going to accept pages that use 'standard' academic format, since that is a format rarely questioned in its effects and history; instead, I want you to present this page in a way that demonstrates your serious and thoughtful attentions.*

ACTIVITY 4

DESIGNING TO HELP OTHERS FEEL SMART

TEACHER NOTES

GOALS

In the course of this activity, students:

- Examine concrete examples of visual composition that encourages or discourages learning.

- Get practice in compositional practices that consider the relationships (visual) texts build with audiences.

TIME

This activity takes place over 3 class meetings.

LEVEL

This is an activity for advanced undergraduates or graduate students.

SEQUENCE

1   I ask people to bring in to the following class "textbooks or manuals they think suck—or that they love." I don't have to say more than that: as soon as I say that, eyes light up, and people in class start talking about a thermodynamics or grammar text with which they have had to fight—or with which they are fighting in a current class.

2   In that following class session, I ask people to talk about the textbooks or manuals they have brought in. I ask them to describe what about the books supports them—or not—in their learning. The discussion weaves quality of writing back and forth through layout and visual presentation.

People in class question why so much information is crammed onto so few pages, why there is so little use of color, why charts and graphs and other illustrations are not on the page where they are discussed, etc.— which brings up issues of the economics and planning and (non)testing of design.

People who bring in texts or manuals they like talk about feeling respected by design, how design can encourage them to feel that they are competent as they approach a subject or appliance.

3   People in class pair up, and then as an assignment choose 4 representative pages from one of the textbooks or manuals that has been criticized in class, and redesign those pages together.

(I recommend that people who have a text in a current class that is giving them trouble redesign the text—I have seen this been a very useful way to study: people in class learn that you design cannot be separated from understanding... and this will bring up in class discussion of why textbooks writers have not 'traditionally' designed their own texts.)

4   In the next class, we put all the redesigns up on the wall and discuss them. People in class then rework their redesigns based on feedback.

5   The last part of the assignment is that people in class write up guidelines for "Designing to Help People Feel Smart": they summarize the strategies and approaches they have observed and used that go into making design that is responsive to and respectful of audiences. I encourage them to focus on the design process as well as on the design product, so that they consider incorporating audience into the design and testing of any materials they make.

ACTIVITY 5

MAKING AN UGLY WEB PAGE

TEACHER NOTES

Use this assignment early-on as students are learning to design Web pages.

GOALS

In the course of this activity, students:

- Enjoy breaking many rules
- Come to understand that qualities like "ugliness" or "unfriendliness" do not inhere in texts but are the results of a text's contexts.

TIME

This activity starts with a homework assignment and then requires a full class for discussion and reflection.

LEVEL

This is an activity for advanced undergraduates or graduate students who know how to build even the most basic Web pages.

SEQUENCE

1   Give students the following assignment:

THE UGLIEST WEBPAGE

I want this assignment to help you think about the relationships you establish with your audience through the shapes of what you make online. In this case, I want you to make something that turns its back on its audience—if not screams at them—as a way of starting to determine, by negation, what design strategies—and why—help your audiences see that you are a designer to be trusted and respected.

As homework—using whatever Web page building strategies you know—build a Web page that you think will completely alienate your audience (which in this case is the class). The topic of the page can be anything.

2   In class, look together at all the pages, and keep a running list of the various strategies people use to make their pages ugly.

3   Go back through the list item by item and ask students to imagine cases in which the strategy would be rhetorically useful, that is, would help them achieve some particular purpose with a particular audience. For example, bright clashing colors or no contrast between text and background can make text hard to read but sometimes (as with the warning messages on the sides of cigarette packages) a text's creators need for text to be present but not necessarily readable.

ACTIVITY 6

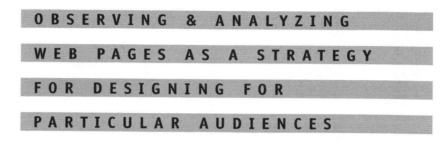

OBSERVING & ANALYZING WEB PAGES AS A STRATEGY FOR DESIGNING FOR PARTICULAR AUDIENCES

TEACHER NOTES

GOALS

In the course of this activity, students:

- Develop their own lists of design guidelines for Web pages for particular audiences and purposes, based on observation of other Web pages for that audience and purpose.
- Learn that appropriate design guidelines can be developed—and modified—through observation.

TIME

The homework assignment described below required a weekend; the assignment was part of a larger activity—designing Web sites for faculty members—that took place over 2 months (for a process of initial discussion, preliminary design, feedback, revision, further feedback, and students teaching the faculty how to update their Web pages).

LEVEL

This is an activity for advanced undergraduates or graduate students who know how to build even the most basic Web pages.

NOTE

What is below is an assignment almost exactly as I presented it to a particular class who were just learning to build Web pages; in the context of the class and our school, it made sense for students to build very straightforward Web pages for faculty in our department who did not yet have Web pages. You can, obviously, modify this assignment so that students observe and build pages to teach elementary school students basic science principles (for example) or observe and build pages for Web essays.

The assignment below is pretty much as the students received it, on a course Web page. After students drew up their lists of observations, and we discussed in class why the observations they made might be pertinent for the audiences and contexts they described, we developed together a list of considerations they should keep in mind as they designed.

Only after developing these lists did students meet with the faculty members for whom they were designing. They discussed with the faculty what the faculty had in mind for their Web pages, and they also showed faculty their observational lists, which helped some faculty better define what they wanted. Then students went through a reiterative process of design, showing thumbnail sketched to faculty for feedback, and only then starting to work developing pages. Most faculty were quite pleased with the process and with the results.

STUDENT ASSIGNMENT

THE PURPOSE OF THIS ASSIGNMENT

You are going to build a Web page for a faculty member within the next few weeks. The intention of this assignment is to help you determine what makes an effective Web page for a faculty member—in general, as well as for faculty in a particular discipline.

WHAT YOU'LL BE DOING

First, I'm asking you to do a bit of thinking about why a university's faculty members would have individual Web pages. Then you're going to go out on the Web and look at lots of different Web sites for faculty members in lots of different disciplines in many different schools. Then I'm going to ask you to write about what you have observed, how your initial thoughts about faculty Web pages have changed, and to draw up a preliminary set of guidelines for building an effective Web page for someone who teaches at a university like ours.

WHAT TO DO ...

FIRST, write a little bit, informally: In class, we talked a bit about the purposes of faculty Web pages. I want you to write up a list of the different kinds of audiences a faculty Web page must address, and the sorts of expectations those different audiences will bring to looking at a faculty member's Web page. Describe to yourself, in words on a page, in as much detail as possible, what you think should be on a faculty member's Web page and how that page should look and function—and why.

SECOND, look... a lot, and closely: Now spend some time looking at faculty Web pages. As you look, test your expectations against the pages you see. Which pages meet your expectations, and how? Which pages disrupt your expectations—but in good directions? Which disrupt your expectations in not so good ways? (Another way to think of this: Which faculty members look as though they really know what they teach? Which faculty members look like people from whom you'd want to take classes? Which faculty members look as though they're attached to schools you'd want to attend? In each of these cases—figure out WHY.)

In each case, note as many details as you can about what on the site worked to satisfy, exceed, or fail your expectations. Be attentive to the overall presentation of a page, how the page is arranged, what you learn from the page, and so on.

I want you to look at the Web pages for at least 12 faculty members from different departments and different schools. As part of that 12, you can look at 8 sites linked below—but you need to find at least 4 other sites on your own. (Please list the sites you observe—and be sure you look at sites of people who teach the same kinds of things as the faculty member with whom you'll be working. You can learn about your faculty members by reading about them on the Humanities Department's Faculty pages.)

Start by checking out how faculty in MTU's Humanities Department present themselves (go to http://www.hu.mtu.edu/, and then click the "Faculty & Staff" link at the top right). Then check out the links for these college faculty:

[here there was a listing—with links to actual Web sites—of approximately 40 different Web sites from faculty across a wide range of Humanities disciplines]

THIRD, write up what you have observed...

Look back at what you wrote before you looked at faculty Web sites, and at all the notes you took while looking. By analyzing what you've observed and written, draw up guidelines to help you make the most effective Web site possible for the faculty member with whom you'll be working.

You can present your guidelines in any way you like, as long as someone else in class will be able to understand them easily (without you hanging over their shoulder to explain what you've written). Your guidelines should make specific reference to sites you observed, so that you use the sites as examples to support your reasoning. Be sure also, as you make recommendations for faculty Web pages, that you explain your recommendations: just what purpose is your recommendation to serve, and for what audience? (And do not feel you have to make recommendations for "conservative" Web sites: if you can give solid reasons for recommending something "unusual", then please do so.)

Be as detailed as you can: address color choice as well as whether you think photographs should be included, and how much and what text, and how elements should be aligned, and what sorts of links, and what kinds of typefaces, and so on, and so on. The more details to which you attend, the easier your job will be in working with your faculty member.

And as you write, keep in mind our conversations about interest, fascination, and delight.

It will probably take you a minimum of three typed pages to do enough analysis and make enough supported recommendations to be useful.

ACTIVITY 7

DESIGNING OTHER VALUES

TEACHER NOTES

GOALS

In the course of this activity, students:

• Consider how to vary the values that design shapes.

TIME

This activity is, minimally, a homework assignment followed by class discussion. It can be broadened to spread over several classes of revision, discussion, and reflection.

LEVEL

This is an activity for students who have some familiarity with Web page or page-layout software.

NOTE

This activity works best at the end of a course that has considered how the material shapes of the communications we give each other take part in shaping the values we take from texts.

ACTIVITY

After you have done any activities that ask students to identify values they see at work in the design of pages (on screen or on paper), ask them to identify values they don't see (values that rarely show up in page or screen design are, for example, generosity, sharing, humility, justice, and quiet). Ask them, as part of a final paper or project for class, to design a text that visually and interactively incorporates one (or more) of the missing values they identified.

THE DATABASE AND THE ESSAY

Understanding Composition as Articulation

Johndan Johnson-Eilola

Do we think we know what writing is?

James E. Porter, *Rhetorical Ethics and Internetworked Writing* 9

Almost without our realizing it, writing is changing. Over the last few decades, the fields of literature and rhetoric and composition have more or less agreed that authors are not omnipotent (except as literary devices). We are comfortable with unreliable narrative. We speak of texts as intertextual networks of citation, reference, and theft. We observe how different readers make different meanings from identical texts. We understand reading and writing subjects as ongoing, contingent constructions, never completely stable or whole. In short, we're at ease with postmodernism.

Or so the story goes.

But while we live in a time of contradictions and contingency, we often fail to recognize these features in the worlds we live in day-to-day, in our classrooms and offices. We tend, despite all of our sophisticated theorizing, to teach writing much as we have long taught it: the creative production of original words in linear streams that some reader receives and understands.

In the series (or network) of pieces that follow, I'll attempt to frame some different ways of understanding textuality and literacy, exploring (and embracing) some of the contradictions and contingencies that we often gloss over or treat as isolated special cases.

I need to make clear at the outset that I'm not after a completely dispersed subjectivity, an utterly fragmented landscape, or the destruction of our current methods of teaching writing. I still use first-person pronouns. Instead, I'm interested in a rough deconstruction of writing practices—not a breakdown or simple taking apart (as the term seems to be commonly used today) but an activity of exploring contradictions as necessary conditions of existence.

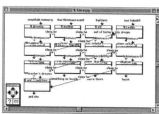

REDEFINING COMPOSITION: DATABASE AND ESSAY

I want to start with a brief background, because much of what I'll say later isn't anything new. But I want to start with the background so I can identify the need to reiterate and rethink our situation.

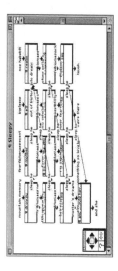

The key issue here is addressing the question, **Where does writing come from?** Contemporary ideas in our field indicate that writing is not a solely (or even largely) individual act, but a social one; new ideas and texts do not spring from the brow of isolated writers, but are developed intertextually from bits and pieces already out there. "Not infrequently, and perhaps ever and always," Jim Porter once wrote, "texts refer to other texts and in fact rely on them for their meaning. All texts are interdependent: We understand a text only as far as we understand its ancestors" ("Intertextuality" 34). But this interdependence of texts is not without its own rifts, ruptures, and politics. In a bizarre way, the very interconnected nature of texts holds them apart.

To open that issue, I want to propose two tentative methods for understanding textuality in our postmodern culture, symbolic-analytic work and articulation theory. Neither of these methods seems all that revolutionary on its own, since each has been used to analyze work and culture for a decade or more. But I'm going to twist them slightly, asking how they might be used to describe writing practices in concrete rather than abstract ways.

METHOD 1:
WRITING AS SYMBOLIC-ANALYTIC WORK

> [R]eality must be simplified so that it can be understood and manipulated in new
> ways. The symbolic analyst wields equations, formulae, analogies, models, con-
> structs categories and metaphors in order to create possibilities for reinterpreting,
> and then rearranging, the chaos of data that are already swirling around us. (Reich
> 229)

As intellectual work begins to replace industrial work in our economy, labor
theorist Reich identifies a new job classification, one in which people manipulate information, sorting, filtering, synthesizing, and rearranging chunks of
data in response to particular assignments or problems. This job classification
includes members from knowledge work fields including architecture, system
administration, and research science.

Symbolic-analytic work focuses on the manipulation of information and
suggests connections to a new form of writing or a new way of conceiving of
writing in response to the breakdown of textuality. Obviously, most symbolic-
analytic workers engage in relatively traditional writing tasks—they write
reports, they take notes, they make presentations. But the key focal point of
their work lies not in simply having good traditional communication skills.
Instead, symbolic-analytic workers are valued for their ability to understand
both users and technologies, bringing together multiple, fragmented contexts
in an attempt to broker solutions.

The production of "original" text will continue to be an important activity,
but the cultural and economic power of that activity is on the wane. In other
words, basic traditional communication skills will continue to be a fundamental functional literacy, but we will increasingly need to teach forms of
symbolic-analytic work.

In many of our classes we already teach things that are typical of symbolic-
analytic work, but so far we've avoided connecting that education up very well
to labor theory in ways that will give us a better structure to what we do (and,
not incidentally, allow us to justify our new methods/goals of teaching to the
public).

METHOD 2:
WRITING AS ARTICULATION

> An articulation is […] the form of the connection that can make a unity of two dif-
> ferent elements, under certain conditions. It is a linkage that is not necessary, deter-
> mined, and essential for all time. (Hall 54)

Articulation involves the idea that ideology functions like a language, being
constructed contingently across groups of people over time and from context
to context. Like language, objects—concrete objects like texts or motor scoot-
ers or conceptual things like the words—objects "mean" not because they

inherently, automatically mean something, but because of what other objects they're connected to. And, like language—often, as language—people can attempt to forge new connections in certain situations; they can connect objects together in various ways to shift the meanings. Importantly, in most cases it involves groups of people and is a struggle against other meanings and other groups.

As cultural theorist Larry Grossberg puts it, with articulation "Meaning is not the text itself, but is the active product of the text's social articulation, of the web of connotations and codes into which it is inserted." Importantly, articulation attempts to move beyond the relatively modernist sender ➤ transmission ➤ receiver model of communication and toward a "theory of contexts." (qtd. in Slack 112). Articulation provides a model for a postmodern practice because it situates itself within a postmodern context and accepts postmodernism (breakdown, fragmentation) as a cultural situation. At the same time, though, articulation attempts to move beyond postmodernism, not by negating postmodernism or rejecting it but by building culture out of what's left over. As Hall once put it, "[H]ow long can you live at the end of the world, how much bang can you get out of the big bang?" ("On Postmodernism and articulation" 131).

Articulation theory provides a way for thinking about how meaning is constructed contingently, from pieces of other meanings and social forces that tend to prioritize one meaning over another. Because articulation conceives meaning as a contingent play of existing forces rather than a traditional "creation" and "reception," the perspective can be useful in helping us understanding writing as a process of arrangement and connection rather than simply one of isolated creative utterance.

METHOD 1 + METHOD 2

We see symbolic-analytic and articulation work happening all the time: Politicians spin events slightly by rearticulating them; students and researchers alike navigate information spaces and construct arguments from various bits of previously dispersed research. But our recognition often applies only abstractly to linear narratives and texts. What happens when our culture takes those methods to the next level. What conditions enable the emergence of a new form of textuality, one that founds itself on fragments and circulation rather than authorial voice? And would writing teachers recognize it if they saw it?

In their College English article of several years ago, Martha Woodmansee and Peter Jaszi argue a point that I think is indicative of our current understanding of what "counts" as writing:

> After the divergence of literary and legal theory it was possible to overlook the substantial contribution of Romantic aesthetics to our law of texts, with the result that while legal theory participated in the construction of the modern 'author', it has yet to be affected by the structuralist and poststructuralist critique of authorship that we have been witnessing in literary and composition studies for decades now. (Woodmansee and Jaszi 771)

According to Woodmansee and Jaszi—and many others—the whole idea of intellectual property (IP) is based on a Romantic notion that ideas spring full-blown from the imagination of single individuals. In our postmodernist or social constructionist cultures, though, we in rhet/comp understand ideas as forming in contexts, in social situations. It's difficult or even impossible to find completely original ideas. So, the argument goes, what right should any single person have over an idea?

Which is all well and good—I agree with this, but only to a point. That point is the deconstructive hinge around which this chapter revolves: For at the same time as Woodmansee and Jaszi (and all the rest of us) claim that the author is dead, we ignore the fact that contemporary IP law is catching up to postmodernism. And here's the deconstructive hinge: in the same article, Woodmansee and Jaszi (and all the rest of us) bemoan the decline of Fair Use rights that educators have long relied on in order to allow us to copy work for free, to use photocopied essays in our coursepacks without paying reprinting fees to "original" authors.

But, as I'll demonstrate in a moment, the decline of fair use rights is firmly linked to a postmodern turn in intellectual property law—for the rise of postmodernism in general is tied to the loss of original context noted in fields as diverse as labor theory, management, literary theory, architecture, and film. From the IP perspective, as I discuss in more detail in another section, textual content has become commodified, put into motion in the capitalist system, forced to earn its keep by moving incessantly. Indeed, in order to facilitate movement, texts are increasingly fragmented and broken apart so that they will fit into the increasingly small micro-channels of capitalist circulation. Publishers, for example, now routinely collect permission fees for chapters photocopied for academic coursepacks, a practice unheard of twenty years ago.

Several years ago, I called the permissions department of a major academic publisher to find out the fees required to reprint a four-hundred word extract from a work in their catalogue. The fees vary, obviously, from publisher to publisher as well as the nature of the quoted work, among other things. Most publishers also only require permissions when quotations exceed a certain (but variable) length, usually several hundred words. When I inquired about the general guidelines as to length, the publisher's representative said, "You need to seek permission to quote even a single word from one of our texts." I thought he was joking (in fact, I laughed out loud), but I soon realized he was serious. I asked for clarification several times, and he would only repeat the single sentence over and over.

While the enforceablity of such a policy is, at best, questionable, the spirit of the policy is increasingly common. Twenty years ago, short selections from longer texts were invisible to the capitalist network of large objects. But in a postmodern economy, objects are actually easier to deal with when they are fragmented into smaller bits, allowing them to be sold as commodities, reassembled and repurposed into new forms over and over again. In one sense, the explosion of "meaning" from a single, monolithic, textual object into a network of intertextual reference didn't (as we earlier thought) create a liberating and communal web of shared experiences. Although we don't realize it yet, that explosion was the start of a supernova, of breakdown and incessant movement and recombination, each slippage and recombination now generating surplus value to be captured as profit.

TEXT AS INTELLECTUAL PROPERTY

In the sections that follow, I'm going to provide a very quick and loose sketch of several important intellectual property issues. I am not interested here in providing a definitive overview of everything to do with IP law or even a coherent picture of how IP law applies to rhetoric and composition. Instead, my goal is to use recent developments in IP law to suggest shifts in how our culture thinks about text and communication. Following this brief set of analyses, I'll attempt to play this breakdown in IP through the lenses of articulation theory and symbolic-analytic work to describe some emerging forms of writing. These new forms of writing are interesting because they take the generally debilitating trends of IP law (the fragmentation of content, the commoditization of text, the loss of context) and make something useful. In a recuperative move, the new forms of writing use fragmentation, loss of context, and circulation as methods for creating new structures.

Few would argue with the proposition that contemporary culture often places a low value on traditional composition skills such as elegant writing, carefully and complex argumentation, sustained attention span on the part of committed readers immersed in a mediasphere dominated by sound bites and flashing lights. Both cultural conservatives and leftist academics agree in principle on this if not on particulars. Rather than lamenting this shift, however, I want to trace a just-emerging sense of text that can, with careful rethinking, occupy an important place in our classrooms.

In understanding what counts as writing, it's useful to look at the legal aspects, particularly those related to intellectual property. IP is near and dear to many of us because we simultaneously own intellectual property—our textbooks, essays, syllabi, Web sites, etc.—and we also use intellectual property in coursepacks, Web sites, and student texts. As many of us have found, recently, the legal issues are pretty complicated. Increasingly, we feel pressured by corporate interests that seem intent on increasing the amount of information we must pay for.

The bulk of this chapter deals with the separation we—I mean "we" as rhet/comp academics, but also, in this particular case, "we" as the general public—have constructed between "writing" and "compilation". In questioning this division, I'm trying to get at an understanding of writing more properly suited to the role writing plays in our culture.

I'll begin by describing the case of *Matthew Bender v West Publishing*, a legal debate over what counts as "originality" in copyrighted texts. This case, I should note at the outset, does not turn traditional understandings of creativity on their head. Indeed, the eventual rulings end up being extremely conservative on that point. But the case itself lays the groundwork for a later series of challenges and rulings that do dramatically affect simple, traditional notions like "creativity" and "writing." Following *Bender v West Publishing*, we'll move to a discussion of U.S. House Resolution 3531, often referred to as the Database Anti-Piracy Act (itself part of the broader World Intellectual Property Office's work to standardize an industrial and post-industrial model of intellectual property on a global scale). Finally in the intellectual property section of this chapter, I'll briefly note several arguments about the legal and ethical status of linking among Web sites, particularly the case of "deep" linking, a term describing links made from one person's site to a particular node deep within another person's site. The legal statutes and cases I cover here are one particular, historical slice of an ongoing postmodern shift. The specific bills passed or defeated do not, in general, seem likely to have radically changed the general trend I'm analyzing, the breakdown of "text" as a coherent and privileged object (a trend that we've long talked about from a literary and psychological perspective but rarely from an economic one).

These three sections, as I said, do not exhaust or even scratch the surface of how intellectual property relates to rhetoric and composition. Rather, they suggest the shape of a trajectory that we must follow and respond to in order to work productively with our students in contemporary cultures.

BENDER V WEST PUBLISHING

Interpreting legal decisions is extremely complicated and, it should go without saying, *I Am Not a Lawyer*. My purpose here is not to dispense legal advice, but to note some cultural trends that impact what it means to write. In order to make some of those trajectories clearer, I want now briefly to examine a case that, on the surface, seems to contradict the enforcement of copyright.

I'd like to examine one particular case, *Matthew Bender v West Publishing*, that surfaces some important issues pertaining to our discussion about what counts as writing, about what we are willing to value. In particular, this case demonstrates developments in the legal status of "originality". For contemporary capitalism, originality typically involves the production of novel texts (no pun intended). We do not typically encourage our students to compose texts simply from fragments of other texts. Even in research papers, we require our students (and ourselves) to produce "new" (original) text that summarizes and paraphrases other texts even as it quotes them—to simply quote texts wouldn't be "writing". *Bender v West Publishing* challenges our notions of what counts for creativity and, in turn, what creativity counts for in the marketplace. In one way of considering *Bender v West Publishing* marks a trend toward postmodern fragmentation and a fetishization of the traditional rhetorical arts of arrangement (nearly to the exclusion of all else).

Legal scholars and practicing lawyers in the U.S. rely heavily on legal decisions published by West Publishing. Formally, these U.S. federal and state proceedings are in the public domain. West, however, claimed copyright of the legal decisions because West added and sometimes edited the original text or added citations to other legal documents. Furthermore, West claimed ownership of the numbering system used in its own publication. This last fact may seem minor—after all, a page numbering system seems pretty trivial. However, because the West publications were the industry standard, common references to legal decisions were based on this pagination system. Several companies challenged West's claims of intellectual property, largely unsuccessfully. But in 1998, the U.S. 2nd Circuit Court of Appeals ruled in favor of one publisher, Matthew Bender and Co. In its judgment, U.S. 2nd Circuit Court of Appeals Judges Cardamone and Jacobs firmly delineate the requirement for creativity in terms of copyright protection:

> It is true that neither novelty nor invention is requisite for copyright protection, but minimal creativity is required. […]

> [C]reativity in the task of creating a useful case report can only proceed in a narrow groove. Doubtless, that is because for West or any other editor of judicial opinions for legal research, faithfulness to the public-domain original is the dominant editorial value, so that the creative is the enemy of the true. (Bender v. West Publishing, 158 F.3d 1693 [2d Cir. 1998]).

Notably, Cardamone and Jacobs separate "creativity" from "truth"—the more factual something is, the less creative it is. I would suggest that the assenting judges here held what's a common view of creativity and writing: mere reportage and selection are not frequently original and should not be protected; what is creative is the production of unique text—a conception that still grounds most writing pedagogy and practice in rhetoric and composition.

On first glance, the *Bender v. West Publishing* ruling seems to uphold our common ideas about what counts as creativity. As the judges point out, we traditionally require an intentionality going beyond arbitrary pagination. In a real sense, they argue for a notion of creativity that is valued precisely because it is not real. Creativity in the traditional sense lies in the ability of an author or inventor to produce something that did not exist before in the world.

I am interested in this case, though, not because of its outcome but because it signals the start of a trend away from valuing creativity in intellectual property and one valuing fragmentation and arrangement. As *Bender v. West Publishing* makes clear, the business of information is both lucrative and competitive. The weight of this market has begun slowly to shift legal opinion. Taken as a whole, this body of legal developments has begun to change how our culture thinks about texts, about creativity.

But given our current understandings of language as a closed system—is there any text that's "truly" creative? In an odd way, we might compare the "arbitrary" pagination in West's books to the arbitrary nature of language, where the "meaning" of words isn't set in stone as it were but is very much arbitrary. In fact, just as West's pagination system became, socially, the standard way of referring to cases, the ongoing social construction of language is what keeps it going—arbitrary doesn't mean without value. Saussure showed us how language functions in society precisely because it's arbitrary: because it's impossible to trace a definitive link from any object to the word describing it, people within cultures must agree, usually implicitly, on the meanings of terms. To some extent, this looks like a magic trick: If we can never really make a firm, stable connection between a word and its object, why does language work at all?

The meaning of any particular term grows out of, among other things, how that particular term relates to other terms within that culture's language. For example, the term "dog" is linked to a community's general concept of what a dog is. Sometimes this is traced formally, as in contemporary biological classification into type specimens; more often, it's a process of formal and informal education that teaches children and others to connect the word "dog" up to examples of dogs. Importantly, "dog" retains its general cultural meaning by opposing "dog" to other similar but different terms such as "cat" or "wolf." (But consider debates over wolf/dog hybrids, which often cannot be placed definitively in one category or the other—the line between the two is not as impermeable as we would like to think.) As Hall points out, the admonition that no meaning is guaranteed doesn't mean that no meanings are possible. So while a number of postmodern theorists have stepped off the cliff that negates any connection between word and image, Hall argues that communities create contingent meanings through a process of negotiation, with specific articulations made real only in concrete, specific contexts. So common meanings arise through shared usage, but those meanings are also open to debate and change (which is often difficult but always possible).

I'm not arguing that this postmodern shift erases traditional texts or narratives. Instead, I'm trying to make clear that our traditional texts are changing, whether we like this our not. We must work to understand the transformations and fragmentations taking place so that we can work within them.

However, after *Bender v West Publishing*, IP regulation takes a decidedly postmodern turn. Two key cases (in an intertextual web of IP law texts) have begun to reshape the terrain of intellectual property in the United States and elsewhere. I want to make clear that I am not concerned very much with the specific legal mechanisms and language, but with how these cases connect up to much larger, cultural shifts in the ways that we produce, consume, and circulate texts: For better or worse—or, in fact, for better and worse—texts no longer function as discrete objects, but as contingent, fragmented objects in circulation, as elements within constantly configured and shifting networks. The point is not that all texts are completely fragmented and resist connection. Instead, texts are broken down in order to reconnect them, over and over again.

From one perspective, this development threatens traditional educational ideas about text and learning; from another, less common perspectives, these developments open up an entirely new terrain in which rhetoric and composition might productively move. We spend our time bemoaning the death documented in the first instance at the cost of the possibilities contained within the second.

Two recent sets of cases signal the movement toward postmodernist understandings of text in culture. In the first set below, I'll consider recent cases involving the use of coursepacks, primarily from the perspective of *Princeton University Press v Michigan Document Service*. In this case, as well as the earlier *Basic Books, Inc. v Kinko's Graphics Corp.*, legal decisions have greatly restricted the Fair Use guidelines that educators have traditionally used in compiling, then having copying shops reproduce and sell coursepacks for their courses. In the second set of cases, recent legislative actions related to the Database Antipiracy Act and the Digital Millenium Copyright Act place explicit emphasis on the idea that texts are databases.

COPYRIGHT, COURSEPACKS, AND THE MARKET

U.S. courts have ruled increasingly against the practice of producing coursepacks—anthologies of previously published (and still under copyright) material in small runs for academic courses. In general, educators and copying shops acted under the notion that such educational uses were protected by Fair Use doctrine which, among other things, placed educational reproduction of copyright material in a special, protected category. But findings such as those in *Basic Books, Inc. v Kinko's Graphics Corporation* and *Princeton University Press v Michigan Document Services* have served to greatly restrict the freedom educators have in reproducing copyrighted works in their classes.

Importantly, these cases seem to have shifted the terrain of decisions away from the commonly used "four factors" (which include key concerns such as purpose and character of the reproduced work, nature of the work (factual versus fictional), the amount and sustainability of the reproduced work) and focused primarily on the last factor, the effect of the reproduction on potential markets for the copyrighted work. As Kenneth Crews notes,

Large-scale reproduction of copyrighted works has become easier and cheaper with newer technologies, leading to arguments that fair use ought to encompass the practical realities of photocopying for classroom use. Technology, on the other hand, has increased the feasibility of implementing licensing for photocopying. The ease of offering and securing a license through Internet-based transactions and the like has bolstered arguments that fair use ought to be diminished to reflect a profitable market that may now be more realistically captured. (n. pag.)

This shift is extremely important,

because it opens a path away from
thinking of intellectual property as a "work"
—as a relatively extended, coherent whole—
and toward thinking of it as marketable chunks.

Oddly, although we frequently lament the fact that our students must now pay copyright permission fees for material in the coursepacks we ask them to purchase for our classes, we don't often think about the postmodern shift that resulted in this situation. So while we've come to grips with postmodernism as a literary movement, we seem surprised when the same phenomena surfaces in the economic realm.

And despite the realization that our culture increasingly values texts that are broken down, rearranged, recombined, we rarely teach forms of writing that support such production. We unwittingly (or sometimes consciously) still think of writing as a way to help the self become present to itself, as a method for personal growth and discovery.

DATABASE ANTIPIRACY ACT AND THE
WORLD INTELLECTUAL PROPERTY
ORGANIZATION

The idea that texts are modular collections of information rather than unified, coherent creative wholes is most directly addressed, from a legal standpoint, in recent legislation and case law regarding databases.

Companies that compile and sell access to online databases—which is an enormously profitable enterprise for companies like Lexis/Nexis and others— began jealously to guard both the structure and content of those databases. A related set of legislative and legal discussions and activities has supported this concept, beginning with cases such as the earlier cited *West Law v. HyperLaw* (which indicated collections of facts were not creative documents) through HR 2652 (the "Collections of Information Antipiracy Act") and its resurfacing in the form of HR 354. Although the future shape and trajectory of these developments are by no means certain, in general they point toward a society in which "writing" as we know it is no longer the premier textuality.

In essence, what supporters of these bills are contesting is the division between "creative" works like novels and "non-creative" works like databases. Dissolving this boundary would undo the notion that ideas develop out of the "genius" of the lone individual and that the whole notion of creativity is contingent (and shifting).

I don't want to be seen as saying that this sort of greed is good—only that we should have been able to predict it. Furthermore, despite whatever might happen with single specific pieces of legislation, we're moving slowly toward a situation where corporations will hold proprietary rights to collections of information.

WIPO PROTESTS

As consumer advocate James Love argues, these new types of legislation will tend to change how we think about intertextuality and writing:

> The [WIPO] treaty seeks, for the first time, to permit firms to 'own' facts they gather, and to restrict and control the redissemination of those facts. The new property right would lie outside (and on top) of the copyright laws, and create an entirely new and untested form of regulation that would radically change the public's current rights to use and disseminate facts and statistics. (n. pag.)

Views on both sides of this issue are polarized; in general, legislation has given special rights to scientific research and journalism, so that news reporting will still have some leeway (not that we should be complacent—I assume that many corporations would also like those rights removed). But most of the corporations that are vocally opposed to this legislation do so on the grounds that they should be able to copy whole-cloth the products of other corporations and remarket them, in the way that HyperLaw wanted to be able to directly copy West Laws books and sell them. So it's difficult to decide who to cheer for here.

The opponents of the HR 2652 were largely successful in getting the database protection language removed from Digital Millennium Copyright Act that was eventually passed. However, the bill itself resurfaced shortly thereafter as HR 354. Occasional reversals aside, the collection of pre-existing content, even relatively fine-grained and factual content such as sporting events scores, is increasingly considered to be a creative act, at least in terms of legal and financial aspects.

DEEP LINKING ON WEB SITES

Finally, perhaps more closely linked to our own traditional concerns, there has grown a bitter debate on the World Wide Web and in the courts about whether or not people need permission to link to someone else's pages. Tradition, growing out academic ideas about scholarship and science, has said that citation should be free, that pointing to the works of others is a necessary and socially valuable thing.

At the same time, companies complaining about the practice of linking to pages point out that their economic model relies on assuming users of their site move top-down through the site, often viewing advertisements on the way. If users jump directly to a page on the site five levels down, then the advertisements won't be seen—and the Web site owner won't be compensated.

So many sites, such as InfoWorld (which I'll discuss in another section) have begun experimenting with "linking policies" that attempt to require users to request permission before linking to material on the site.

This whole debate illustrates another of the contradictions between two models of practice: academic/scientific citation (which holds that knowledge should be free) and economic models (which holds that information should be in circulation, but it must earn money in doing so).

In 1999, the popular print- and Web-based trade magazine InfoWorld posted this linking policy on their Web site:

> Like most online publications, InfoWorld Electric has a policy regarding links. When we refer to a link, we mean a hypertext link, where you post the URL (Uniform Resource Locator) of some content on our site to your site. This can be simply including the link in text form or attaching a URL to one of our logos for the reader to click on.
>
> To link to an article on InfoWorld Electric, send an e-mail request to Meera Srinivas with the URL of the InfoWorld content you want to link to. If your request is approved, we will ask you to confirm back to us the exact URL of the place on your site where we can find the link. (n. pag.)

As you can see, what they're doing here is attempting to regulate who points to subpages on their site. The regulation can be seen as serving several purposes, one of which is to discourage rampant linking; in addition, the policy helps InfoWorld track where users may be entering the site in order to maximize advertising exposure (and to improve demographic data collection). InfoWorld's Web site, like many similar sites, exchanges "free" news about the information economy for "eyeballs". Web communication has been referred to as "narrowcasting" in its ability to target well defined and discrete demographic groups. Advertisers, the argument goes, can pitch their wares to carefully selected audiences, groups that are more likely than the general population to respond by purchasing a product. At a broader level, InfoWorld's policy represent a general and increasing tendency on the part of contemporary corporations to control information without much regard to current value.

After a great deal of public protest, InfoWorld rescinded the policy, although I think—taken in light of the earlier IP legal developments—it signals a trend in understanding how and why people cite each other.[1]

I'm a little leery of the model that says we cite only to earn money, but it's important that we recognize that trend in order to better deal with it. Information increasingly holds value in a commodity sense, not for its ability to get anything done or produce value.

---

[1] National Public Radio, for example, briefly issued a linking policy in 2002 that, like InfoWorld's earlier policy, required users to request permission before linking. After protests, NPR adjusted the policy so that users could link to NPR's site as long as they didn't suggest NPR supports any third party or attempt to generate profit.

So we have here two oddly similar but oddly contradictory trajectories: scholars in rhet/comp, propounding the decline of the unified subject while simultaneously saying that text is outside of the economic sphere. On a second set of not-quite-as-contradictory trajectories, we have postmodern capital continually fragmenting "text" into its most discrete components in order to put them in motion—because movement is what they extract value from. But what seems clear is that this fragmentation and circulation is postmodernism.

Where that leaves us, then, is in a very difficult—but also very exciting—situation, one in which we have to both participate and resist. We cannot just give ourselves over to maximizing capital or completely fragmenting the self. I don't have to rehearse the problems with that route; even the most pomo among us has tried it only to find out it doesn't work. Instead, I would argue, what we have to do is understand this system better, to participate in it, but critically.

NEW RESPONSIBILITIES IN CONSTRUCTION

I want to make two quick points, then move into some examples. This new understanding of writing can lead us to some important considerations for teaching writing.

1 We can't separate writing from the economic sphere. We can attempt to keep access open, but we can no longer ignore intellectual property laws and pretend that they will go away. Just as importantly, an expanded notion of writing will serve to help us have a voice in the types of writing that go on outside our classroom—not just the essays or poetry that a handful of students will write, but in the Web pages they design, in the databases they build. So this should act to give us a broader sphere to address rather than a narrower one.

2 This new notion of writing as at least partly—perhaps primarily—about valuing connection will let us argue to our students that information is not neutral. Collection is a social and political act; there are not mere disembodied facts, but choices. I'll return to this idea later in a brief discussion of articulation theory, but I'd like to show some examples first.

I admit that I find the incessant commodification of knowledge a depressing trend. And a part of me would agree that the recent move toward extending copyright apparently indefinitely, toward making text a terrain for profit and little else, will often make the rich richer and the poor poorer. I also, though, have to admit that our field's insistence on thinking of texts as "free" and articulating creativity as the production of "original" text have often blinded us to enormous cultural shifts. More importantly, our participation within the capitalist system as teachers and textbook authors often makes our protests over IP law a little disingenuous.

In the following sections, I'll attempt to outline some of the more productive implications of shifts in textuality, ways of writing and teaching writing that are emerging from the same conditions of fragmentation and recombination. For while some of the implications of postmodernism are problematic, that does not exhaust the trend. Indeed, once we begin to understand and teach forms of writing that value contingency and arrangement, we will begin to see that the positive cultural and educational aspects of this shift hold a great deal of potential.

WEB LOGS

Web Logs (or "blogs" as they're often called) have existed in various forms since nearly the beginning of the Web, although they've risen dramatically in popularity starting in 2002. As a genre, they're relatively straightforward: in essence, a blog is a frequently updated Web site consisting primarily of short posts by someone. Somewhat like a Web browsing diary, blogs typically include brief summaries or mentions of other sites on the Web, with links to the sites described. New entries to the blog are placed near the top, pushing old entries down (eventually moving off the main page to archive pages). Weblogs are sometimes dismissed as diaries—and in some instances, that's all they are. But as I'll describe in another section, blogs differ in some key ways from simple diaries (not the least of which is that they're aggressively public).

In this screen, one of the first to popularize and evangelize the genre, software industry insider Dave Weiner arranges a series of very brief observations, comments, and—especially—links to other sites in a reverse chronological format. Down the middle of the page, each paragraph (or occasionally more than one paragraph) forms an entry, most of which are previews or teasers linked to other Web pages, most of which aren't authored by Weiner. In reading this, one gets the sense of massive and ongoing interconnection; there's the chatty voice—I'm not sure if it's a "true" voice, but that's a moot point—the voice of Dave Winer connecting us up to all he knows; at the same time, there's the distinct sense that Dave himself is con-structed by these con-

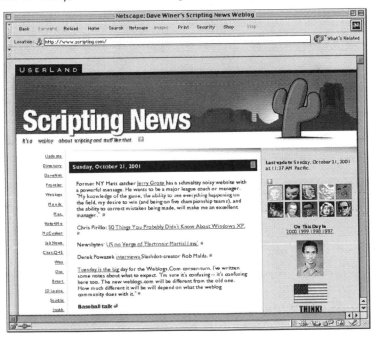

nections over time and across space. The text-that-is-Dave (or at least "Userland" Dave) is not a unified voice, but a dispersed and changing Web.

This is a relatively common and non-shocking analysis, but it's a starting point at how we might value writing in our classes and our scholarship. Although at first glance, weblogs may appear to be a trivial genre—a laundry list of events and observations elevated to a public spectacle—they exhibit some key characteristics that rhetoric and composition teachers frequently search for in writing and reading assignments.

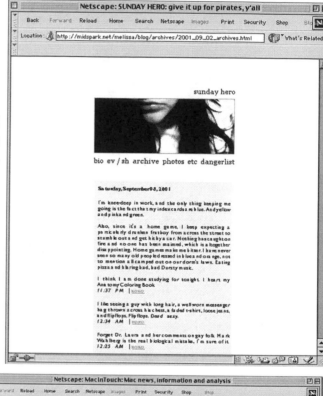

They exist and interact with complex rhetorical situations, ranging from public/private diaries:

to consumer-lead support systems for computer systems: They make concrete intertextual connections and analyses. They provide interaction among multiple authors in a community,

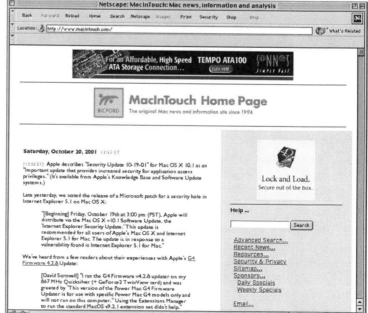

face-to-face and/or virtual:

Weblogs such as these require authors to read other texts, to analyze those texts, and respond to those texts in writing.

Not incidentally, weblogs also provide a useful working example of—and space for communication within—a postmodern textuality that most current pedagogical work in rhetoric and composition has problems approaching. In several ways, weblogs provide a complement to Web site authoring, an activity increasingly used in rhetoric and composition courses. In many ways, though, weblogs push more insistently at the postmodern tendencies of text: they are by definition fluid and shifting; they are so easy to produce and modify as to seem nearly disposable (but never really disappearing, with old text being archived to create a searchspace of shadow information).

Weblogs represent a symbolic-analytic form of writing: authors scan the Web, culling out interesting bits of information, rearranging them, posting pointers to them on blogs. They speak to varied audiences, but typically some group loosely organized around a set of common topics. Recursively, weblogs become terrain for a second tier of activities, with weblog authors reading each other's blogs, commenting on them, scavenging new stories from each other in a system of mutual self-reference. Meta-browsing tools like NetNewsWire provide weblog readers and authors with tools to assist in managing large amounts of information spread across multiple weblogs.

All of this raises, then, a host of additional important questions: *What defines a weblog compared to the more general Web site? What is the structure of a weblog (both internally and externally)? How do particular weblogs generate and hold readers? How do readers of a log become participants?* All these are issues that bear importance for rhetoric and composition as we attempt to find a place in the online world.

COMMUNITY WEBLOGS
To some extent, many early and current

weblogs could be framed as linear, individual voices, the diaries I alluded to earlier. From a postmodern perspective, though, their incessant dispersal—the constant centrifugal force that encourages readers to click links and move away from their current location—suggests an ironic reversal of a traditional diary's attempts to unify the writing subject by making the subject both speaker and listener. In a weblog, the subject is composed of exterior texts, constantly moving outward.

But another type of weblog pushes the dispersal even farther. Communal sites such as Slashdot and Plastic construct a social, dispersed subjectivity that constantly deconstructs narrative, presenting the self as an ongoing amalgam of multiple voices. In the Plastic screenshot shown here, the weblog itself has been broken down, made intensely multiple and fragmented. The individual stories, summaries, and links to other sites are contributed by members of the community. Each story on the main page links to subpages for discussion and debate by the community.

Although we have often thought of online spaces as supporting various levels of community, one interesting feature here is the way in which the landscape has been surfaced. If this is a city, it would be Tokyo or Los Angeles rather than Paris or Detroit. Each discussion competes for attention, the lead stories near the left and top cycling in and out, constantly rearranging. Plastic is, in effect, a fragmented database of community. Is Plastic a text? Most of us would provisionally say yes, but with reservations. We would be more likely to think of the individual stories and responses as texts because they are something more like what we teach our students to write. But I would like to argue that these gathered texts themselves compose a larger text that challenges our ideas about what it means to write. It might be comforting to think of Plastic as an edited collection, but there are several key distinctions. First, Plastic is not a stable collection but an ongoing and contingent set of texts that swim in and out of existence (most stories begin and then ebb away within a handful of days). Second, Plastic is not edited in the traditional sense. Most edited works rely on a small number of gatekeepers to select texts for inclusion (often only a single editor).

But on Plastic, after participants reach a certain level of experience as members of the community, they are allowed to vote on (and suggestion revisions to) short pieces submitted by any member of the community. In this sense, Plastic is edited by itself. Third, we would have to agree that "writing" Plastic involves key activities beyond the production of text, ranging from the programming of a database system that allows the site to change over time as new stories move in and old ones move out. And the interface to the site itself constitutes another important form of writing, given how it influences how much content will fit into a single story, how stories are arranged in relation to each other, and more. Participants in Plastic, like most community discussants, engage in ongoing articulation and rearticulation, disputing, bringing in references to other Web resources to illustrate points, constantly negotiating contingent meanings. For example, in 2003 the following story was posted for discussion on Plastic:

Dubya Will Give Peace A Chance (In N. Korea)
found on AP via Yahoo
edited by John (Plastic)
written by kilroy

"How is North Korea's nuclear program different from Iraq, you might ask? Well, for one thing, North Korea's is much, much farther along. In addition to being on the verge of possessing nuclear technology (they already have material a-plenty), North Korea is currently developing long-distance missile technology... apparently those missiles they shot over Japan in '98 don't have quite the range they're looking for," kilroy writes. "And unlike Iraq, which at least has the decency to lie about its nuclear intentions, Kim Jong Il has announced he has no intention of stopping his program. For a minute, I was worried we might have to delay that whole invade-Iraq-tomorrow thing, but luckily Bush is seeking diplomatic solutions, and Japan (which is looking more like Kuwait by the day) has begun negotiations. (55 comments - all new)

[join the discussion]

As is standard on Web sites, each of the underlined pieces of text indicates a link to another source on the Web (eleven separate links in the brief write-up), ranging from stories on CNN and Yahoo News through email addresses of participants. In the discussion linked to the brief story, participants ask questions, offer opinions and resources, and challenge each other over a range of issues, including the 1994 negotiation of the Nuclear Freeze Agreement, Selig S. Harrison's book *Korean Endgame*, and other geopolitical issues and (rare on semi-anonymous discussion boards), changes of opinion and negotiated agreements.

None of these features are markedly unique or revolutionary. For despite my distinctions between traditional editing and the production of Plastic, there are similarities between the two. I'm suggesting, though, that the form of writing that is Plastic is part of a larger trend away from traditional ideas about text and writing. The postmodernization of text should encourage us to see something like Plastic as more than an interesting exception to or special case of writing; instead, these texts are increasingly the more commonly used object. Hypertext pioneer Ted Nelson once claimed that hypertext, the structure of nodes connected by links, was actually the more general form of text; linear text was a special case. In this way, we might come to think of these fragmented and multiple texts as the norm, and traditional essays and narratives being special cases.

DATABASE DESIGN AND WEB SEARCH ENGINES

In terms of influence, database and Web search engine design are two primary forms of online writing. Rhetoric and composition, however, pay little attention to such activities, ceding them to computer programming and software engineering. There are, obviously, some aspects of these activities that fall outside the expertise of most rhetoric and composition teachers. However, by ignoring them as forms of writing, we make their influence invisible. In addition, we often fail to take from them important methods for thinking about communication and work, things that could influence our own work in useful ways.

First, like Plastic and Slashdot, the space of a search engine screen has itself been painstakingly designed, with various sections written to satisfy an extremely large number of audiences (this is a text read by millions of people a day—we should all hope for such an audience). And, as with traditional texts, the writers have thought very hard about their audience, addressing them, persuading them, moving them. The screen may seem a touch dense to our "refined" aesthetic tastes ("less is more"), but in the next ten years, this sort of jammed interface will be the norm; it's a new aesthetic ("more is more"). In fact, the very act of disobeying this aesthetic will itself be a marketing ploy, as in the case of Google's site:

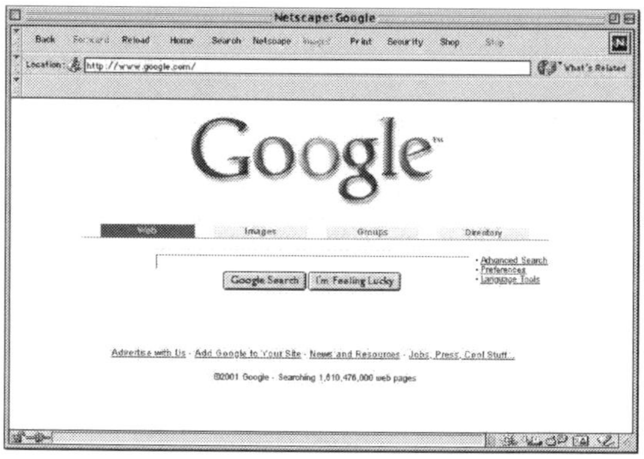

Google, unlike most other search engines, relies heavily on sales of search engine software rather than advertising for revenue. Even Google has, over the last year, begun integrating additional text into their search engine interface; what once held a handful of links now holds thirteen different text entry or interaction elements. Additionally, Google now includes…

specialized search engines for Usenet discussion groups:

images:

a fee-based service for web research:

a news page automatically generated by analyzing news links on the Web:

and a hierarchically organized index of the Web:

These texts are collaboratively written from both pictures and words, not only in the traditional sense of a number of people at the search engine HQ deciding what words to put where.

Databases and search engines are also collaborative in the radically post-modernist sense that each individual user rewrites the space as they enter search terms and the text reorganizes its billions of bits of information around that specific query.

Importantly, if we value this search engine—which is in effect the front end to a database—if we value this as a form of writing, then we can then begin to argue that the sorts of choices one makes in writing the database—for example, what categories to include, what to exclude; which category to put first; etc.—we can start to argue that these choices involve responsibilities to the reader and to society, just as we now do in other, more traditional forms of writing. In fact, I would argue that the sorts of writing that goes on in the examples I've covered here will have much broader social effects than what we currently teach. Hypertext theory and practice suggested some of these possibilities, but in the long run the forms of hypertext that we ended up with looked a lot like slightly more complex versions of traditional texts.

For example, searching on the phrase "human rights" gives differing results on Yahoo, Lycos, and Ask. On Yahoo and Ask, Amnesty International and Human Rights Watch Web sites score the number one and two positions respectively. However, Amnesty does not appear in the top ten cites on Lycos (although Human Rights Watch is in the number one spot). Additionally, both Lycos and Yahoo include three sites in the "Sponsored" section that occurs above the standard Web search results (sponsored sites pay an advertising fee to show up at the top of searches on specific terms): ECHR Fraud (a site about alleged fraud in the European Court of Human Rights), Ideal Works (a catalogue of human rights issues related to specific brands of products), and the Web site for H. Victor Conde, a human rights lawyer. Ask includes a sponsored link as well, but to Questia, an online library.

Although we now commonly help our students look critically at the results they receive from searches on the Web as well as methods for evaluating resources, our thinking about search engines tends to stop there.

In the classroom, search engines can provide us with points of departure, beyond the obvious questions I raised above. In an important sense, understanding the search engine as itself a form of writing helps us understand the relationship between composition and programming: a search engine works by automatic, contingent rhetorics.

A user's query operates a machine that develops a unique textual space, one shifting and reordering itself based on the changing volumes of the World Wide Web in conjunction with the specifics of the query and the engine's inherent qualities (method of indexing, search space, rotating banner ads and paid site placements, user screensize and resolution, etc.). The ubiquity and power of search engines makes it difficult to dismiss as a serious form of text.

Although they may seem trivial to us, the complexities of search engine design suggest writing as not merely the static arrangement of text—something that even those richest standard hypertexts can escape—but an active artifact, one put into motion by interaction with others. Indeed, search engines make concrete and visible many of the things that hypertext theorists have long argued for: contingent, networked texts, composed with large and shifting social spaces out of the literally millions of voices.

That is not to say that programming search engines should, itself, become a primary activity for writing teachers and students. Instead, we can take observations about search engines—analyses, observations of real users, etc.— and apply them to text in order to create related spaces that challenge our notions of what text means. The accumulated social text of error 404, for example, was drafted in a graduate computers and composition seminar I taught. The "text" represents an accumulation and structuring of massive sets of quotations gathered from theoretical and practical course readings during the semester. As part of that course, we discussed the texts, wrote traditional papers interpreting and challenging those texts, designed Web sites, and completed the sorts of assignments typical of such a seminar.

In order to challenge ourselves to investigate the permeable boundaries of the concept of "text" or "essay", we decided to write an essay that included almost no "original" text or linear thread. Drafted initially in Storyspace over the course of several weeks by the class and then translated into HTML for interface design and Web access, error 404 functioned as a hypertext about our course readings. But unlike a more traditional text, error 404 includes no explicit apparatus that interpreted either the text (that is, we never explicitly wrote text about the texts in the network); in addition, error 404 contained no explicit critical framework apparatus that interpreted the network text. Instead, the text is set into action by user clicks as they navigate a contingent space of multiply juxtaposed other texts. But unlike "traditional" hypertext, error 404 explicitly avoids any "original" text, working more like a symbolic-analytic collage than an essay or story.

From a traditional composition perspective, error 404 is not, itself a text, a creative act composed by an individual or a community. In fact, when we submitted the text to an online journal, the reviews came back split, with a hypertext theorist praising the innovation in form while two other reviewers pointedly requested an essay "framing" the work. The critical framework is implied of course, made explicit only in verbal discussions in the class ("What should we link to this chunk of text in order to challenge it or argue against it? What other texts does this text suggest?") or in book chapters or essays like one I wrote for a collection on computers and postmodernism (Taylor and Ward) or the text you're currently reading. Or in the reader's mind and actions. But to traditional readers (even avowed literary postmodern theorists), error 404 is not a text without the traditional, creative framework.

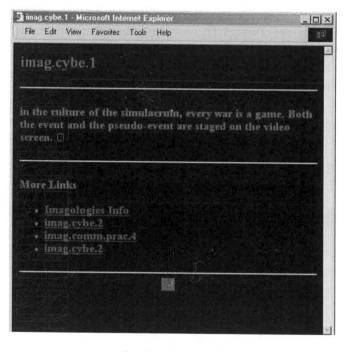

From a database perspective, error 404 is a framework for producing meaningful interactions. The interface provides a surface onto which changing pieces of information are arranged and rearranged in response to user's actions. As with many complex hypertexts (and a database might be conceived of an n-to-n connected hypertext), the "text" does not exist except as interaction with reader. In this way (and also like other interpretations of hypertext), texts are fluid, contingent, and constantly changing. Authors are more like designers or deconstructivist information architects.

Is error 404—or a search engine—merely a derivative work? Only in the sense that it is composed of pieces of other texts. But that is true of any text—work on intertextuality has taught us that all texts are composed of numerous other texts. Are these sorts of texts merely functional? Only in the sense that the text must be operated or started and run by someone. But that is also true of any text—work on reader response, cultural studies, usability studies, and a whole host of theoretical and practical fields has taught us that meaning does not inhere in a static text.

NONLINEAR MEDIA EDITING

And with guitars it's a lot about getting layers, which is great with ProTools. We would sit and track two hours worth of guitars and cut them up and loop them and build a whole wall of sound, which was the approach with the whole album. (Ray DiLeo, Engineer/Programmer, Filter, Title of Record)

And these new forms of writing have moved on—way ahead of nearly all of us—into other spheres of mediated life. Nonlinear video and audio production systems such as Avid and ProTools are radically affecting the ways people in video and audio approach their work.

As noted by Ray DiLeo, an engineer and programmer who worked with the alt-rock group Filter notes, writing and recording a song is frequently no longer about a group of musicians gathering around a single microphone (a method surviving in and revived in bluegrass and folk artists such as the Del McRoury Band). It's not even simply the use of multiple tracks pioneered Les Paul that combine the work of single, isolated musicians into one apparently simultaneous song. We're not even talking about "tweaking" a finished product to add in a new rhythm track, something musicians such as Steely Dan began doing obsessively many decades ago. Over the last century, the virtual space of music performance has mutated, shifting from on-the-spot, realtime performance toward a recursive, manipulation, filtering (no pun intended), translation, and reorganization of information apart from the bodied constraints of live performance. An environment like ProTools still allows realtime performance, but it also opens a radically different space for composition.

In the Spring of 2001, I began working with David Dies, a graduate student in Crane School of Music at SUNY Potsdam, who worked extensively with ProTools to design commissioned pieces. During one of my observations, David worked on a six-minute piece designed to be played from CD as accompaniment to a live trumpet. Here are some selections from the observation log I created during one session, in which David worked on what he called "precomposition".

time	video/audio
3:20	D explains he's created a new file in ProTools with 8 blank tracks It's "a canvas ... and palette in one" accumulating a mass of information on which to draw during composition
8:20	d gets paper, explains that he doesn't do a lot of sketch work, but is going to write down notes about interesting tambres that he can come back to later. begins actively moving among three MIDI keyboards, Mac ProTools workstation, and pad of paper (multiple sources and spaces for information)
25:25	after long sequence of tones, "I have half a mind to capture this" "I'm not wild about the initial [...] I want to capture that second half to see if I still like it when it's isolated. [plays tone]. See? That's cool." actively fragmenting existing sounds
30:20	"once this is captured, I tend to not come back to the keyboard" "It's so manipulable there" (in ProTools). Says in a previous composition he created melodies from a scale (by cutting up). explains why he's recording source tones that he's played. typically likes to work from the virtual palette of sounds during composition rather than moving back to MIDI keyboard. composition for D emphasized rearrangement, selection rather than production.

In these transcripts, we begin to see evidence of a new sort of writing—composing processes (the phrase arcing over both music and text) supporting work as experimentation, arrangement, filtering, movement, rehearsal and reversal. These terms will be familiar to writing teachers—they're what we often struggle to push students towards in their own composing process, with varying levels of success. ProTools reminds us of the potential (as yet largely untapped) in nonlinear writing spaces such as Storyspace or Dreamweaver. The cultural and technological forces contributing to the development and use of those writing environments align with those surrounding ProTools. But I want to suggest that ProTools represents the next step (to call it an evolutionary step would to posit an unsupportable teleology), a picture of where composition may be headed. Reflecting about and acting within that picture can help us develop our own productive, critical responses.

One key aspect of ProTools is the way in which it deconstructs the separation between artifact and performance, long a stumbling block for composition.

WEB ARCHITECTURES

Here's a second example of a new sort of text, one that some of you are probably familiar with, the MOO. This is the ProNoun MOO which I worked with for several years (or, depending on who you ask, should take the blame for). In addition to serving twenty or thirty sections a semester of business writing and tech writing courses, we also allow other classes and projects to use it. Here, Teena Carnegie and others have constructed spaces for a conference they held in 2000, attended (virtually) by people from all over the US and Canada.

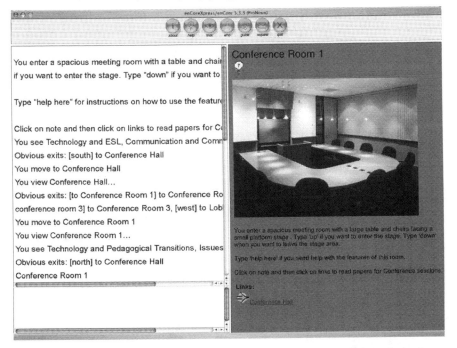

MOO spaces hold two types of writing, one familiar to us and the other relatively unknown. In one instance, we have the texts written in the space—the paper icons on the right side, for example, hold draft conference presentations that participants will read prior to the session so that they can discuss the texts in realtime. And there are the numerous words on the screen describing the room and actions one can take in the room or on one of the objects in the room.

But those spatial words are actually part of a different order of text in ProNoun, the architecture of the space. If we want to value texts that are constructed, accumulated, arranged, then we need to think about architecture as a form of writing. Numerous philosophers have noted the connection between architecture and philosophy; I think, following Derrida, that we need to start to thinking of writing as architecture. I won't go into a lot of details about this right now, but just want to suggest that there is much in architectural theory that can help us think about writing at a number of levels. Jay Bolter claimed that texts have always constructed different spaces; today, we more frequently think of ourselves as moving within texts—we navigate Web sites, surf channels, browse and manipulate, remake. And lest we consider architecture too functionalist, we should also follow the movement into deconstructivist and postmodernist architecture in order to begin understanding texts that are postmodernist but still function.

FORESTALLING CLOSURE

Important to my overall project here are the ways that articulation theory and symbolic-analytic work moves through fragmentation. They don't deny the force of postmodernism or postmodern capitalism. Instead, articulation theory requires a responsible stance toward contingency and fragmentation. From an articulation theory stance, writers—or designers, more accurately—actively map fragments back into contexts recursively. There aren't any guaranteed social meanings or knowing authorial asides. There are only social struggles, uneven forces, the incessant act of connecting and disconnecting the local and the global.

If we start to understand connection as a form of writing, then articulation theory can offer us a way to understand the "mere" uncreative act of selection and connection as very active and creative. Perhaps as importantly, it moves the idea of database construction—or any sort of connective writing, like hypertext—away from technical/functional skills only and toward the sense that making decisions about how to arrange "facts" is a very important process, one that involves ethical responsibilities on the part of the writer/designer.

And in the here-now of the World Wide Web, of the blipvert soundbite, of the writing that is no longer writing as we once knew it, we are all finding ourselves responsible for making connections, for finding ways to learn and to teach new forms of making cultural meanings.

ACTIVITY 1

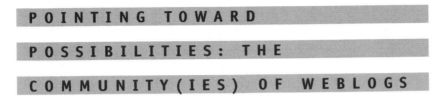

POINTING TOWARD POSSIBILITIES: THE COMMUNITY(IES) OF WEBLOGS

TEACHER'S NOTES

The weblog assignment provides students with opportunities to think about writing as an activity that's simultaneously social and individual. In some ways, authoring a weblog will seem similar to designing a Web site, another useful student assigment; weblogs are, in most cases, actually a subtype of Web site. They include, however, specific characteristics than can help students understand intertextuality and new forms of writing. By asking students to produce a steady stream of material over time, writing a weblog requires them to see the log as more integrated into their lives. And the insistence on writing as a form of quotation-—weblogs invariably include a mix of "original" text and text copied from other weblogs or sites—students (and teachers) learn to question the "original"/"copied" dichotomy.

TIME FRAME

Four weeks:

Week 1	Students read one or two weblogs, discuss characteristics and variations in class.
Week 2 and 3	Students begin a weblog, posting an average of once per day. Amount of in-class discussion can vary depending on level of students, how weblogs are working, etc. Also, students read at three or more other student weblogs and refer to them in their own.
Week 4	Students discuss weblog experiences, draft brief report.

The timeframe can be expanded for full semester, with weblog threaded throughout their work. Can also be contracted if the amount of weblog authoring is reduced.

POSSIBLE VARIATIONS

The weblogs can be collaborative (from two to six students per weblog).

ACTIVITY

OVERVIEW FOR STUDENTS

Weblogs, or "blogs" as they're sometimes called, offer a new form of writing on the World Wide Web. Unlike traditional Web sites, blogs usually require very little in the way of technical expertise. Many blog sites even offer free onsite hosting and Web-based editing features that make writing a blog a very simple process.

But like many simple technologies, blogs come in an enormous range of classifications and uses. There are blogs for independent music groups, disaffected college students, professional organizations, and more. Some rely heavily on uploaded Webcam shots while others exist as scrolling words on a screen. Some are individually authored; others are collaborative works; still others combine a "main" author page with extensive collaborative discussion pages. Analyzing and designing blogs can help you think about how people read texts, how people author texts, and how different texts function for different groups of users.

ANALYZE A WEBLOG

Begin by selecting a blog to analyze. To find examples, you can go to any large search engine and search on "weblog" or "blog". Alternatively, you can find a site that hosts weblogs, such as http://www.blogger.com/, and search lists of different blogs on that site.

After you've selected a site, answer the following questions:

1   Who reads this site?

2   Are the readers of the site "present" in the site somehow? (Are they referred to by the writer? Is there a discussion section?)

3   What is the "grain size" of the posts on the site? What is the shortest entry? What is the longest?

4   Does the site have a history? Are older posts moved to an archive that can be read somehow?

5   How do you think the writer envisions the site? What does it mean to them? Why are they writing the site?

6   If the site includes images, what are the image of? What are they supposed to mean?

7   Does the writer belong to a larger weblog community?

8   How does this site differ from other sites in the Web, in general?

9   Are blogs more like journals, newspapers, Web sites, tv shows, radio shows, novels, or what?

After you've analyzed the weblog, share your reports with other people in class and compare your findings. Are there common aspects running through the analyses of blogs? Which blogs seem the most interesting to your class? Which seem the least?

RUNNING A WEBLOG

Either as a class or individually, locate a site that provides free hosting for weblogs or locate a solution that will let you host a site on your own server.

1   Decide on a topic and scope for your blog. What will it cover? Who will the readers be?

2   Select a name and a theme or look and feel if one is available. Think about both your purpose and your audience as you determine names and themes, because these will both affect how your audiences see your site.

3   Begin your blog.

4   Either in the blog or in a separate, private journal (depending on whether or not personal notes seem to be appropriate in the blog itself), track your thoughts about the act of writing the blog. Does it feel weird? Do you have a hard time writing? Why?

FINAL ANALYSIS

After writing the blog for at least two weeks, report back to the class on your experiences. How do your experiences compare with others?

ACTIVITY 2

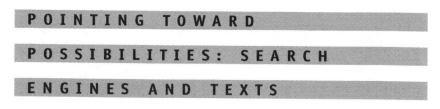

POINTING TOWARD POSSIBILITIES: SEARCH ENGINES AND TEXTS

TEACHER'S NOTES

The first phase of the search engine and text assigment begins with a commonly used method for helping students understand the importance of looking critical at Web (and other) resources. By comparing the varying results they receive from search engines on the same query, students will learn valuable background information about search engines and indices. The goal of this portion of the assignment isn't to get them to pick the "best" search engine—there is no single best; there are only different types. So although students (and nearly everyone) may have a favorite search engine, students (and nearly everyone) needs to learn both how that search engine works as well as instances in which using a different search engine would be helpful. Comparing reports and findings will help them flesh out this understanding.

The second part of the assignment asks students to look a little deeper, at the notion that search engines are, in a sense, texts to be analyzed: what does it mean, culturally, politically, economically, ideologically, for one type of result to come up higher in a search engine hit list than another site? Who made decisions that affected how the results looked—and why?

TIMEFRAME

From one day to one week, depending on the complexity of the final report.

VARIATION

This activity can be either collaborative or individual work. In classes emphasizing or experimenting with creative writing, a "found art" sort of project could be added near the end, that asked students to select and interpret the search engine texts as creative documents.

ACTIVITY

OVERVIEW FOR STUDENTS

For many users, search engines of one form or another are a primary point of entry into the Web. They structure the Web in both predetermined and contingent ways: Yahoo organizes the Web into a hierarchy of categories; Google crawls the Web and indexes key terms in a searchable database. Different search engines offer different—sometimes dramatically different—responses to the same search query.

ASSIGNMENT

As a class, list as many search engines as possible. Then, randomly assign three search engines to each student (most search engine will be assigned more than once, which is fine—it'll give you something to compare in the final reports).

Also as a class, come up with three different types of search queries. Which three depends on your class, but try to come up with three that are very different in terms of who might type them in or what topics they apply to. For example, here are three examples:

- weezer
- discount paperclips
- discrimination

For each search and each search engine, record the following information

1 How many hits did the search engine find?

2 What were the top ten hits?

3 Did all the hits seem related?

4 Were there hits that seemed to make no sense?

ANALYSIS

Write or present a brief report summarizing your findings. Be sure to provide concrete examples to illustrate your findings. How did each search engine organize the information? Were there entries on the list that were included because someone had paid to have them there (sometimes called "sponsored")?

In comparing findings with your classmates, were there major differences between what each search engine found?

ACTIVITY 3

WHO'S VISIBLE ON THE WEB:
THE POLITICS OF SEARCH
ENGINES

TEACHER'S NOTES

Although the World Wide Web is often characterized as a democractic, equal-izing space, access to the Web—particularly to Web-authoring tools—remains unequal, drawn along rather predictable lines of race, gender, and wealth. In addition, the Web itself—for a variety of important reasons—represents itself as predominantly monocultural.

The "Who's Visible" assignment asks students to look hard at how different demographic (social, gender, racial, etc.) are constructed visibly on the World Wide Web. The goal of the assignment is not to place blame for constructing certain subjectivities, but to understand the complexity of the topic. In addi-tion, as students themselves begin authoring Web sites they will need to make conscious decisions about who is represented in their own work, and how they represent others.

Note: This exercise requires students to enter racial and gendered terms into search engines. It is likely that some of these terms will be linked to sexually explicit and/or offensive sites. This is entirely part of the goal of the exercise, which is to link racial and gender terms to their presentation on the Internet. However, students will need to be given the option to opt out of that portion of the assignment for personal reasons. In addition, we would discourage against demonstrating this activity in a public computer lab in order to avoid subjecting participants to potentially harassing sites.

TIMEFRAME

One day to one week (depending on complexity of report)

VARIATIONS

To minimize potentially explicit or offensive search results, instructors can assignment specific search terms and/or engines (after testing them to vet results). Could concentrate on subset of possible terms—who is represented, graphically or textually in searches on specific occupational titles, for example?

ACTIVITY

OVERVIEW FOR STUDENTS

Although the Web was originally created as a relatively specialized network for publishing scientific work, it is rapidly becoming a major cultural force. As the Web becomes more common, the presence or absence of different types of people within the Web becomes a political issue. If the Web is represented as the domain of a particular group or subgroup of people based on their race, color, sex—or whatever—then, in a recursive way, users outside of that group are implicitly discouraged from using the Web.

The majority/minority distinction is, in some ways, a culturally relative construction: consider the majority/minority faces you would see at a meeting of the Boy Scouts of America versus the local National Organization of Women chapter versus the playground at your local elementary school. In each of those contexts, majority/minority divisions differ dramatically.

ASSIGNMENT

In order to help you think about who is present and who is absent on the Web, choose a search engine and enter your own name into the query. Do you find many hits? Are there other people with your name?

Next, come up with a set of demographic terms that describe yourself – race, ethnicity, gender, age, etc. Enter those terms into a search engine: what types of entries come up? How many?

Finally, come up with a set of "Other" terms—for each of your own demographic terms, list a common term used to describe people unlike you. Try to avoid relying on derogatory terms.

For more information about Web demographics, see the following sites:

- Basic, long-term WWW user demographic surveys:
  <http://www.cc.gatech.edu/gvu/user_surveys/>
- Domain name registration demographics:
  <http://www.domainstats.com/>
- Early MIT article on measuring the growth of the Web:
  <http://www.mit.edu/people/mkgray/growth/>
- Nua's massive database of Internet surveys and reports:
  <http://www.nua.ie/surveys/index.cgi>.

ACTIVITY 4

ONLINE COMMUNITIES AND ARCHITECTURES

TEACHER'S NOTES

The Online Communities project helps students understand and practice multiple online communication skills, from simple navigation and interpersonal communication within a MOO environment through various levels of programming (the degree of which depends on the specific form of assignment chosen as well as the student's interests). Although in one sense, MOOs seem like a very simple (almost cartoonish) technology, that initial simplicity brings with it a relatively short learning curve but robust long-term experiences. And if the learning curve of the technology itself is relatively simple—a handful of commands will be enough to get started in nearly any MOO—the impact of that technology on communication patterns and structures is relatively high, making MOOs a useful forum for understanding communication as a contingent, socially situated, and ever-changing activity.

TIMEFRAME

Because students are being asked to join an external community, it is important to let them move slowly into that community, observing for the most part at the start. Only after getting a sense of the lay of the land should they begin participating at the level of constructing spaces. Shorter assigments could be created by working with an in-house MOO that the teacher has set up for local students, although this would also create a relatively homogenous and isolated environment (one of the benefits of the assignment is that it requires them to go out and find other communities). Very brief (one or two hour) assignments could be constructed by the teacher bringing in transcripts and other documents from a MOO that will let students answer the questions in the assignment without actually participating in the MOO (a valuable experience, but time intensive).

VARIATIONS

Students could examine other forms of online community using similar sets of questions: weblogs, instant messaging programs, bulletin boards, etc..

ASSIGNMENT OVERVIEW

MOO communities represent a popular line in the development of online collaborative spaces that reaches back over a decade. In a MOO (which, confusingly and recursively, stands for "MUD, Object Oriented," a term in which

MUD stands for "Multi-User Dimension"), users occupy virtual spaces in which they interact with each other, move around, communicate, and more. Although usually MOOS are text-based (so that users actually read textual descriptions of the spaces), newer MOOs are Web-based and provide users with a more visual interactive space.

ACTIVITY

Begin by locating resources on MOOs by entering MOO into a search engine or by visiting one of these sites:

- The MOO-Cows FAQ: http://www.moo.mud.org/moo-faq/
- The Lost Library of MOO: http://www.hayseed.net/MOO/
- LinguaMOO home page: http://lingua.utdallas.edu/

ANALYSIS

Read accounts of MOO users in order to gain some background on how MOOs work. Then, locate a public MOO that you can join. Try to pick one that's either very general or one that appeals to a specific interest of yours. Join the MOO and spend at least a week getting familiar with the MOO, including its purpose, the users in the MOO, and its history. Analyze community in the MOO—are there communal places? Are they inhabited? When and by whom? Who gets to build in the MOO you occupy?

ANALYSIS, PART 2

After you're comfortable communicating and navigating in the MOO you've chosen, build yourself a space within the MOO: an office, a park, whatever.

1   What regulations govern building/digging in the MOO? Who decides who else can build, and where?

2   Are there certain types of rooms that are common in the MOO?

3   Is the architecture of the MOO based on one or more real-world architectures? Is it a schoolhouse? An office? A subway?

4   How would use be affected if the MOO was translated into a different sort of architecture? Could it be an airport? A machine shop? A hospital?

4   How is building in the MOO like writing? How is it different than writing? Is a room a text?

5   Do other people enter your space? Are you encouraged to enter others?

a bibliography of print resources

FOR WORKING WITH THE VISUAL &
INTERACTIVE ASPECTS OF TEXTS,
WHETHER THE TEXTS BE ON SCREEN OR
ON PAPER

The texts in this bibliography have been categorized according to the following scheme:

Ad	Advertising
An	Animation
B	History/Consequences of the Book and/or writing (which includes how the visual presentation of pages contributes to interpretation)
C	Comics
Com	Composing visual texts: hands-on/practical/sometimes theoretic background & guidelines for how to arrange texts visually
CW	Computers & Writing
E	Examples of academic texts whose visual presentation questions (not necessarily explicitly) the ideologies of the "standard" visual presentation of academic texts
F	Film studies (both the theoretic as well as the applied—and just a few 'classics')
G	Gender
H	Hypertext
Im	"Images"
In	Interactivity
L	Literacy, Visual Literacy
M	Media
N	Narrative issues related to how texts can be organized online
NM	Texts that specifically address questions/issues in new media
P	Pedagogical issues in teaching with new media/the visual aspects of texts
Ps	Psychoanalytic approaches (mostly used in film theory)
R	Rhetoric: Visual Rhetoric, Rhetorics of Interactivity
S	Seeing, Sight, Vision, Perception, and the History and/or Science thereof…
T	Typography
V	Visual Communication, Visual Rhetoric, Graphic Design, Design: theory and practice
VC	Visual Culture
WI	Word/Image issues

CW,H Aarseth, Espen J. *Cybertext: Perspectives on Ergodic Literature.* Baltimore: The Johns Hopkins Press, 1997.

G,Ps Adams, P. *The Emptiness of the Image: Psychoanalysis and Sexual Differences.* New York: Routledge, 1996.

CW,Im,WI Allen, Nancy, ed. *Working with Words and Images.* Westport, CT: Ablex, 2002.

M Allen, R., ed. *Channels of Discourse, Reassembled: Television and Contemporary Criticism.* Chapel Hill: University of North Carolina Press, 1992.

CW Anson, Chris. "Distant Writing: Teaching Writing in a Culture of Technology." *College English* 61.3 (January 1999): 261–80.

S,V Arnheim, Rudolf. *Visual Thinking.* Berkeley: University of California Press, 1969.

Com,V ———. *The Power of the Center: A Study of Composition in the Visual Arts.* Berkeley: University of California Press, 1982.

Im,S Aumont, Jacques. *The Image.* London: British Film Institute, 1997.

B Baker, Nicholson. "The History of Punctuation." *The Best American Essays 1994.* Ed. Tracy Kidder and Robert Atwan. New York: Houghton Mifflin, 1994.

Com,V Bang, Molly. *Picture This: Perception & Composition.* Boston: Little Brown & Company, 1991.

VC Banham, Reyner. *Theory and Design in the First Machine Age.* Second Edition. Cambridge: The MIT Press, 1999.

CW,H Barrett, Edward, ed. *Text, Context, and Hypertext: Writing With and For the Computer.* Cambridge: The MIT Press, 1988.

V,VC Barton, Ben and Marthalees Barton. "Ideology and the Map: Toward a Postmodern Visual Design Practive." *Professional Communication: The Social Perspective.* Eds. Nancy Roundy Byler and Charlotte Thralls. Newbury Park: Sage, 1993. 49–78.

R,V ———. "Toward a Rhetoric of Visuals for the Computer Era." *Technical Writing Teacher* 12 (Fall 1985): 126–45.

F,M Bazin, Alfred. *What Is Cinema?* Vols. I & II. Berkeley: University of California Press, 1967.

T,V,WI Beirut, Michael, William Drenttel, Steven Heller, and DK Holland, eds. *Looking Closer: Critical Writings on Graphic Design.* New York: Allworth Press, 1994.

T,V,WI ———. *Looking Closer 2: Critical Writings on Graphic Design.* New York: Allworth Press, 1997

V,VC Bierut, Michael, Jessica Helfland, Steven Heller, and Rick Poynor, eds. *Looking Closer 3: Classic Writings on Graphic Design.* New York: Allworth Press, 1999.

L,V,WI Berger, Arthur Asa. *Seeing is Believing: An Introduction to Visual Communication.* Mountain View, CA: Mayfield Publishing, 1998.

An,E,S,VC   Berger, John. *About Looking.* New York: Pantheon Books, 1980.

Ad,E,S,VC   ———. *Ways of Seeing.* London: Penguin, 1972.

CW,V   Bernhardt, Stephen A. "Seeing the Text." *CCC* 37 (1986): 66–78.

WI   Bernstein, Charles. *My Way: Speeches and Poems.* Chicago: University of Chicago Press, 1999.

H   Bernstein, Mark. "The Hypertext Patterns of Scrutiny in the Great Round." *Hypertext Now.* 12 December 2003. <http://www.eastgate.com/HyperTextNow/archives/Scrutiny.html>.

H   ———. "The Navigation Problem Reconsidered." *Hypertext/Hypermedia Handbook.* Ed. Emily Berk and Joseph Devlin. New York: McGraw-Hill, 1991.

E,R,VC   Blakesley, David and Collin Brooke, eds. *Enculturation* 3.2 (2001). (Special issue on visual rhetoric). 12/15/03. <http://enculturation.gmu.edu/3_2/toc.html>.

R   Blair, Carole, Marsha S. Jeppeson, and Enrico Pucci, Jr. "Public Memorializing in Postmodernity: The Vietnam Veterans Memorial as Prototype." *Quarterly Journal of Speech* 77 (1991): 263–88.

R   Blair, Carole, and Neil Michel. "Reproducing Civil Rights Tactics: The Rhetorical Performances of the Civil Rights Memorial." *Rhetoric Society Quarterly* 30.2 (2000), 31–55.

R,V   Blair, J. Anthony. "The Possibility and Actuality of Visual Arguments." *Argumentation and Advocacy* 33 (Summer 1996): 23–39.

VC   *The Block Reader In Visual Culture.* London; New York: Routledge, 1996.

Com,F,V   Block, Bruce. *The Visual Story: Seeing the Structure of Film, TV, and New Media.* Boston: Focal Press, 2001.

M,VC   Bolter, Jay David and Richard Grusin. *Remediation: Understanding New Media.* Cambridge: MIT Press, 1999.

H,L   Bolter, Jay David. "Hypertext and the Question of Visual Literacy." *Handbook of Literacy and Technology: Transformations in a Post-Typographic World.* Eds. David Reinking, Michael C. McKenna, Linda D. Labbo, and Ronald D. Kieffer. Mahwah, NJ: Lawrence Erlbaum, 1998. 3–14.

H,L   ———. "Literature in the Electronic Writing Space." *Literacy Online: The Promise (and Perils) of Reading and Writing with Computers.* Ed. Myron C. Tuman. Pittsburgh: University of Pittsburgh Press, 1992. 19–42.

H,L,M   ———. *Writing Space: The Computer, Hypertext, and the History of Writing.* Hillsdale, NJ: Lawrence Erlebaum Associates, 1991.

G,V   Bosley, Deborah. "Gender and Visual Communication: Toward a Feminist Theory of Design." *IEEE Transactions on Professional Communication.* 35 (1992): 32–40.

L,P,V   Brasseur, Lee. "Visual Literacy in the Computer Age: A Complex Perceptual Landscape." *Computers and Technical Communication: Pedagogical and Programmatic Perspectives.* Ed. Stuart Selber. Greenwich, CT: Ablex, 1997. 75–96.

S   Brennan, Teresa and Martin Jay, Eds. *Vision in Context: Historical and Contemporary Perspectives on Sight.* New York: Routledge, 1996.

R,H,L   Brent, Doug. "Rhetorics of the Web: Implications for Teachers of Literacy. *Kairos: A Journal for Teachers of Writing in Webbed Environments.* 2.1 (1997). 12 December 2003. <http://english.ttu.edu/kairos/2.1/features/brent/bridge.html>.

B,T   Bringhurst, Robert. "The Typographic Nude." *Critique* 4 (Spring 1997): 87–91.

T   ———. *The Elements of Typographic Style.* Point Roberts, WA: Hartley & Marks, 1992.

H,R   Brook, Collin Gifford. "Making Room, Writing Hypertext." *JAC* 20.2 (2000): 349–89.

L   Bruce, Bertram C., and Maureen P. Hogan. "The Disappearance of Technology: Toward an Ecological Model of Literacy." *Handbook of Literacy and Technology: Transformations in a Post-Typographic World.* Eds. David Reinking, Michael McKenna, Linda Labbo, and Ronald Kieffer. New Jersey: Lawrence Erlbaum, 1998. 269–81.

M,S,VC   Brunette, P. and D. Wills, eds. *Deconstruction and the Visual Arts: Art, Media, Architecture.* Cambridge: Cambridge University Press, 1994.

Im,S,VC,WI   Bryson, Norman, Michael Holly, and Keith Moxey, eds. *Visual Culture: Images and Interpretations.* London: Wesleyan University Press, 1994.

R,V   Buchanan, Richard. "Declaration by Design: Rhetoric, Argument, and Demonstration in Design Practice." *Design Discourse: History, Theory, Criticism.* Ed. Victor Margolin. Chicago: University of Chicago Press, 1989. 91–109.

S,VC   Buck-Morss, Susan. *The Dialectic of Seeing: Walter Benjamin and the Arcades Project.* Cambridge: MIT Press, 1995.

VC   Burgin, Victor. *Indifferent Spaces: Place and Memory in Visual Culture.* Berkeley: University of California Press, 1996.

Im,VC   Burnett, R. *Cultures of Vision: Images, Media & the Imaginary.* Bloomington: Indiana University Press, 1995.

L,P   Burniske, R.W., Lowell Monke, and Jonas F. Soltis. *Breaking Down the Digital Walls: Learning to Teach in a Post-Modem World.* (SUNY Series, Education and Culture). Albany: State University of New York Press, 2001.

T   Byrne, Chuck. "Jack W. Stauffacher, Printer, Etc." *Emigre* 45 (Winter 1998): 16–29.

B,WI   Carruthers, Mary. *The Book of Memory: A Study of Memory in Medieval Culture.* Cambridge: Cambridge University Press, 1990.

B,WI ———. *The Craft of Thought: Meditation, Rhetoric, and the Making of Images, 400–1200.* Cambridge: Cambridge University Press, 1998.

B,T Chappell, Warren. *A Short History of the Printed Word.* Second Edition. Vancouver: Hartley and Marks, 1999.

H,In,L Charney, Davida. "The Effect of Hypertext on Processes of Reading and Writing." *Literacy and Computers: The Complications of Teaching and Learning with Technology.* Eds. Cynthia L. Selfe and Susan Hilligoss. New York: The Modern Language Association, 1994. 238–63.

B Chartier, Roger. *The Order of Books.* Stanford: Stanford University Press, 1994.

B ———. *Forms and Meanings: Texts, Performances, and Audiences from Codex to Computer.* Philadelphia: University of Pennsylvania Press, 1995.

S Classen, Constance. *Worlds of Sense: Exploring the Senses in History and Across Cultures.* London: Routledge, 1993.

T Cole, Gregory. "Towards a New Arabic Typography." *PRINT* 52.3 (May/June 1998): 112–15, 126.

L,P Cope, Bill, and Mary Kalantzis, eds. *Multiliteracies: Literacy Learning and the Design of Social Futures.* New York: Routledge, 2000.

S,VC Crary, Jonathan. *Suspensions of Perception: Attention, Spectacle, and Modern Culture.* Cambridge: MIT Press, 2000.

S ———. *Techniques of the Observer: On Vision and Modernity in the Nineteenth Century.* Cambridge: MIT Press, 1995.

T Crawford, Alisdair. "Bilingual Typography." *Visible Language* 21.1 (Winter 1987): 42–65.

L, WI Cummins, Tom. "Representation in the Sixteenth Century and the Colonial Image of the Inca." *Writing Without Words: Alternative Literacies in Mesoamerica and the Andes.* Eds. Elizabeth Hill Boone and Walter D. Mignolo. Durham: Duke University Press, 1994. 188–219.

F Dancyger, K. *The Technique of Film and Video Editing.* Boston: Focal Press, 1993.

NM,VC Darley, Andrew. *Visual Digital Culture: Surface Play and Spectacle in New Media Genres.* London: Routledge, 2000.

B,L,WI Deibert, Ronald J. *Parchment, Printing, and Hypermedia: Communication in World Order Transformation.* New York: Columbia University Press, 1997.

E Derrida, Jacques. *Glas.* Trans. John P. Leavey, Jr. and Richard Rand. Lincoln: University of Nebraska Press, 1986.

B Diringer, David. *The Book Before Printing: Ancient, Medieval, and Oriental.* New York: Dover Publications, 1982.

Com,L,V Dondis, Donis. A. *A Primer of Visual Literacy.* Cambridge: MIT Press, 1993.

V,VC	Doordin, Dennis P., ed. *Design History: An Anthology.* Cambridge: MIT Press, 1995.
H,N	Douglas, J. Yellowlees. *The End of Books—Or Books without End?: Reading Interactive Narratives.* Ann Arbor: University of Michigan Press, 2001.
H,In	———. "'How Do I Stop This Thing?': Closure and Indeterminacy in Interactive Narratives." *Hyper/Text/Theory.* Ed. George P. Landow. Baltimore: Johns Hopkins University Press, 1994. 159–88.
H,In	———. "Wandering through the Labyrinth: Encountering Interactive Fiction." *Computers and Composition* 6.3 (August 1989): 91–103.
H,In	———. "What Hypertexts Can Do That Print Narratives Cannot." *Reader* 28 (Fall 1992): 1–22.
H,In	———. "Gaps, Maps, and Perception: What Hypertext Readers (Don't) Do." *Perforations* 3.
T	Dowding, Geoffrey. *Finer Points in the Spacing and Arrangement of Type.* Point Roberts, WA: Hartley & Marks, 1996.
B,WI	Drucker, Joanna. *The Visible Word: Experimental Typography and Modern Art, 1909–1923.* Chicago: The University of Chicago Press, 1994.
B,WI	———. *Figuring the Word: Essays on Books, Writing, and Visual Poetics.* New York: Granary Books, 1998.
B	———. *The Alphabetic Labyrinth: The Letters in History and the Imagination.* London: Thames and Hudson, 1995.
In,M	Druckery, Timothy, ed. *Ars Electronica: Facing the Future.* Cambridge: MIT Press, 2001.
V	Druin, Allison and Cynthia Solomon. *Designing Multimedia Environments for Children.* New York: John Wiley & Sons, 1996.
L,P	Druin, Allison, ed. *The Design of Children's Technology.* San Francisco: Morgan Kauffman, 1999.
B	Eisenstein, Elizabeth. *The Printing Press as an Agent of Change.* Vols. I & II. Cambridge: Cambridge University Press, 1979.
C,VC	Eisner, Will. *Comics and Sequential Art.* Tamarac, FL: Poorhouse Press, 1985.
WI	Elkins, James. *On Pictures and the Words that Fail Them.* Cambridge: Cambridge University Press, 1998.
Im,WI	———. *The Domain of Images.* Ithaca: Cornell University Press, 1999.
Im,S,WI	———. *The Object Stares Back: On the Nature of Seeing.* New York: Simon & Schuster, 1996.
Im,S,WI	———. *The Poetics of Perspective.* Ithaca: Cornell University Press, 1995.

In Ellsworth, Elizabeth. "A Fourth Paradox: Teaching as Performance Suspended in Time—Interactive Pedagogy in New Media." *Teaching Positions: Difference, Pedagogy, and the Power of Address.* New York: Teachers College Press, 1999. 165–73.

H,In Ess, Charles. "The Political Computer: Hypertext, Democracy, and Habermas." *Hyper/Text/Theory.* Ed. George P. Landow. Baltimore: Johns Hopkins University Press, 1994. 225–67.

VC Evans, Jessica and Stuart Hall. *Visual Culture: The Reader.* London: Sage, 1999.

P Evard, Michele. "A Community of Designers: Learning Through Exchanging Questions and Answers." *Constructionism in Practice: Designing, Thinking, and Learning in a Digital World.* Eds. Yasmin Kafai and Mitchel Resnick. Mahwah, NJ: Lawrence Erlbaum, 1996. 223–39.

S,WI Farnell, Brenda. *Do You See What I Mean? Plains Indian Sign Talk and the Embodiment of Action.* Austin: University of Texas Press, 1995.

B Febvre, Lucien, and Henri-Jean Martin. *The Coming of the Book.* Trans. David Gerard. London: Verso, 1976.

L,WI Fleckenstein, Kristie S. "Images, Words, and Narrative Epistemology." *College English* 58.8 (December 1996): 914–33.

L,P,WI Fleckenstein, Kristie S., Linda T. Calendrillo, and Demetrice A. Worley, eds. *Language and Image in the Reading-Writing Classroom: Teaching Vision.* Mahwah, NJ: Lawrence Erlbaum Associates, 2002.

B Foot, Mirjam M. "Bookbinding and the History of Books." In *A Potencie of Life: Books in Society.* Ed. Nicolas Barker. London: The British Library, 1993. 113–26.

R,V Foss, Sonja K. "The Construction of Appeal in Visual Images: A Hypothesis." *Rhetorical Movement.* Ed. David Zarefsky. Evanston: Northwestern University Press, 1993.

R,V ———. "Rhetoric and the Visual Image—A Resource Unit." *Communication Education* 31:1 (1982)

S,VC Foster, Hal, ed. *Vision and Visuality* [Dia Art Foundation, #2]. Seattle: Bay Press, 1998.

L,P,WI Garrett-Petts, W.F. and Donald Lawrence, eds. *Integrating Visual and Verbal Literacies.* Winnepeg: Inkshed Press, 1996.

In,R Gasperini, Jim. "Structural Ambiguity: An Emerging Interactive Aesthetic." *Information Design.* Ed. Robert Jacobson. Cambridge, MA: MIT Press, 1999. 301–15.

T Gill, Eric. *An Essay on Typography.* Boston: David R. Godine, 1988.

M,P Goldfarb, Brian. *Visual Pedagogy: Media Cultures in and beyond the Classroom.* Durham: Duke, 2002.

S   Gombrich, E.H. *Art and Illusion: A Study in the Psychology of Pictorial Representation.* Princeton: Princeton University Press, 1969.

H   Graver, Bruce E. "This is Not a Hypertext: Scholarly Annotation and the Electronic Medium." *Profession* 1998: 172–78.

T   Gray, Nicolette. *A History of Lettering: Creative Experiment and Letter Identity.* Boston: David R. Godine, 1986.

E,L   Grimm, Nancy M., Anne Frances Wysocki, Marilyn M. Cooper. "Rewriting Praxis (and Redefining Texts) in Composition Research." *Under Construction: Working at the Intersections of Composition Theory, Research, and Practice.* Eds. Christine Farris and Chris M. Anson. Logan, UT: Utah State University Press, 1998. 250–81.

L,P   Gruber, Sibylle, ed. *Weaving a Virtual Web: Practical Approaches to New Information Technologies.* Urbana, IL: NCTE, 2000.

B,M   Gumbrecht, Hans Ulrich and K. Ludwig Pfeiffer, eds. *Materialities of Communication.* Stanford: Stanford University Press, 1994.

H   Guyer, Carolyn. "Along the Estuary." *Tolstoy's Dictaphone: Technology and the Muse.* Ed. Sven Birkerts. St. Paul: Graywolf Press, 1996. 157–64.

B,M,CW   Haas, Christina. *Writing Technology: Studies on the Materiality of Literacy.* Mahwah, NJ: Lawrence Erlbaum, 1996.

S   Haraway, Donna. "Situated Knowledges: The Science Question in Feminism and the Privilege of Partial Perspective." *Simians, Cyborgs, and Women: The Reinvention of Nature.* New York: Routledge, 1991. 183–201.

H   Harpold, Terence. "Conclusions." *Hyper/Text/Theory.* Ed. George P. Landow. Baltimore: The Johns Hopkins University Press, 1994. 189–222.

In,NM,VC   Harries, Dan. *The New Media Book.* London: British Film Institute, 2002.

CW,P   Hawisher, Gail and Paul LeBlanc, eds. *Re-imagining Computers and Composition: Teaching and Research in the Virtual Age.* Boynton/Cook, 1992.

CW,P   Hawisher, Gail and Cynthia Selfe, eds. *Critical Perspectives on Computers and Composition Instruction.* New York: Teachers College Press, 1989.

CW   ———. *Evolving Perspectives on Computers and Composition Studies: Questions for the 1990s.* Urbana: NCTE and Computers and Composition, 1991.

CW,L   ———. *Passions, Pedagogies, and 21st Century Technologies.* Logan: Utah State Univerity Press, 1999.

B   Hayes, Kevin J. "The Book in American Utopian Literature, 1883–1917." *Visible Language* 31.1 (1997): 64–85.

P,NM,V,VC   Heller, Steven, ed. *The Education of an E-Designer.* New York: Allworth Press, 2001.

P,V,VC	———, ed. *The Education of a Graphic Designer.* New York: Allworth Press, 1998.
A,G,VC	———. *Sex Appeal: The Art of Allure in Graphic and Advertising Design.* New York: Allworth Press, 2000.
A,VC	Heller, Stephen and Marie Finamore, eds. *Design Culture: An Anthology of Writing from the AIGA Journal of Graphic Design.* New York: Allworth Press, 1997.
B,T,V	Heller, Stephen and Philip B. Meggs, eds. *Texts on Type: Critical Writings on Typography.* New York: Allworth Press, 2001.
L,V,VC	Heller, Stephen and Karen Pomeroy, eds. *Design Literacy: Understanding Graphic Design.* New York: Allworth Press, 1997.
B	Hellinga, Lotte. "The Codex in the Fifteenth Century: Manuscript and Print." *A Potencie of Life: Books in Society.* Ed. Nicolas Barker. London: The British Library, 1993. 63–88.
B,Com,T,V	Hendel, Richard. *On Book Design.* New Haven: Yale University Press, 1998.
S,VC	Heywood, Ian and Barry Sandywell, eds. *Interpreting Visual Culture: Explorations in the Hermeneutics of the Visual.* London: Routledge, 1999.
B,Com,T,V	Hochuli, Jost and Robin Kinross. *Designing Books: Theory and Practice.* London: Hyphen Press, 1996.
Im,In,B,NM	Hocks, Mary, and Michelle Kendrick, eds. *Eloquent Images: Visual Literacy and New Media.* Cambridge: MIT Press, 2003.
S	Hoffman, Donald D. *Visual Intelligence: How We Construct What We See.* New York: Norton, 1998.
E,VC	Holland, Jeanne. "Scraps, Stamps, and Cutouts: Emily Dickinson's Domestic Technologies of Publication." *Cultural Artifacts and the Production of Meaning: The Page, the Image, and the Body.* Eds. Margaret J. M. Ezell and Katherine O'Brien O'Keeffe. Ann Arbor: University of Michigan Press, 1994. 139–81.
E	Howe, Susan. *The Birth-mark: Unsettling the Wilderness in American Literary History.* Hanover, NH: Wesleyan University Press, 1993.
S	Howes, David, ed. *The Varieties of Sensory Experience: A Sourcebook in the Anthropology of the Senses.* Toronto: University of Toronto Press, 1991.
In,NM	Huhtamo, Erkki. "From Cybernation to Interaction: A Contribution to the Archaeology of Interactivity." *The Digital Dialectic: New Essays on New Media.* Ed. Peter Lunenfeld. Cambridge, MA: MIT Press, 1999. 96–110.
B,WI	Hunter, J. Paul. "From Typology to Type: Agents of Change in Eighteenth-Century English Texts." *Cultural Artifacts and the Production of Meaning: The Page, the Image, and the Body.* Eds. Margaret J. M. Ezell and Katherine O'Brien O'Keeffe. Ann Arbor: University of Michigan Press, 1994. 41–70.

B,WI — Illich, Ivan, and Barry Sanders. *ABC: The Alphabetization of the Popular Mind.* New York: Vintage Books, 1988.

I,VC — Ivins, W. M. *Prints and Visual Communication.* Cambridge: MIT Press, 1953, 1996.

S,VC — Jay, Martin. *Downcast Eyes: The Denigration of Vision in Twentieth-Century French Thought.* Berkeley: University of California Press, 1994.

S,VC — Jenks, Chris, ed. *Visual Culture.* New York: Routledge, 1995.

B — Johns, Adrian. *The Nature of the Book: Print and Knowledge in the Making.* Chicago: University of Chicago Press, 1998.

H,L — Johnson-Eilola, Johndan. *Nostalgic Angels: Rearticulating Hypertext Writing.* Norwood, NJ: Ablex, 1997.

H — ———. "Reading and Writing in Hypertext: Vertigo and Euphoria." *Literacy and Computers: The Complications of Teaching and Learning with Technology.* Eds. Cynthia L. Selfe and Susan Hilligoss. New York: The Modern Language Association, 1994. 195–219.

H — Johnson, Robert. "Romancing the Hypertext: A Rhetorical/ Historiographical View of the Hyperphenomenon." *TCQ* 4.1 (1995): 11–22.

H,In,L — Joyce, Michael. *Of Two Minds: Hypertext Pedagogy and Poetics.* Ann Arbor: University of Michigan Press, 1995.

H — Kahn, Paul and George Landow. "The Pleasures of Possibility: What is Disorientation in Hypertext?" *Journal of Computing in Higher Education* 4.2 (Spring 1993): 57–78.

B,CW,P — Kalmbach, James. *The Computer and the Page: Publishing, Technology, and the Classroom.* Norwood, NJ: Ablex, 1997.

B,L — Kaplan, Nancy. "Literacy beyond Books: Reading when all the World's a Web." *The World Wide Web and Contemporary Cultural Theory.* Eds. Andrew Herman and Thomas Swiss. New York: Routledge, 2000.

S — Keller, Evelyn Fox and Christine R. Grontkowski. "The Mind's Eye." *Discovering Reality: Feminist Perspectives on Epistemology, Metaphysics, Methodology, and the Philosophy of Science.* Eds. Sandra Harding and Merrill B. Hintikka. Dordrecht: D. Reidel Publishing, 1983. 207–24.

An,VC — Kenner, Hugh. *Chuck Jones: A Flurry of Drawings.* Berkeley: University of California Press, 1994.

B,WI — King, Mark B. "Hearing the Echoes of Verbal Art in Mixtec Writing." *Writing Without Words: Alternative Literacies in Mesoamerica and the Andes.* Eds. Elizabeth Hill Boone and Walter D. Mignolo. Durham: Duke University Press, 1994. 102–36.

L,VC,WI — Kinross, Robin. "The Rhetoric of Neutrality." *Design Issues* II.2: 18–30.

B,T ————. *Modern Typography: An Essay in Critical History.* London: Hyphen Press, 1992.

H,In Kirschenbaum, Matthew. "Machine Visions: Towards a Poetics of Artificial Intelligence." *Electronic Book Review* 6 (Winter 1997-1998). 12 December 2003. <http://www.altx.com/ebr/ebr6/6kirschenbaum/6kirsch.htm>.

B,M Kittler, Friedrich A. *Gramophone, Film, Typewriter.* Trans. Geoffrey Winthrop-Young and Michael Wutz. Stanford: Stanford University Press, 1999.

An,VC Klein, Norman M. *Seven Minutes: The Life and Death of the American Animated Cartoon.* London: Verso, 1993.

VC Koerner, Joseph Leo. "Hieronymus Bosch's World Picture." *Picturing Science / Producing Art.* Eds. Caroline A. Jones and Peter Galison. New York: Routledge, 1998. 297–323.

S,VC Kofman, Sarah. *Camera Obscura of Ideology.* Trans. Will Straw. Ithaca: Cornell University Press, 1999.

Com,V Kostelnick, Charles, and David D. Roberts. *Designing Visual Language: Stategies for Professional Communicators.* Boston: Allyn and Bacon, 1998.

Ps,S Krauss, Rosalind. *The Optical Unconscious.* Cambridge: MIT Press, 1994.

L,VC Kress, Gunther and Theo van Leeuwen. *Multimodal Discourse: The Modes and Media of Contemporary Communication.* London: Edward Arnold, 2001.

L,V,WI Kress, Gunther, and Theo van Leeuwen. *Reading Images: The Grammar of Visual Design.* London: Routledge, 1996.

Com,L,WI Kress, Gunther. "Visual and Verbal Modes of Representation in Electronically Mediated Communication: The Potentials of New Forms of Text." *Page to Screen: Taking Literacy into the Electronic Era.* Ed. Ilana Snyder. London: Routledge, 1998. 53–79.

L,Im Kress, Gunther. *Literacy in the New Media Age.* New York: Routledge, 2003.

G,E Kristeva, Julia. 1985. "Stabat Mater." *Poetics Today* 6.1–2 (1985): 135–52.

Com,NM,V Kristof, Ray and Amy Satran. *Interactivity by Design: Creating & Communicating with New Media.* Mountain View, CA: Adobe Press, 1995.

B,H,In Landow, George P. *Hypertext 2.0: The Convergence of Contemporary Critical Theory and Technology.* Baltimore: The Johns Hopkins University Press, 1997.

H,In ————. "The Rhetoric of Hypermedia: Some Rules for Authors." *Hypermedia and Literary Studies.* Eds. Paul Delany and George P. Landow. Cambridge: MIT Press, 1991. 81–104.

H   ———. "What's a Critic to Do?" *Hyper/Text/Theory.* Ed. George P. Landow. Baltimore: Johns Hopkins University Press, 1994: 1–48.

L,R,WI   Lanham, Richard A. "Digital Rhetoric: Theory, Practice, and Property." *Literacy Online: The Promise and Perils of Reading and Writing with Computers.* Ed. Myron C. Tuman. Pittsburgh, PA: University of Pittsburgh Press, 1992. 221–43.

L,R,VC,WI   ———. *The Electronic Word: Democracy, Technology, and the Arts.* Chicago: University of Chicago Press, 1993.

In,NM,V   Laurel, Brenda. *Computers as Theatre.* Reading, MA: Addison-Wesley, 1991.

V, VC   Lavin, Maud. *Clean New World: Culture, Politics, and Graphic Design.* Cambridge: MIT Press, 2001.

VC   ———. "Photomontage, Mass Culture, and Modernity." In *Montage and Modern Life,* 1919–1942. Ed. Matthew Teitelbaum. Cambridge: MIT Press, 1992. 36–59.

I,VC   Leppert, Richard. *Art and the Committed Eye: The Cultural Functions of Imagery.* Boulder, CO: Westview Press, 1996.

V   Lester, P. M. *Visual Communication: Images With Messages.* New York: Wadsworth, 1995.

B   Levarie, Norma. *The Art & History of Books.* New Castle, DE: Oak Knoll Press, 1995.

S   Levin, David Michael, ed. *Modernity and the Hegemony of Vision.* California: University of California Press.

S   ———. *Sites of Vision: The Discursive Construction of Sight in the History of Philosophy.* Cambridge: MIT Press, 1997.

NM   Lievrouw, Leah A. and Sonia M. Livingstone, eds. *Handbook of New Media Social Shaping and Consequences of ICTs.* London: Sage, 2002.

I,VC   Lister, Martin, ed. *The Photographic Image in Digital Culture.* London: Routledge, 1995.

WI   Lubell, Stephen. "Bilingualism in the Hebrew Text." *Visible Language* 27.1–2: 162–204.

I,R   Lucaites, John Louis and Robert Hariman. "Dissent and Emotional Management in a Liberal-Democratic Society: The Kent State Iconic Photograph." *Rhetoric Society Quarterly* 31.3 (2001): 37–43.

In,NM   Lunenfeld, Peter, ed. *The Digital Dialectic: New Essays on New Media.* Cambridge: MIT Press, 2000.

In,NM   Lunenfeld, Peter. *Snap to Grid: A User's Guide to Digital Arts, Media, and Culture.* Cambridge, MA: MIT Press, 2000.

VC,WI   Lupton, Ellen and J. Abbott Miller. "Deconstruction and Graphic Design: History Meets Theory." *Visible Language* 28.4 (Autumn 1994): 346–66.

B,V,VC,WI   ———. *Design Writing Research: Writing on Graphic Design.* New York: Princeton Architectural Press, 1996.

Com,V	Lynch, Patrick. "Yale Style Manual." 28 April 2003. 12 December 2003. <http://info.med.yale.edu/caim/manual/contents.html>.
C,VC	Magnussen, Anne and Hans-Christian Christiansen, eds. *Comics and Culture: Analytical and Theoretical Approaches to Comics.* Copenhagen: Museum Tuscalanum Press, 2000.
B	Manguel, Alberto. *A History of Reading.* New York: Viking, 1996.
In,NM	Manovich, Lev. *The Language of New Media.* Cambridge: MIT Press, 2001.
V,VC	Margolin, Victor, ed. *Design Discourse: History, Theory, Criticism.* Chicago: University of Chicago Press, 1989.
V,VC	Margolin, Victor and Richard Buchanan, eds. *The Idea of Design: A Design Issues Reader.* Cambridge: MIT Press, 1998.
In,V	Marra, Rose. "Human-Computer Interface Design." *Hypermedia Learning Environments: Instructional Design and Integration.* Eds. Piet A. M. Kommers, Scott Grabinger, and Joanna C. Dunlap. Mahwah, NJ: Lawrence Erlbaum, 1996. 115–35.
B,Com,V	Martin, Douglas. *An Outline of Book Design.* London: Blueprint, 1989.
H,In	Maso, Carole. "Rupture, Verge, and Precipice/Precipice, Verge, and Hurt Not." *Tolstoy's Dictaphone: Technology and the Muse.* Ed. Sven Birkerts. St. Paul: Graywolf Press, 1996. 50–72.
C,VC,WI	McCloud, Scott. *Understanding Comics.* New York: HarperPerennial, 1993.
B,L,VC,I	McGann, Jerome. "Composition as Explanation (of Modern and Postmodern Poetries)." *Cultural Artifacts and the Production of Meaning: The Page, the Image, and the Body.* Eds. Margaret J. M. Ezell and Katherine O'Brien O'Keeffe. Ann Arbor: University of Michigan Press, 1994. 101–38.
B,L,VC,I	———. *Black Riders: The Visible Language of Modernism.* Princeton: Princeton University Press, 1993.
B,L,VC,I	———. *The Textual Condition.* Princeton: Princeton University Press, 1991.
S	McHugh, Heather. "A Stranger's Way of Looking." In *Broken English: Poetry and Partiality.* Hanover, NH: Wesleyan University Press, 1993. 41–67.
B,V	McLean, Ruari. *Modern Book Design.* London: Longmans, Green, and Co., 1951.
B,VC,WI	McLuhan, Marshall. *The Gutenberg Galaxy.* Toronto: University of Toronto Press, 1962.
A,B,VC,WI	———. *The Mechanical Bride: Folklore of Industrial Man.* Boston: Beacon Press, 1951.

R,V   McQuarrie, Edward F. and David Glen Mick. "Visual Rhetoric in Advertising: Text-Interpretive, Experimental, and Reader-Response Analyses." *The Journal of Consumer Research.* 26:1, 1999.

T,V   Meggs, Phillip. *Type and Image: The Language of Graphic Design.* New York: Van Nostrand Reinhold, 1992.

V   ———. *A History of Graphic Design.* Third Edition. New York: John Wiley & Sons, 1998.

L,VC   Messaris, Paul. *Visual Literacy: Images, Mind & Reality.* Colorado: Westview Press, 1994.

Ad,I,VC   ———. *Visual Persuasion: The Role of Images in Advertising.* Thousand Oaks, CA: Sage, 1997.

A,V,WI   Meyers, Greg. *Words in Ads.* New York: St. Martins Press, 1994.

B,L,WI   Mignolo, Walter D. "Literacy and the Colonization of Memory: Writing Histories of People without History." *Literacy: Interdisciplinary Conversations.* Ed. Deborah Keller-Cohen. Cresskill, NJ: Hampton Press, 1994.

B,L,WI   ———. "Signs and Their Transmission: The Question of the Book in the New World." *Writing without Words: Alternative Literacies in Mesoamerica and the Andes.* Eds. Elizabeth Hill Boone and Walter D. Mignolo. Durham, NC: Duke University Press, 1994. 220–270.

VC   Mirzoeff, Nicholas. *The Visual Culture Reader.* London: Routledge, 1998.

Im,WI   Mitchell, WJT. *Iconology: Images, Texts, Ideology.* Chicago: University of Chicago Press, 1986.

Im,WI   ———. *Picture Theory: Essays on Verbal and Visual Representation.* Chicago: University of Chicago Press, 1994.

Im,M   ———. *The Reconfigured Eye: Visual Truth in the Post-photographic Era.* Cambridge: MIT Press, 1996.

WI   ———. "Word and Image." *Critical Terms for Art History.* Eds. Robert S. Nelson and Richard Shiff. Chicago, University of Chicago Press, 1996. 47–57.

Com,V   Mok, Clement. *Designing Business: Multiple Media, Multiple Disciplines.* San Jose: Adobe Press, 1997.

In,NM   Moser, Mary Anne and Douglas Macleod, eds. *Immersed in Technology: Art and Virtual Environments.* Cambridge: MIT Press, 1996.

H   Moulthrop, Stuart. "The Politics of Hypertext." *Evolving Perspectives on Computers and Composition Studies: Questions for the 1990s.* Eds. Gail E. Hawisher and Cynthia L. Selfe. Urbana, IL: NCTE, 1991. 253–71.

I,VC   Moxey, Keith. "Hieronymous Bosch and the 'World Turned Upside Down': The Case of The Garden of Earthly Delights." *Visual Culture: Images and Interpretations.* Eds. Norman Bryson, Michael Ann Holly, and Keith Moxey. Hanover, NH: Wesleyan University Press, 1994. 104–40.

H,N   Murray, Janet. *Hamlet on the Holodeck: The Future of Narrative in Cyberspace.* Cambridge, MA: MIT Press, 1998.

Com,NM,V   Mullet, Kevin and Darrell Sano. *Designing Visual Interfaces: Communication-Oriented Techniques.* Mountain View, CA: Sun Microsystems, 1995.

L,P   Mullin, Joan A. "Alternative Pedagogy: Visualizing Theories of Composition." *ARTiculating: Teaching Writing in a Visual World.* Eds. Pamela B. Childers, Eric H. Hobson, and Joan A. Mullin. Portsmouth, NH: Boynton/Cook, 1998. 57–71.

Im   Nichols, B. *Ideology and the Image.* Bloomington: Indiana University Press, 1981.

H,in,V   Nielsen, Jakob. *Hypertext & Hypermedia.* San Diego: Academic Press, 1990.

B,H,L   Nunberg, Geoffrey, ed. *The Future of the Book.* Berkeley: University of California Press, 1996.

WI   Nuyen, A.T. "The Rhetoric of Feminist Writing." *Philosophy and Rhetoric* 28.1 (1995): 69–82.

F,L,S   Olin, Margaret. "Gaze." *Critical Terms for Art History.* Eds. Robert S. Nelson and Richard Shiff. Chicago: The University of Chicago Press, 1996.

B,M,WI   Ong, Walter J. *Orality and Literacy: The Technologizing of the Word.* London: Routledge, 1982.

    Packer, Randall and Ken Jordan. *Multimedia: From Wagner to Virtual Reality.* New York: W. W. Norton, 2001.

B   Parkes, M. B. *Pause and Effect: An Introduction to the History of Punctuation.* Berkeley: University of California Press, 1993.

B,H   Parkes, Malcolm. "Folia Librorium Quaerere: Medieval Experience of the Problems of Hypertext and the Index." *Fabula in Tabula: Una Storia degli Indici dal Manoscritto al Testo Electronico.* Eds. Claudio Leonardi, Marcello Morelli, and Francesco Santi. Spoleto: Centro Italiano di Studi Sull'Alto Medioevo. 23–41.

G,F,Ps   Penley, Constance, ed. *Feminism and Film Theory.* New York: Routledge, 1988.

In,NM   Penny, Simon, ed. *Critical Issues in Electronic Media.* Albany: State University of New York Press, 1995.

S,VC   Perkins, David N. *The Intelligent Eye: Learning to Think by Looking at Art.* Santa Monica: The Getty Center for Education in the Arts, 1994.

B,L,VC   Perloff, Marjorie. *Radical Artifice: Writing Poetry in the Age of Media.* Chicago: University of Chicago Press, 1991.

An,VC   Pilling, Jane, ed. *A Reader in Animation Studies.* Sydney: John Libbey, 1997.

WI   Poggenpohl, Sharon. "More Than a Book Review of The Electronic Word." *Visible Language* 28.2 (Spring 1994): 172–92.

S   Pomian, Krzysztof. "Vision and Cognition." *Picturing Science, Producing Art.* Eds. Caroline A. Jones and Peter Galison. New York: Routledge, 1998. 211–31.

R,V   Porter, James. and Patricia A. Sullivan. "Repetition and the Rhetoric of Visual Design." *Advances in Discourse Processes.* 48 (1994).

E   Rasula, Jed and Steve McCaffery, Eds. *Imagining Language: An Anthology.* Cambridge: MIT Press, 1998.

L,P   Reinking, David, Michael C. McKenna, Linda D. Labbo, and Ronald D. Kieffer, eds. *Handbook of Literacy and Technology: Transformations in a Post-Typographic World.* Mahwah, NJ: Lawrence Erlbaum, 1998.

F   Renov, M. and Suderburg, E. *Resolutions: Contemporary Video Practices.* Minneapolis: University of Minnesota Press, 1996.

T   Riedinger, Edward A. "The Tales Typography Tells." *Visible Language* 23.4 (Autumn 1989): 369–74.

In, NM   Rieser, Martin and Andrea Zapp, eds. *New Screen Media: Cinema/Art/Narrative.* London: British Film Institute, 2002.

VC   Rogoff, Irit. *Terra Infirma: Geography's Visual Culture.* London: Routledge, 2000.

In   Rokeby, David. "Transforming Mirrors: Subjectivity and Control in Interactive Media." *Critical Issues in Electronic Media.* Ed. Simon Penny. Albany: State University of New York Press, 1995: 133–58.

S   Romanyshn, Robert. "The Despotic Eye and Its Shadow: Media Image in the Age of Literacy." *Modernity and the Hegemony of Vision.* Ed. David Michael Levin. Berkeley: University of California Press, 1993. 39–360.

S,VC   ———. *Technology as Symptom and Dream.* London: Routledge 1989.

E   Ronell, Avital. *The Telephone Book: Technology, Schizophrenia, Electric Speech.* Lincoln: University of Nebraska Press, 1989.

L,R,V   Root, R.L. "Imagining Visual Literacy: The Poetics and Rhetoric of the Image." *CEA Critic,* 58.3 (1996): 60–71.

P,Ps,VC   Rose, Gillian. *Visual Methodologies.* London: Sage, 2001.

G,S   Rose, Jacqueline. *Sexuality in the Field of Vision.* New York: Routledge, 1986.

S   Rosen, P., ed. *Narrative, Apparatus, Ideology.* New York: Columbia University Press, 1986.

H   Rosenberg, Martin. "Physics and Hypertext: Liberation and Complicity in Art and Pedagogy." *Hyper/Text/Theory.* Ed. George P. Landow. Baltimore: Johns Hopkins University Press, 1994. 268–97.

Ad,G,V   Rothschild, Joan, et al., eds. *Design and Feminism : Re-Visioning Spaces, Places, and Everyday Things.* Piscataway, NJ: Rutgers University Press, 1999.

NM	Rush, Michael. *New Media in Late 20th-Century Art.* London: Thames and Hudson, 1999.
H, In, L	Ryan, Marie-Laure, ed. *Cyberspace Textuality: Computer Technology and Literary Theory.* Bloomington: Indianda University Press, 1999.
H, In, N	Ryan, Marie-Laure. "Beyond Myth and Metaphor: The Case of Narrative in Digital Media." *Game Studies* 1 (July 2001) <http://www.gamestudies.org/0101/ryan/>.
H, In, L	———. *Narrative as Virtual Reality: Immersion and Interactivity in Literature and Electronic Media.* Baltimore: The Johns Hopkins University Press, 2001.
S	Sacks, Oliver. *An Anthropologist on Mars: Seven Paradoxical Tales.* New York: Vintage, 1996.
S	———. *Seeing Voices: A Journey into the World of the Deaf.* New York: HarperCollins, 1990.
B,L,M	Saenger, Paul. *Space Between Words: The Origins of Silent Reading.* Stanford: Stanford University Press, 1997.
Ad,R,V	Scott, Linda M. "Images in Advertising: The Need for a Theory of Visual Rhetoric." *The Journal of Consumer Research.* 21.2 (September 1994).
CW,L	Selfe, Cynthia. *Technology and Literacy in the Twenty-First Century: The Perils of Not Paying Attention.* Carbonale, IL: Southern Illinois University Press, 1999.
CW,L	Selfe, Cynthia and Susan Hillgoss, eds. *Literacy and Computers: The Complications of Teaching and Learning with Technology.* New York: MLA, 1994.
CW,L	Selfe, Cynthia and Gail Hawisher, eds. *Literate Lives in the Information Age: Stories from the United States.* Mahwah, NJ: Lawrence Erlbaum (forthcoming).
CW,In,NM	Selfe, Cynthia L. and Richard J. Selfe. "The Politics of the Interface: Power and its Exercise in Electronic Contact Zones." *CCC* 45.4 (December 1994): 480–504.
T	Shaw, Paul. "Lead Soldiers." *Print* 52:4 (July/August 1998): 96–103, 226.
R	Shelley, Cameron. "Rhetorical and Demonstrative Modes of Visual Argument." *Argument and Advocacy* 33 (Fall 1996): 53–68.
Com,R,V	Shriver, Karen A. *Dynamics in Document Design.* New York: John Wiley & Sons, 1997.
Com,V	Siegel, David. *Creating Killer Web Sites: The Art of Third-Generation Web Sites.* Second Edition. Indianapolis: Hayden Books, 1997.
B,T,V,WI	Smith, Keith A. *Text in the Book Format.* Rochester, NY: Keith A. Smith Books, 1995.
I,F	Smith, Terry, ed. *Impossible Presence: Surface and Screen in the Photogenic Era.* Chicago: University of Chicago Press, 2001.

H,In,NM,V   Snyder, Ilana, ed. *Page to Screen.* London: Routledge, 1998.

S   Snyder, Joel. "Visualization and Visibility." *Picturing Science/Producing Art.* Eds. Caroline A. Jones and Peter Galison. New York: Routledge, 1998. 379–97.

B   Solomon, Martin. "The Power of Punctuation." *The Idea of Design: A Design Issues Reader.* Eds. Victor Margolin and Richard Buchanan. Cambridge: MIT Press, 1998. 113–17.

I,L,VC   Stafford, Barbara Maria. *Artful Science: Enlightenment Entertainment and the Eclipse of Visual education.* Cambridge: MIT Press, 1994.

I,VC   ———. *Good Looking: Essays on the Virtue of Images.* Cambridge: MIT Press, 1996.

I,S,VC   ———. *Visual Analogy: Consciousness as the Art of Connecting.* Cambridge: MIT Press, 1999.

B   Steinberg, S.H. *Five Hundred Years of Printing.* Revised by John Trevitt. London: The British Library and the Oaknoll Press, 1996.

WI   Steiner, Wendy. *The Colors of Rhetoric: Problems in the Relation between Modern Literature and Painting.* Chicago: University of Chicago Press, 1982.

L,WI   Stephens, Mitchell. *The Rise of the Image, the Fall of the Word.* New York: Oxford University Press, 1998.

B   Stewart, Susan. *Crimes of Writing: Problems in the Containment of Representation.* Durham: Duke University Press, 1994.

L,WI   Street, Brian V. *Literacy in Theory and Practice.* Cambridge: Cambridge University Press, 1984.

T,V   Swanson, Gunnar, ed. *Graphic Design & Reading: Explorations of an Uneasy Relationship.* New York: Allworth Press, 2000.

H,N,NM   Swiss, Thomas, ed. *Unspun: Key Concepts for Understanding the World Wide Web.* New York: New York University Press, 2000.

VC   Tagg, J. *The Burden of Representation: Essays on Photographies and Histories.* Minneapolis: University of Minnesota Press, 1988.

VC   Taylor, Lucien, ed. *Visualizing Theory: Selected Essays From V.A.R. 1990–1994.* New York: Routledge, 1994.

E   Taylor, Mark. *Hiding.* Chicago: University of Chicago Press, 1997.

E,P   Taylor, Mark and Esa Saarinen. *Imagologies.* London: Routledge, 1994.

L,P   Taylor, Todd and Irene Ward, eds. *Literacy Theory in the Age of the Internet.* New York: Columbia University Press, 1998.

B,L,R,V   Tebeaux Elizabeth. "Ramus, Visual Rhetoric, and the Emergence of Page Design in Medical Writing of the English Renaissance—Tracking the Evolution of Readable Documents." *Written Communication,* 8.4 (1991): 411–45

V	Thomson, Ellen Mazur. *The Origins of Graphic Design in America 1870–1920*. New Haven: Yale University Press, 1997.
NM	Trumbo, Jean. "The Spatial Environment in Multimedia Design." *Design Issues*. 13.3 (Autumn 1997): 19–28.
B,V	Tschichold, Jan. *The Form of the Book: Essays on the Morality of Good Design*. Trans. Hajo Hadeler. Point Roberts, WA: Hartley & Marks, 1991.
B,Com,T,V	————. *The New Typography: A Handbook for Modern Designers*. Trans. Ruari McLean. Berkeley: University of California Press, 1995.
L,V	Tufte, Edward R. *Envisioning Information: Narratives of Time and Space*. Chesire, CT: Graphics Press, 1997.
L,V	————. *The Visual Display of Quantitative Information*. Second Edition. Chesire, CT: Graphics Press, 2001.
L,V	————. *Visual Explanations: Images and Quantities, Evidence and Narrative*. Chesire, CT: Graphics Press, 1997.
L	Tuman, Myron. *Word Perfect: Literacy in the Computer Age*. Pittsburgh: University of Pittsburgh Press, 1992.
E	Urion, Marilyn Vogler. "Public Text/Private Text: Making Visible the Voices that Shape Our Social Conscience." *Computers and Composition* 12.1 (1995): 3–13.
VC	Venturi, Robert, Denise Scott Brown, and Steven Izenour. *Learning from Las Vegas*. Revised Edition. Cambridge: MIT Press, 1997.
S	Virilio, Paul. *War and Cinema: The Logistics of Perception*. London: Verso, 1989.
S	————. *The Vision Machine*. Bloomington: Indiana University Press, 1994.
S	————. *The Art of the Motor*. Minneapolis: University of Minnesota Press, 1995.
VC	Votolato, Gregory. *American Design in the Twentieth Century*. Manchester: Manchester University Press. 1998.
B,T,V	Warde, Beatrice. *The Crystal-Goblet: Sixteen Essays on Typography*. Ed. Henry Jacob. London: Sylvan, 1955.
	Wardrip-Fruin, Noah and Nick Montfort, eds. *The New Media Reader*. Cambridge, MA: MIT Press, 2003.
R,NM	Warnick, Barbara. "Rhetorical Criticism in New Media Environments." *Rhetoric Review*. 20.1-2 (2001): 60–65.
L,P,V	Wilde, Judith, and Richard Wilde. *Visual Literacy: A Conceptual Guide Approach to Graphic Problem Solving*. New York: Watson-Guptill, 2000.
F,G	Williams, Linda, ed. *Viewing Positions: Ways of Seeing Film*. New Jersey: Rutgers University Press, 1994.
Com,V	Williams, Pamela. "The Complete Design Library." *Critique* 4 (Spring 1997): 65–80.

Com,V   Williams, Robin. *The Non-Designer's Design Book: Design and Typographic Principles for the Visual Novice.* Berkeley: Peachpit, 1994.

Ad,WI   Williamson, Judith. *Decoding Advertisements: Ideology and Meaning in Advertising.* London: Marion Boyars, 1978.

B,Com,V   Wilson, Adrian. *The Design of Books.* San Francisco: Chronicle Books, 1993.

H   Woodland, J. Randal. "Spider Webs, Symphonies, and the Yellow-Brick Road: Form and Structure in Electronic Texts." *The New Writing Environment: Writers at Work in a World of Technology.* Eds. Mike Sharples and Thea van der Geest. London: Springer-Verlag, 1996. 183–203.

L,P,S   Woolsey, Kristina Hooper, Scott Kim, and Gayle Curtis. *Vizability: Change the Way You See the World.* Boston: PWS Publishing, 1996.

I,V   Worth, Sol. *Studying Visual Communication.* Ed. Larry Grossberg. 1981. 12 December 2003. <http://astro.temple.edu/~ruby/wava/worth/svscom.html>.

V,VC   Wurman, Richard Saul. *Information Anxiety 2.* Indianapolis: Que, 2000.

NM,R,WI,E   Wysocki, Anne Frances. "Impossibly Distinct: On Form/Content and Word/Image in Two Pieces of Computer-Based Interactive Multimedia." *Computers & Composition* 18 (2001): 137–62.

Com,NM,R   ———. "The Multiple Media of Texts: How Onscreen and Paper Texts incorporate Words, Images, and Other Media." *What Writing Does and How It Does It: An Introduction to Analysis of Text and Textual Practices.* Eds. Charles Bazerman and Paul Prior. Mahwah, NJ: Lawrence Erlbaum and Associates, 2003. 123-163.

H,Im,In,NM   ———. "Seriously Visible." *Eloquent Images: Visual Literacy and New Media.* Eds. Mary Hocks and Michelle Kendrick. Cambridge: MIT Press, 2003. 37-59.

B   Yates, Frances. *The Art of Memory.* Chicago: University of Chicago Press, 1966.

Com,F,V   Zettl, H. *Sight, Sound, Motion: Applied Media Aesthetics.* New York: Wadsworth, 1990.

works cited

Applen, J. D. "Encountering Hypertext Technology: Student Engineers Analyze and Construct Web Pages." Gruber 14–24.

Ardener, Shirley. "The Partition of Space." *Gender, Space, Architecture*. Eds. Jane Rendell, Barbara Penner, and Iain Borden. London: Routledge, 2000. 112–117.

Armstrong, Elizabeth and Joan Rothfuss. *In the Spirit of Fluxus*. Minneapolis: Walker Art Center, 1993.

Arnheim, Rudolf. *The Power of the Center*. Berkeley: University of California Press, 1982.

Ashton, Dore. *A Joseph Cornell Album*. New York: Viking Press, 1974.

Auping, Michael. *Jenny Holzer*. New York: Universe, 1992.

Bang, Molly. *Picture This: Perception & Composition*. Boston: Little, Brown and Company, 1991.

Barber, John F., and Dene Grigar, eds. *New Worlds, New Words: Exploring Pathways for Writing About and In Electronic Environments*. Cresskill, NJ: Hampton Press, 2001.

Bartholomae, David. "What is Composition and (if you know what that is) Why Do We Teach It?" Bloom et al. 11–28.

Bartholomae, David and Anthony Petrosky. *Ways of Reading: An Anthology for Writers*. 2nd ed. Boston: Bedford Books of St. Martin's, 1990.

Barton, David and Mary Hamilton. *Local Literacies: Reading and Writing in One Community*. London: Routledge, 1998.

Basic Books, Inc. v. Kinko's Graphics Corp. 758 F. Supp. 1522, 1530. S.D.N.Y. 1991.

Baudrillard, Jean. *Simulations*. Trans. Paul Foss, Paul Patton, and Philip Beitchman. New York: Semiotext(e), 1983.

Benjamin, Walter. *The Arcades Project*. Trans. Howard Eiland and Kevin McLaughlin. Cambridge: Belknap Press of Harvard University Press, 1999.

———. *Charles Baudelaire: A Lyric Poet in the Era of High Capitalism*. London : Verso, 1997.

———. "Unpacking My Library." *Illuminations*. Ed. Hannah Arendt. New York: Schocken Books, 1968. 59–67.

Block, René. Curator's Statement for the exhibit "Lost and Found." Apexart. New York, 23 May–23 June 2001. <http://www.apexart.org/exhibitions/block.html>

Bloom, Lynn Z., Donald A. Daiker, and Edward M. White, eds. *Composition in the Twenty-First Century: Crisis and Change*. Carbondale: Southern Illinois University Press, 1996.

Bolter, Jay David. *Writing Space: The Computer, Hypertext, and the History of Writing*. Hillsdale, NJ: Lawrence Erlbaum, 1991.

Bourdieu, Pierre. *Outline of a Theory of Practice*. trans. Richard Nice. Cambridge: Cambridge University Press, 1977.

Brandt, Deborah. "Literacy Learning and Economic Change." *Harvard Educational Review*. 69.4 (1999): 373–94.

———. "Sponsors of Literacy." *College Composition and Communication* 49 (1998): 165-185.

Brennan, Teresa and Martin Jay, eds. *Vision in Context: Historical and Contemporary Perspectives on Sight.* New York: Routledge, 1996.

Brodkey, Linda. *Writing Permitted in Designated Areas Only.* Minneapolis: University of Minnesota Press, 1996.

Bryson, Norman, Michael Ann Holly, and Keith Moxey, Eds. *Visual Culture: Images and Interpretations.* Hanover, NH: Wesleyan University Press, 1994.

Buell, Thomas C. "Notes on Keeping a Journal." *College Composition and Communication* 20 (Feb. 1969): 43–46.

Cassirer, Ernst. *Kant's Life and Thought.* New Haven: Yale University Press, 1981.

Castells, Manuel. *The Information Age: Economy, Society, and Culture.* 3 vols. Malden, MA: Blackwell, 1996–98.

Classen, Constance. *Worlds of Sense: Exploring the Senses in History and Across Cultures.* London: Routledge, 1993.

Crain, William. "Open Admissions at the City University of New York." *Academe.* 89:4 (July-August 2003): 46–49.

Crews, Kenneth. "Not the 'Last Word' on Photocopying and Coursepacks: The Sixth Circuit Rules Against Fair Use in the MDS Case." 30 October 2002. <http://www.iupui.edu/~copyinfo/mdscase.html>.

Csomay, Eniko and Sibylle Gruber. "Changing Economies, Changing Politics, and the Web: a Hungarian Perspective." *Global Literacies and the World-Wide Web.* Eds. Gail Hawisher and Cynthia L. Selfe. London: Routledge, 2000. 21-51.

Debes, John L. and Clarence M. Williams. "Chapter Five." *Visual Literacy, Languaging, and Learning, Provocative Paper Series #1.* 8 July 2001. Benedict Visual Literacy Collection, Arizona State University Libraries. <http://www.asu.edu/lib/archives/vlhist.htm>.

Deibert, Ronald J. *Parchment, Printing, and Hypermedia: Communication in World Order Transformation.* New York: Columbia University Press, 1997.

de Duve, Thierry, ed. *The Definitively Unfinished Marcel Duchamp.* Cambridge, MA: MIT Press, 1993. 187–230.

Drew, Julie. "Cultural Composition: Stuart Hall on Ethnicity and the Discursive Turn." *JAC* 18.2 (1998): 172–196.

Duchamp, Marcel. *Salt Seller: The Writings of Marcel Duchamp.* Ed. Michel Sanouillet and Elmer Peterson. New York: Oxford University Press, 1973.

Eagleton, Terry. *The Ideology of the Aesthetic.* Oxford: Blackwell, 1990.

Eiland, Howard, and Kevin McLaughlin. Translators' Foreword. Benjamin, *The Arcades Project* ix–xiv.

Elbow, Peter. "Reflections on Academic Discourse." *College English* 53 (Feb. 1991): 135–155.

Elkins, James. *The Object Stares Back: On the Nature of Seeing.* New York: Simon & Schuster, 1996.

Faigley, Lester. "Material Literacy and Visual Design." *Rhetorical Bodies.* Eds. Jack Selzer and Sharon Crowley. Madison, WI: University of Wisconsin Press, 1999. 171–201.

Feenberg, Andrew. *Alternative Modernity.* Berkeley: University of California Press, 1995.

————. *Critical Theory of Technology.* New York: Oxford University Press, 1991.

Fleming, David. "The Streets of Thurii: Discourse, Democracy, and design in the Classic Polis." *Rhetoric Society Quarterly* 32.3 (Summer 2002): 5–32

Foster, Hal. *The Return of the Real.* Cambridge: MIT Press, 1996.

Friere, Paulo. *Pedagogy of the Oppressed.* Trans. Myra Bergman Ramos. New York: The Continuum Publishing Company, 1990.

Gee, James. *Social Linguistics and Literacies: Ideology in Discourses.* Brighton, GB: Falmer Press, 1990.

George, Diana. "From Analysis to Design: Visual Communication in the Teaching of Writing." *College Composition and Communication* 54.1 (2002): 11–39.

Gillette, David. "When Media Collide." Gruber 3–13.

Graff, H. J. *The Legacy of Literacy: Continuities and Contradictions in Western Culture and Society.* Bloomington, IN: Indiana University Press, 1987.

Grossberg, Lawrence. "Cultural Studies and/in New Worlds." *Critical Studies in Mass Communication* 10 (1993): 1–22.

Gruber, Sibylle, ed. *Weaving a Virtual Web: Practical Approaches to New Information Technologies.* Urbana: National Council of Teachers of English, 2000.

Haacke, Hans. "School for Scandal." Interview with Deborah Solomon. *The New York Times Magazine* 26 Mar. 2000: 23.

Haas, Christina. *Writing Technology: Studies on the Materiality of Literacy.* Mahwh, NJ: Lawrence Erlbaum, 1996.

Hall, Stuart. "On Postmodernism and Articulation: An Interview with Stuart Hall." Ed. Lawrence Grossberg. *Journal of Communication Inquiry* 10.2 (1986): 45–60.

Hawisher, Gail. "Accessing the Virtual Worlds of Cyberspace." *Journal of Electronic Publishing.* 6.1 (2001). 10 July 2001. <http://www.press.umich.edu/jep/06-01/hawisher.html>.

Hawisher, Gail E., and Cynthia L. Selfe. "Dispatches from the Middlewor(l)ds of Computers and Composition: Experimenting with Writing and Visualizing the Future." Barber & Grigar 185–209.

————, eds. *Passions, Pedagogies, and 21st Century Technologies.* Logan: Utah State Univerity Press, 1999.

Hawisher, Gail E., and Patricia Sullivan. "Women on the Networks: Searching for E-Spaces of Their Own." *Feminism and Composition Studies: In Other Words.* Eds. Susan Jarratt and L. Worsham. New York: Modern Language Association, 1998. 172–197.

Hayles, N. Katherine. *Writing Machines.* Cambride: MIT Press, 2002.

Hendricks, Jon. "Uncovering Fluxus—Recovering Fluxus." Kellein 119–135.

Hiassen, Carl. *Stormy Weather.* New York: Alfred A. Knopf, 1995.

Higgins, Dick. "Statement on Intermedia." Armstrong & Rothfuss 172–173.

Hilligoss, Susan. *Visual Communication.* New York: Longman, 1999.

Hoffman, Donald D. *Visual Intelligence: How We Construct What We See.* New York: Norton, 1998.

Holland. Jeanne. "Scraps, Stamps, and Cutouts: Emily Dickinson's Domestic Technologies of Publication." *Cultural Artifacts and the Production of Meaning: The Page, the Image, and the Body*. Eds.Margaret J. M. Ezell and Katherine O'Brien O'Keeffe. Ann Arbor: University of Michigan Press, 1994. 139-181.

Horner, Bruce. *Terms of Work for Composition: A Materialist Critique*. Albany: State University of New York Press, 2001.

Howes, David, ed. *The Varieties of Sensory Experience: A Sourcebook in the Anthropology of the Senses*. Toronto: University of Toronto Press, 1991.

Infoworld Electric. "Using Copyrighted Material from InfoWorld." 12 August 1999. <http://www.infoworld.com/cgibin/displayStat.pl?/readerservices/permissions.htm>.

Jameson, Frederic. *Postmodernism or the Cultural Logic of Late Capitalism*. Durham, NC: Duke University Press, 1991.

Janangelo, Joseph. "Joseph Cornell and the Artistry of Composing Persuasive Hypertexts." *College Composition and Communication* 49 (Feb. 1998): 24–44.

Jay, Martin. *Downcast Eyes: The Denigration of Vision in Twentieth-Century French Thought*. Berkeley: University of California Press, 1993.

Julier, Laura. "Community-Service Pedagogy." *A Guide to Composition Pedagogies*. eds. Gary Tate, Amy Rupiper, and Kurt Schick. New York: Oxford University Press, 2001: 132–148.

Kant, Immanuel. *Critique of Judgment*. Trans. J. H. Bernard. New York: Hafner Publishing Company, 1966.

Kellein, Thomas, ed. *Fluxus*. London: Thames and Hudson, 1995.

Kirschenbaum, Matthew. "Machine Visions: Towards a Poetics of Artificial Intelligence." *Electronic Book Review* 6 (Winter 1997-1998). 12 December 2003. <http://www.altx.com/ebr/ebr6/6kirschenbaum/6kirsch.htm>.

Kitalong, Karla Saari and Tino Kitalong." Complicating the Tourist Gaze: Literacy and the Internet as Catalysts for Articulating a Postcolonial Palauan Identity." *Global Literacies and the World-Wide Web*. Eds. Gail Hawisher and Cynthia L. Selfe. London: Routledge, 2000. 95-113.

Kress, Gunther. "'English' at the Crossroads: Rethinking Curricula of Communication in the Context of the Turn to the Visual." Hawisher and Selfe, *Passions and Pedagogies* 66–88.

———. *Literacy in the New Media Age*. London: Routledge, 2003.

Kress, Gunther and Theo van Leeuwen. *Multimodal Discourse: The Modes and Media of Contemporary Communication*. London: Edward Arnold, 2001.

———. *Reading Images: The Grammar of Visual Design*. London: Routledge, 1996.

Leppert, Richard. *Art and the Committed Eye: The Cultural Functions of Imagery*. Boulder, CO: Westview Press, 1996.

Love, James. "Government Proposes New Regulation of Sports Statistics and Other 'Facts'." *CNI Roundtable*. 10 November 1996. <http://www.cni.org/Hforums/roundtable/1996-04/0086.html>. 15 April 2003. Rpt. from Information Policy Notes. 10 November 1996.

Lutz, William D. "Making Freshman English a Happening." *College Composition and Communication* 22 (Feb. 1971): 35–38.

Macrorie, Ken. *Searching Writing*. Rochelle Park, NJ: Hayden, 1980.

Manovich, Lev. *The Language of New Media*. Cambridge: MIT Press, 2001.

Matthew Bender v. West Publishing. 158 F.3d 1693. 2d Cir. 1998. <http://laws.find-law.com/2nd/977910.html>.

McGann, Jerome. "Composition as Explanation (of Modern and Postmodern Poetries)." *Cultural Artifacts and the Production of Meaning: The Page, the Image, and the Body*. Eds. Margaret J. M. Ezell and Katherine O'Brien O'Keeffe. Ann Arbor: University of Michigan Press, 1994. 101-138.

———. *The Textual Condition*. Princeton: Princeton University Press, 1991.

McShine, Kynaston, ed. *Joseph Cornell*. New York: MOMA, 1980.

Mead, Margaret. *Culture and Commitment: The New Relationships between the Generations in the 1970s*. New York: Doubleday, 1970.

Mekas, Jonas. "The Invisible Cathedrals of Joseph Cornell." Ashton 162–167.

Mirzoeff, Nicholas, Ed. *The Visual Culture Reader*. London: Routledge, 1998.

Mitchell, WJT. *Picture Theory*. Chicago: University of Chicago Press, 1994.

New London Group. "A Pedagogy of Multiliteracies: Designing Social Futures." *Harvard Education Review* 66.1 (1996): 60–92.

O'Doherty, Brian. *American Masters: The Voice and the Myth*. New York: Universe Books, 1988.

The On-line Visual Literacy Project. Ed. Stonehill, Brian. 1994. 8 July 2001. <http://www.pomona.edu/Academics/courserelated/classprojects/Visual-lit/intro/intro.html>.

Pijnappel, Johann. "Fluxus: Today and Yesterday." *Art & Design* No. 28 (1993).

Porter, James. "Intertextuality and the Discourse Community." *Rhetoric Review* 5.1 (1986): 34–47.

———. "Legal Realities and Ethical Hyperrealities: A Critical Approach toward Cyberwriting." *Computers and Technical Communication: Pedagogical and Programmatic Perspectives*. Ed. Stuart Selber. Greenwich, CT: Ablex, 1997. 45–73.

———. *Rhetorical Ethics and Internetworked Writing*. Greenwich, CT: Ablex, 1998.

Princeton University Press v. Michigan Document Services, INC. 1996 FED App. 0357P. 6th Cir. 12 July 2001. <http://laws.findlaw.com/6th/960357p.html>

Ratcliff, Carter. "Joseph Cornell: Mechanic of the Ineffable." McShine 43–67.

Reich, Robert B. *The Work of Nations: Preparing Ourselves for 21st-Century Capitalism*. New York: Alfred A. Knopf, 1991.

Romano, Susan. "The Egalitarianism Narrative: Whose Story? Which Yardstick?" *Computers and Composition* 10.3: 5–28.

Romano, Susan, Barbara Field, and Elizabeth de Huergo. "Web Literacies of the Already Accessed and Technically Inclined: Schooling in Monterrey, Mexico." *Global Literacies and the World-Wide Web*. Eds. Gail Hawisher and Cynthia L. Selfe. London: Routledge, 2000. 189-216.

Rose, Gillian. *Visual Methodologies*. London: Sage, 2001.

Rosenberg, Harold. "Object Poems." In *Artworks and Packages*. Chicago: University of Chicago Press, 1969. 75–87.

Selfe, Cynthia L. *Technology and Literacy in the Twenty-First Century: The Importance of Paying Attention.* Carbondale: Southern Illinois University Press, 1999.

Selfe, Cynthia L. and Gail E. Hawisher. *Literate Lives in the Information Age: Narratives on Literacy in the United States.* Mawah, NJ: Lawrence Erlbaum Publishers. Forthcoming.

Selfe, Cynthia L. and Richard J. Selfe. "The Politics of the interface: Power and its Exercise in Electronic Contact Zones." *College Composition and Communication* 45.4 (1994) 480–504.

Selfe, Richard. "What Are We Doing to Ourselves? (Some Material Practices of Digital Publishing)." Barber & Grigar 307–348.

Shoos, Diane and George, Diana. "Dropping Bread Crumbs in the Intertextual Forest: Critical Literacy in a Postmodern Age." Hawisher and Selfe, *Passions and Pedagogies* 115–127.

Simic, Charles. *Dime-Store Alchemy: The Art of Joseph Cornell.* Hopewell, NJ: Ecco Press, 1992.

Sirc, Geoff. "Virtual Urbanism." *Computers and Composition* 18(1), 11–19.

Slack, Jennifer Daryl. "The Theory and Method of Articulation in Cultural Studies." *Stuart Hall: Critical Dialogues in Cultural Studies.* Eds. David Morley and Kuan-Hsing Chen. New York: Routledge, 1996. 112–130.

Spinuzzi, Clay. "'Light Green Doesn't Mean Hydrology!': Toward a Visual Rhetorical Framework." *Computers and Composition* 18.1: 39–54.

Stiles, Kristine. "Between Water and Stone: Fluxus Performance: A Metaphysics of Acts." Armstrong and Rothfuss 62–99.

Stone, Allucquére Rosanne. *The War of Desire and Technology at the Close of the Mechanical Age.* Cambridge: MIT Press, 1995.

Street, Brian V. *Social Literacies: Critical Approaches to Literacy in Development, Ethnography, and Education.* London: Longman, 1995.

Stroupe, Craig. "Visualizing English: Recognizing the Hybrid Literacy of Visual and Verbal Authorship on the Web." *College English* 62.5 (May 2000): 607–632.

Sturken, Marita and Lisa Cartwright. *Practices of Looking: An Introduction to Visual Culture.* Oxford: Oxford University Press, 2001.

Suquet, Jean. "Possible." de Duve 85–111.

Takayoshi, Pamela. "Building New Networks from the Old." *Computers and Composition* 11(1): 21–35.

Ulmer, Gregory L. *Heuretics: The Logic of Invention.* Baltimore: Johns Hopkins University Press, 1994.

Weil, Bruce. Lecture. Walker Art Center, Minneapolis. 7 Apr. 2000.

Wijers, Louwrien. "Fluxus Yesterday and Tomorrow." Pijnappel 7–13.

Williams, Emmett, and Ann Noël, eds. *Mr. Fluxus.* London: Thames and Hudson, 1997.

Williams, Robin. *The Non-Designer's Design Book.* Berkeley, CA: Peachpit Press, 1994.

Williams, Sean. "Part 1: Thinking Out of the Pro-Verbal Box." *Computers and Composition* 18.1 (2001): 21–32.

Woodmansee, Martha and Peter Jaszi. "The Law of Texts: Copyright in the Academy." *College English* 57 (1995): 769Ω–87

Wysocki, Anne Frances and Johnson-Eilola. "Blinded by the letter: Why are we using literacy as a metaphor for everything?" Hawisher and Selfe, *Passions and Pedagogies* 349–368.

Wysocki, Anne. "Impossibly Distinct: On Form/Content and Word/Image in Two Pieces of Computer-Based Multimedia." *Computers and Composition* 18.2 (2001): 137–162.

———. "with eyes that think, and compose, and think: on visual rhetoric." *Teaching Writing with Computers: An Introduction.* Eds. Pamela Takayoshi and Brian Huot. Boston: Houghton-Mifflin, 2003. 182–201.

about the authors

Johndan Johnson-Eilola works as a Professor of Technical Communications at Clarkson University, teaching courses in information architecture, technical communication, usability, and mass communication. In addition to numerous journal articles and book chapters, he is the author of *Nostalgic Angels* (Ablex/Greenwood), *Central Works: Landmark Essays in Technical Communication* (Oxford University Press, co-edited with Stuart Selber), and *Datacloud* (Hampton Press), as well as the Web-based textbook *Professional Writing Online* (Longman, with James E. Porter and Patricia Sullivan) and the print textbook *Designing Effective Websites* (Houghton Mifflin).

Geoffrey Sirc works in composition at the University of Minnesota's General College.

Cynthia L. Selfe is Professor of Humanities in the Humanities Department at Michigan Technological University. She is also the founder and co-editor (with Gail Hawisher) of *Computers and Composition* and of the *Computers and Composition* book series with Ablex, Greenwood, and Hampton Press. Selfe is past chair of the Conference on College Composition and Communication and of the College section of the National Council of Teachers of English. In 1996, Selfe was recognized as an EDUCOM Medal award winner for innovative computer use in higher education—the first woman and the first English teacher to receive this award. In 2001, Selfe, with long-time collaborator Gail Hawisher (of the University of Illinois) accepted CCCC's Technology Innovator Award. She is the author of numerous articles and books on computers and composition, including *Technology and Literacy in the Twenty-First Century: The Importance of Paying Attention* (Southern Illinois University Press), *Computer-Assisted Instruction in Composition* (NCTE), and *Creating a Computer-Supported Writing Facility* (Computers and Composition Press); she is a co-author with Gail Hawisher of Literate Lives in the Information Age: Narratives on Literacy in the United States. She has also co-edited several collections of essays on computers and composition studies.

Anne Frances Wysocki teaches rhetoric, visual communication, and new media theories and production in the undergraduate Science and Technical Communication and graduate Rhetoric and Technical Communication programs at Michigan Technological University. Her recent publications—both online and print—consider the visual rhetorics and bodily constructions of online and print texts; she has also designed and developed interactive digital learning materials for three-dimensional visualization and for geologic processes. With Dennis Lynch, she is developing a textbook, *compose/design/advocate: A Rhetoric for Integrating Written, Visual, and Oral Communication* (Longman, 2004).

index